Principles &
Practices
of

Biblical
Parenting

Writings also by Paul J. Bucknell

Overcoming Anxiety: Finding Peace, Discovering God

Building a Great Marriage! Faith, Forgiveness, Friendship

Cross Training: Discipling for Change!

Christian Premarital Counseling: Preparing the Two

The Godly Man: When God Touches a Man's Life

Genesis: The Book of Foundations

Reaching Beyond Mediocrity: Being an Overcomer

Godly Beginnings for the Family

Book of Romans: Building a Solid Foundation

Running the Race: Overcoming Sexual Lusts

Walking with Jesus: Abiding in Christ

Find these and many more resources at:

Biblical Foundations for Freedom
www.foundationsforfreedom.net

Principles &
Practices

of

Biblical
Parenting

Raising Godly Children

Paul & Linda Bucknell

Principles & Practices of Biblical Parenting: Raising
Godly Children

Copyright © 2007, 2012 Paul and Linda Bucknell

ISBN 978-1-61993-006-3

www.foundationsforfreedom.net
Pittsburgh, Pennsylvania,15212 USA

Chinese versions available:
    Mandarin (Traditional and Simplified).
Contact info@foundationsforfreedom.net.

Dedication

To God our Father and His Son,

the Lord Jesus Christ,

may praise arise

from whom all wisdom, love,

graciousness and power

unceasingly flow

unto a most unworthy people

that we and many others

might be adopted into His family,

become like Him and

enjoy Him and His blessings

forever.

Appreciation

We are most grateful to our parents and grandparents from whom we have learned endless good and wonderful things. Where would we be without them? We also give thanks to the Lord for raising up godly teachers and families that would further instruct us in the way of truth. Without them, this book would not have been written. Our family would have been numbered as another casualty.

Oh, how much we needed vision, instruction and humility to find, trust and walk on God's noble path. God graciously, though slowly, began to show us His ways and His blessings began to touch our lives. "How blessed are those who trust in the LORD."

And lastly, we are so appreciative of all those who have lived in our home, sat in our classes or who have otherwise refined our perspectives, attitudes, hearts and the words in this book. A great thanks to you all for making a difference in this generation!

TABLE OF CONTENTS

Discipline and the Loving Use of the Rod

Setting Boundaries

Raising Godly Children

Developing Intergenerational Love

Regaining the Trust of Our Teens

Integrating God's Truth into our Families

Preface

Parenting God's way works!

That is certainly what we have found over twenty-plus years of parenting. Like many new parents, we thought that raising children would be easy and natural. After all, we loved them, didn't we? We were very mistaken and had so much to learn!

If we were not naturally good parents, then perhaps being a missionary and pastor would help us have great children? No. This was not the situation either. Our first children, though greatly loved, ended up being the objects of our parenting experiments. Sometime after the third child the Lord graciously began to help us understand His ways.

Principles and Practices for Biblical Parenting shares many things that we have learned from Him and applied to our lives over the years. One would think that they were mysterious truths hidden away. Instead, we have realized that we overlooked the most simple and plain truths of God's Word. Perhaps the principles were so broad or basic that we did not even observe what they had to do with the raising of our children.

We knew these truths. We would agree with them. Only we did not know how to apply them to our lives and parenting in particular. When God began to reveal how they related to our parenting styles and techniques, we could then start implementing these truths. This is what we call practices or applications. In other words, we discovered not only the knowledge of what to do but how to practically carry it out in hundreds of different situations. Instead of being frustrated, we could find solutions that worked!

Now with eight children, we realize how helpful it would have been if someone had told us at the beginning of our parenting experience all the things that we now know. There were no resources back when we started, and although there are many Christian parenting books out on the market, most of them have never integrated God's principles and practices together.

Each chapter is full of parenting principles and practical advice on how to nurture and handle one's children from toddlers up to the teenage years. We deal with the hard cases like tempers, picky eaters and "I don't want to!" We have even shown how to implement God's ways when one has a history of mistakes.

The last chapter is a bit different. That is our story, including our mistakes. If you want to read the last first, that is fine, but make sure you return to the beginning. As you allow God's Word to come into your heart and family more fully, you will be able to train up godly children, children who are thoroughly influenced by God and His Word. We are not ignorant of the troubles that surround us in this increasingly secular society. We show you situation by situation why secular advice fails and God our Designer's plan works.

Just start applying these principles and practices to your family one by one, and you will see how you too can have a godly, happy and loving family.

Rev. Paul Bucknell

August 2007

Chapter #1

GOD'S GOALS FOR THE FAMILY

Purpose: Help parents adopt God's plan for their family by increasing their understanding of God's purpose for the family in His kingdom and the parents' key role in shaping godly children.

A. God's Design for the Family

1) God's design is the best!

The inventor best understands the intricacies of his product. Sure he might explain the functions to others, but in the end only the designer really understands how the individual parts fit in with its complete purpose. When something goes wrong with my printer, I do not turn to my radio owner's manual for help. I look for the printer manual.

The same is true with the family. If we have questions on how to guide the family, whether it be the individual parts or the whole purpose, we turn to God's Word, the Bible, where our Creator Designer has clearly spoken everything we need to know about the family (2 Timothy 3:16-17).

In order for us to understand the family, we need to go back to its creation. God formed and fashioned both man and woman and then organized them into married units. God's blessing upon each of these couples would be seen as they bear forth new individuals that display resemblances of both the father and mother. These children would then not only look like their father and mother but also resemble God in whose image man and woman were made.

And God created man in His own image, in the image of God He created him; male and female He created them. And God blessed

them; and God said to them, "Be fruitful and multiply, and fill the
earth, and subdue it; and rule over the fish of the sea and over the
birds of the sky, and over every living thing that moves on the
earth" (Genesis 1:27-28).

The word 'godly' refers to those people or ways that are in
conformity to God's own desires. A godly family, for instance, would be
a family that is strongly characterized by God's plan and purpose. An
ungodly family has little regard for God's ways.

God encouraged this process of establishing a godly world by
commanding the couples to be fruitful and multiply. This in turn would
create what we now know as societies, cultures and nations. With the
entrance of sin into the human race, man and woman needed not only
have children but needed to train them in God's ways if God's blessing
would spread.

God told us in the above verses that man was made distinctly
different from the other animals. Male and female human beings were
made in God's image. Man was designed to communicate with God
who is a spiritual being.

Man is more than his physical body. He has an invisible part[1] that
is comprised of heart, will, conscience. The heart is where desires
originate. The will is the part that makes decisions. The conscience
helps judge the rightness or wrongness of any given decision. Man also
is set apart from the animals by his self-awareness.

As God has a design for the individual human being, so He has
one for the family itself. Sometimes we are slow to obey God's Word.
We hear so much about caring for the physical or educational needs of
the child that we forget the importance of his or her inner or spiritual
needs. Let's see what a child's spiritual needs might be.

2) Understanding God's Design for the Family

God did not only form male and female individuals, but also shaped the
way that they interact with each other, both publicly and privately.
Their physical bodies largely dictate this interaction, but by no means
stops there. There are also inward desires, insights and needs that arise
in males and females that shape the way they want to relate to each
other. We can see how man and woman naturally pair off and want to
be married.[2]

These built-in differences are further constrained and focused by
the outward structure that God set over mankind. The need for the
oversight of parents makes them guardians, providers and instructors.

The social structure for marriage and family did not need to be explained to Adam and Eve. God inserted significant words early in the scriptures to help mankind affirm that these innate desires were to function within the marital and family bonds. "For this cause a man shall leave his father and his mother, and shall cleave to his wife; and they shall become one flesh" (Genesis 2:24). The Lord carefully designed marriage and family to accomplish His overall good purposes.

The family serves a crucial part in God's plans for His kingdom. God communicates, preserves and further expands His holy influence through the strong family network. The home is the place where His truths are lived out and taught. By visiting a Christian family, one should be able to gain a good glimpse of God's goodness, love, order, communion, provision and law.

Pause for Reflection:
Name three things a person would understand about God and His ways by staying with your family for a week.

3) A Brief History of the Family

God created the first family with Adam as its head and Eve as his helpmate. This couple became the first family and the origin of all the other families on earth. Adam, the male, was responsible for the decisions made in the family. When he made wise decisions, his family prospered. When he chose to disobey God's rules, his family and all the families originating from him were seriously impacted.

> *Therefore, just as through one man sin entered into the world, and death through sin, and so death spread to all men, because all sinned (Romans 5:12).*

Adam's children, then, not only inherited a physical and invisible likeness to their parents, but also a sin nature (a tendency to go against God's way). Furthermore, man's intimate relationship with God was broken. It would seem that God could no longer accomplish His purposes through man, but God did not give up. He could still use His original design to accomplish His purposes. Not only does the Lord restrain evil through the family but even can develop His plans for the world at large through the family.

We begin to see God's plan take shape in Genesis 12 when God started a new family. From the then existing chaotic and rebellious society, God chose a man and his descendants through whom His holy purpose would be preserved and multiplied. God chose Abraham to leave the world he was so familiar with and go where He appointed him. Abraham was not perfect, and yet God was able and willing to use him and his descendants to bring great blessings to the world. Throughout history God has used many families as a platform to expand His holy and good purposes.

Job, Moses, Samuel, Ruth and David are just a few names that remind us of God's ability to use families despite their flaws to strengthen His kingdom. Despite these flaws, however, God used one of these godly families to bring Jesus Christ His only begotten Son into the world. This righteous couple, Joseph and Mary, lived and taught God's Word to Jesus. Later Jesus would mightily use what He had learned as a child to relate to God and to teach many others. God made a new family through Jesus and called it the church. God the Father was so intent on expanding His 'new' family that He sacrificed His own Son so that others like us could be adopted into His family as His children and live out His ways.

> *But as many as received Him, to them He gave the right to become children of God, even to those who believe in His name* (John 1:12).

God has clearly instructed both the church and the family on how to succeed in life and carry out His purposes. Without strong and godly families, the church and society will be weak. When the families are strong, then Christ can develop His wonderful plan for the church. God also used individuals such as Daniel, but we should remember that they also were part of a family that God used to shape that person. God has given us His Holy Spirit and Word by which we can develop godly families and churches. With God's Word in our hands, we can no longer say that God did not tell us how to produce godly families. We will expand on how this works out in the pages that follow.

Pause for Reflection:
What is needed to make a strong and godly family? What are one or two things that your own family needs so that God can better use your family for His purposes?

B. God's Way to Rescue the Family

1) God Can Help Any Family!
God astonishes us by the way He chooses to help our broken families. He combines His wisdom, power and grace to lift a family up and cause His good purpose to be accomplished through them. We hardly know

all of God's plans, but we appreciate how He helps us improve our lives as we determine to work along with Him.

Most families do not have ideal starting situations. When a parent, however, determines to carry out God's purpose, we start to see the wonderful effect God's Word has on the family. What used to be a problem now becomes an opportunity to see God's amazing grace. Timothy, for example, did not have a believing father. His mother was a Jew and his father was evidently an unbelieving Greek. God's grace, however, still shone brightly through the influence of his mother and grandmother. What is it in the following passage that Paul expected Timothy to possess because it was in his mother and grandmother?

> *For I am mindful of the sincere faith within you, which first dwelt in your grandmother Lois, and your mother Eunice, and I am sure that it is in you as well (2 Timothy 1:5).*

This 'sincere faith' was more than words. It was a living faith through which Timothy walked in the presence of God Almighty. When God's Word is lived out, then God's Word has great effectiveness. The same is true with any of our families. Parents have a great impact on their children. When they turn to the Living God, God begins to help their whole family. Or even as in the situation of Timothy's mother, when she set her heart on obeying God, God marvelously worked.

My wife and I are humbled by our mistakes. We see the emotional and behavioral scars from our poor parenting in the lives of our children. We teach parenting seminars and write books so that others do not need to waste twenty years making mistakes on their children! We have had to repent, restudy God's Word and more consistently conform our lifestyle to that of the Lord.[3]

This is, of course, a process. We are still going through it. However, humble hearts persistently seeking help from the Lord greatly speed up this process of learning. Later in the book we will share more of our personal journey.

The key thought here, though, is that God starts where we are at and really desires to work with us and our problems to get us and our children to where we should be.

2) **Problems Creating a Godly Family**

Some Christian parents might think of how they have tried so hard to be good parents and yet are frustrated with the results. Through these chapters we will share important biblical principles that will help correct those situations. There are many difficult situations and questions that parents want help with. By His grace we will teach step by step how God's truths touch on many of these key issues.

One person recently asked about personal evangelism, "What do you say to the non-Christian who says that Christianity was 'his parents' thing and not his?" The question points us to a major problem Christian families are facing. Many Christian parents think they are doing a good job of parenting when they verbally instruct their children to what they should and should not do. The problem is that truth is not primarily passed on through spoken instruction but on how their parents live out their lives.

These young people are not following the Lord because they have found nothing attractive in their parents' lives. Many Christian parents are so influenced by the falsehoods of secularism that the glorious love of God is no longer seen in their lives. Young people reason, "If my parents had such a bad marriage, why should I get married?" They no longer believe the power of the Gospel. They have in a sense been 'de-evangelized' by their parents. Of course, there are other factors, but I have heard young people commonly note this problem.

This means that Christ in His glorious fullness was missing from the home. Wherever we find Jesus in the New Testament, the people flocked to Him so that they could know Him and listen to His teaching.[4] We want to make the home a place our children love to be: a place where God's love, care and forgiveness is so evident, a place they love to be.

Pause for Reflection:
Does your child like to be home with you? Do they tend to bring their friends home to share that love that they find at home with others?

3) 'Caught and Taught': The Problem & the Solution
We need to broaden our minds so that we can understand how basic truths and values are passed on to our children. Some rightly state that truths are 'caught not taught.'[5] This is getting at a significant truth which emphasizes the important impact parents' lifestyles make on their children. (We will expand on this below.) Note the following chart. Teaching and modeling both are key components to passing a love for God on to our children.

God's Word does indeed need to be taught to our children. Families should memorize and meditate on God's Word together. We must not leave our task of teaching God's love to others. Many parents have failed here. Both aspects, however, are needed. Timothy not only had a good example·in his mother and grandmother (see 2 Timothy 3:15) but also was trained with the holy scriptures.

Children imitate what they see their parents doing. If what the parents say is different from what they do, the children will often unconsciously imitate what they do. When children are older, they will not only notice this inconsistency but dismiss and even despise what they had been taught. This is a root cause to many problems in the family today.

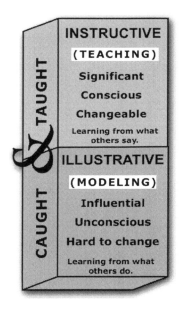

If the father obeys God, then everyone will know how important God is to his daily life. If he, however, looks very spiritual on Sunday but lives in contradiction to what God says through the week, his family will conclude that God is a religious God– for church only. They will think that God does not have much to do with their daily life.[6]

Let us describe why those things that a child sees become so important. Many of these thoughts will be further developed in the following lessons. We will focus on three kinds of learning: positional, relational and responsive. These three points describe how children unconsciously learn from their parents, that is, how they adopt the values of their parents or 'catch' the truth.[7]

(1) Positional Learning   (Responding to authority)

The parents shape a child's understanding of God by the way they live out their God-given roles of father and mother. This can largely be traced back to the fact that the parents are the child's only authority for the first years of his or her life. They learn how to respond to authorities from the way their parents respond to God.

- The father models the authority of God in decision and rule making. The child's first impression of authority comes from how his or her father expresses (or does not express) his authority and responds to the authorities in his life. This modeling of authority

17

largely shapes a child's attitudes toward God. For example, a child might see God as involved in his life or distant from him.

- The mother models the gentle and caring attitudes of God. The child learns how one in control can be strong and forthright as well as tactful, kind and loving.
- The husband by the way he loves his wife shows the way someone in authority loves and cares for those who are under his charge.
- The wife demonstrates how to get along with authority. She faithfully supports her husband even if she disagrees with him.[8] She models how to respect authority.

Positional learning	Relational learning	Responsive learning
Parents respond to authority	Parents react to outside world	Parents handle their child
They learn how to respond to authority.	**They learn how to relate to others.**	**They learn how to deal with others.**

Husbands and wives, then, through the way they interrelate to each other and how they as fathers and mothers treat their children play a foundational part in the building of a child's basic life assumptions. This training starts at a very early age even before the child can talk.

Pause for Reflection:

Many children think of God as distant and uncaring. Could this be because their father has never opened up and shared his life with his children? Does God really like to talk to His children? (See Genesis 3:8). How is Dad involved in the lives of his children in your home?

(2) Relational Learning (Relating to others)

The child also learns how to react to life's circumstances by watching the way his parents respond to the outside world. It matters little what the parents say. The child knows what the parent believes by what his father and mother do. If the life model contradicts the words, the children will ignore the words. Let us look at several of the many scenes that shape the lives and attitudes of our children.

- How does Daddy respond when someone treats him badly? Does he forgive or try to take revenge?
- How does Mommy react to situations that she does not like and cannot control? Does she trust God or worry and complain?
- Is Daddy content with what he has? Does he have to buy many things to be happy?

- Does Mommy change what she might do or say because of what people might say or think? Or does she fear the Lord?

When a child sees God's Word lived out, he or she gains that same faith and understanding on how a righteous life ought to be lived out. This does not make the child a Christian, and yet, he or she becomes comfortable with the wholesomeness of the truth. They see the sweetness of the Christian's trust in God and desire that peace and way of life more than what the world offers.[9] This is what is called relational learning, but there is one more significant way children learn that we would like to discuss.

(3) Responsive Learning (Cultivating morals)

Thirdly, the child learns by the way his parents deal with him. This would include a mother's care for her young child but also the way the father cares for his child. The way a child is handled strongly influences the way a child perceives what is important in life, what is right or wrong. This is where a child learns values.

- What does Mommy do when the baby cries? Does she always pamper the baby or sometimes allow the baby to cry when he or she is only seeking attention?

- What does Daddy do when the baby interrupts Daddy and Mommy's time with his cute antics? Does Daddy forget about Mommy and play with the child or prioritize his relationship with his wife and explain how he will later play with the child?

- What does Mommy do when the baby exasperates her? Does she shun the baby or patiently and kindly deal with him?

> **God designed it so that those who care most for the child should care for the child.**

- What does Daddy do when his son is in a stubborn fit? Does he give in and bribe the child to quietness or calmly sit out the 'storm'?

The child is unconsciously learning many things even from the time he or she is an infant. This is the most important reason parents should care for their little ones themselves. Many parents sincerely believe that children do not learn things when they are small. On the basis of this belief they send their children off to nursery care or far away with others to be raised. They could not be more wrong. God designed it so that those who care most for the child (the parents) should care for the child.

Successful parenting comes about when we combine right living with right instruction. We are cultivating more than the mind; we are shaping the soul or heart of the child. Parents are either creating in their children a distaste for what they say that they believe or a love for what they believe. Through this perspective we can see why God holds the parents responsible for the way they raise their children.

Pause for Reflection:

List one positive and one negative example that you as parents have set for your children.

4) The Pattern of Good Parenting

Children do not consciously reflect on what they are learning from their parents' behavior. They unconsciously observe and imitate their parents. Life's most basic training takes place early in life before children are able to read or write. This is the basic reason the tendency to shift the responsibility of child care from the mother to others can have dire consequences.

Young children should be observing and learning from how well their parents get along. They receive lots of special attention from their parents. This is God's purpose for making children grow up so slowly. He wants them not only to be protected but to learn many good things from their parents. Good parenting involves three basic steps.

- Understanding the truths of God. **(Knowing)**
- Applying God's truths to our lives. **(Modeling)**
- Instructing our children in God's Word.[10] **(Instruction)**

Our children will imitate us for good or for bad! If we do not set a good example of how to resolve personal conflicts, then our children will not know how to resolve personal conflicts. We simply will not have given them the tools, confidence (trust) and knowledge to solve life problems. We will not have given our children the faith that should have been instilled in them.

Parents for the most part rarely think about such matters. They typically think more about getting the child fed and his or her needed rest than the nurturing of their hearts and development of godly values. Let us look more clearly at the goals God has for our families.

Pause for Reflection:
Think about how you resolve conflicts with your spouse and others. How well will your child be able to resolve personal conflicts from observing the way that you handle them?

C. Learning God's Goal for the Family

1) God's Goals are My Goals!

Far too often we fail to accomplish any real long-lasting goals because we are crisis-oriented rather than God-oriented. Of course, we admire ourselves for trying to solve problems regarding the raising of our children, but these attempts fall far short of what God has in store for our families.

The problems that we try to solve more often than not revolve around our points of frustration. Our child cries and disturbs us so we look for a solution. We need to turn our minds and hearts all the way around until we focus on what God wants for our children and families. Look at His standards and the goals He has for our children. It helps if we ask, "What kind of young man or woman does God want of my child?"

Better approach to making goals.

Design

Goal: Live by design!

We can train all sorts of skills into our children, but none compare to the virtues a person needs: goodness, obedience, love, patience, respectful, kindness, self-control, gentleness and wisdom, etc. We might desire to pass on to our children the ability to make much money or run fast, but how tragic it would be not to train their heart. God has given us the needed resources to properly equip each child. Without proper training, possible blessings disappear and harsh consequences from God's judgment appear.

God wants to bless our children so that they will courageously, lovingly and faithfully serve Him and others in this world. God desires to use our families to expand His kingdom of love.

To help us along in thinking about what kind of children God wants us to raise, let us look at a few key passages and thoughts from His Word (the Bible). After all, our goal for our children must be shaped

God's Word provides clear direction for the child to follow.

by God's goal for our children. We do not know how He will specifically use each child, but we want to lay His spiritual foundation in each of their lives so that in whatever area God leads them, they will succeed and pass on His blessings to others.

It is interesting to see how the apostle Paul 'parented' Timothy. Paul often calls Timothy his son (1 Timothy 1:2). Perhaps, Timothy's own father had died at an early age. Whatever the case, Paul acted as a spiritual father to Timothy. Note the three goals listed in the instruction that the Apostle Paul gives to Timothy below.

> *But the <u>goal of our instruction</u> is love from a pure heart and a good conscience and a sincere faith (1 Timothy 1:5).*

In the section below we will focus on these three goals. Paul thinks it is crucial to input them into the believers' hearts. They also serve nicely to help us understand what goals parents should have for their children.

2) The Goal of Parenting

We take these three goals directly from 1 Timothy 1:5 above.

1. Cultivating love from a pure heart (Mark 12:29-31)
2. Developing a good conscience (Proverbs 1:7-8)
3. Forming a sincere faith (Galatians 5:22-23)

Each of them require a little contemplation in order to apply it to our own lives and our process of parenting.

(1) Cultivating love from a pure heart (Mark 12:29-31)

We have no greater purpose than to have our children be like Jesus. Jesus summarized His own heart when He summarized all the commandments in a few lines.

> *Jesus answered, "The foremost is, 'Hear, O Israel! The LORD our God is one Lord; and you shall love the Lord your God with all your heart, and with all your soul, and with all your mind, and with all your strength. The second is this. You shall love your neighbor as yourself. There is no other commandment greater than these" (Mark 12:29-31).*

What word in the above verses is repeated twice and guides us in how we are to respond to God and man? The word is love. We are to love God and to love man. Jesus calls them one commandment because they cannot be separated. Secular man insists on saying a person can love his fellow man without loving God. Jesus says one can love his neighbor only if he loves God.

For our love to be acceptable, it must come from a pure heart. Because God is one, then our devotion cannot be divided. All of our lives need to be spent on doing what pleases the Lord. All our heart, all our soul, all our mind and all our strength is needed to rightly love God and man. The pattern is obvious. A true love is an undivided one requiring all of our affection and purpose. This kind of love is willing to make the kind of sacrifices that are needed in life.

God made everything around us to be enjoyed. God provides for our needs and wants us to be thankful and content with what He provides for us. He wants us to use what we have to care for others. The Lord is desirous of our love. If we love Him, then we will obey Him. We need to point our children to the goal of loving God and man like Jesus did.

(2) Developing a good conscience (Proverbs 1:7-8)

Certain attitudes and perspectives about God are foundational to real learning. The attitude (heart) is the frame where the pieces of truth are placed. This is like the indentations in a Chinese Checker board. They provide a way to set the marbles in order. If there is no order, there are no rules and no game. Proverbs 1:7-8 give us a clear picture of how a good conscience is developed.

> *The fear of the LORD is the beginning of knowledge; fools despise wisdom and instruction. Hear, my son, your father's instruction, and do not forsake your mother's teaching (Proverbs 1:7-8).*

The foundation of a good conscience is the fear of God. The fear of God is more than knowledge. It is the way a person perceives God's true being. Without this spiritual knowledge, our children will not be able to gain the wisdom and instruction necessary for godly living.

Many people believe this fear is not healthy. The fear of the Lord, however, is good and necessary because the God who constantly monitors our lives is real. If God was different than He states or nonexistent, then this fear would not be necessary. But since He is true, then it behooves us to live in light of Him. A fear of gravity helps protect children near a cliff because gravity will bring a child to his death if he goes over the edge. And so, a fear of God helps shape a child's life so that he can live wisely and escape God's judgment.

Children will have a good conscience when they fear God because of two reasons:

1. God's standards will be inscribed on his conscience. He fears God rather than man. God is everywhere so no matter what a child does or where he is, he is compelled to do what is right.[11]

2. A person who fears God is more apt to listen to his conscience. Even when he does wrong, he is still affected by that inner voice. For example, when he does wrong, he is willing and even desirous of putting things right. He is uncomfortable with the guilt. He is concerned with the consequences that God would bring. So those who fear God are wise because they tend to avoid guilt by simply obeying first and are willing to seek forgiveness when guilt has occurred.

The fear of the Lord can be described as an attentive and obedient spirit before the LORD. A person who fears the Lord is aware of the importance of God's commands and desires and so conforms his life to them. A person who fears the Lord allows God's thoughts and purpose to influence what he thinks, does and says. The absence of the fear of the Lord means he does not allow those things to shape his life. He fears no consequence for disobeying God. A person's fear in the Lord is something that can grow or diminish depending on the person's faith.

Parents are to cultivate this fear of the Lord in the lives of their children. We are told how to do this in the very next verse. "Hear, my son, your father's instruction, and do not forsake your mother's teaching" (Proverbs 1:8). God has made the parent the means by which the child gains his or her perception of God and the world. Even Moses, God's great prophet, was nursed by his God-fearing mother during his early years.[12] One can imagine she prayed a lot for Moses and taught him God's ways before releasing him to Pharaoh's daughter.

The way a parent responds to the Lord will greatly influence the child. If the parent fears the Lord, then the child will imitate them in this matter. If not, then the child will not care about God's will. The child will esteem his or her own ideas as more important. Instilling the fear of God into our children is the greatest protection our children will have in this devilish secular world. The world teaches them that their own desires and ambitions should be the motivation to decision making.

Pause for Reflection:
The question rightly deserves asking, "What are we passing on to our children?" How can we pass this fear of God on to them? Have we as

parents really learned to live in the fear of God? List one situation where your child has observed you fearing the Lord. For example, you withstand peer pressure or refrain from doing something to please God.

(3) *Forming a sincere faith (Galatians 5:22-23)*

Parents also should cultivate a sincere faith in their children. A sincere faith in God produces what Paul calls the fruit of the Spirit. These things reflect the simple but genuine faith one has in God. Without faith, none of this fruit would be possible. They depend on our faith in God and our trust in His goodness given to us.

> *But the fruit of the Spirit is love, joy, peace, patience, kindness, goodness, faithfulness, gentleness, self-control; against such things there is no law (Galatians 5:22-23).*

Those who are brought up in God's ways are confident, because they understand how they should rightly relate to God, others and the creation around them.

➢ They are **loving** because by faith they believe others are important and made in God's image.

➢ They are **joyful** because they know that God their Father wonderfully watches over them.

➢ They are **peaceful** because they are confident of God's presence in all sorts of difficult circumstances.

➢ They are **patient** because they trust that God will, in His time, care for all their needs.

➢ They are **kind** because they pass on God's grace and mercy as they were shown in Christ.

➢ They are **good** because they reflect God's goodness in the kind way they treat others.

➢ They are **faithful** because they consistently honor God by imitating God's unchanging good ways to others.

➢ They are **gentle** by rejecting acts of manipulation so that they can tenderly satisfy the needs of others.

➢ They are able to exercise **self-control** because they have learned by faith to rule over their passions.

The more we learn God's ways, the more desirable they are. There are many things that need to be learned about raising our children, but we cannot, dare not, forget God's purposes in what He can do through parents who are keen on raising children His way.

Biblical parenting is simply taking the very best things and passing them on to our precious children. Our goals are high but obtainable. Where they cannot obtain these high principles, we kindly show them their need for Christ. There they discover the fullness of God's love and the power of His Spirit.

3) The Focus on the Heart

God is not merely concerned with modifying the outward behavior of a child. He is concerned with those things that shape who the child is and why the child does certain things. In short, God is concerned with the heart. God expects parents to properly cultivate the love, conscience and faith of their children. We must reject a superficial perspective of parenting that only focuses on the development of certain skills or providing for their physical needs. They are important but fall far short of God's goals for our children. This is the world's common approach to parenting which results in a multitude of sad stories.

If God gave you a way to rightly train the heart of your child, would you not take that opportunity? Through these chapters we will show you how to implement that kind of training, but first we encourage you to make a commitment to do your very best to raise your children with a heart for God. Below is a response form allowing you as parents to commit to properly training your children. As the training continues, you will increasingly understand what practical steps you need to take to carry out this commitment. This commitment will give you a firm foundation upon which to apply all that you learn.

One evening, our family was sitting down together in our living room for family devotions. That night our Bible study was on Christ's royal law of love, "Treat others as you would want to be treated." I asked if anyone kept the law of love that day.

Our little six year-old, named Kathryn, raised her hand and explained. That afternoon she had come home from a friend's birthday party where she got many take-home treats. She had shared her treats with her brothers and sisters (in a large family that is not a small feat!). And indeed, I had seen her siblings especially happy because she had shared her special treats with them during their playtime. Our home was especially happy that day because a little girl got a picture of what it was to be like Jesus.

Pause for Reflection

From reflecting on the above teaching, write down the spiritual goals you want to have for your children. Make sure you discuss them with your spouse. Remember to pray about why you want these goals.

Your Commitment

Sign your name below if you are willing, by His grace and power, to train your children to be like Jesus.

Father: _____

Mother: _____

Summary

All training takes place at home whether we realize it or not. We might be training them for good or for bad, but we **are** training our children. Parental training instills values, attitudes, responses and a general outlook on life in the lives of our children. Home is the training ground for life and in many cases for eternity.

Whatever we pass on to our children, good or bad, is what we will reap. We must constantly ask, "What are we imparting to our children? Do we like the results of what we see?" Many of us have not done very well. In fact, we might be tempted to give up because it seems too late. It is not.

Fortunately, by God's amazing grace, He can change us and therefore change our children. We will need to speed ahead by improving our knowledge of His Word, more intently obeying Him and carefully instructing our children. Our children are looking to see if our beliefs make a good difference. If we model it for them, they find it hard to resist. God's love is always glorious and desirable. We only need to kindly explain the change in our own lives and live out consistently godly lives.

Parenting Principles & Practices

- God has a plan for how parents are to raise their children.

- God largely uses parents to train these children for His purposes.

- God directs parents in the needed training of their children through His Word and the Holy Spirit.

- Young children learn through what a parent says but even more so through what a parent does.

- God wants to train the child's heart through positive instructions in the Bible.

- The ultimate goal for each of our children is that they be like Jesus Christ.

Parenting Questions

1. What place does the family have in God's kingdom today? Why?

2. Why don't many children of Christian parents follow the Lord?

3. What does the phrase 'caught not taught' have to do with parenting?

4. Where do children gain their primary understanding of God?

5. What are the three steps to good parenting?

6. What then is God's goal for our children? Why?

Notes from Chapter #1

---

[1] This invisible part of a human is called a soul. To be fair it is differently understood, but the scripture helps shape our understanding of its operation.

[2] It is true that many individuals are so disillusioned by the troubles of their parents' interaction that they are willing to consider alternatives other than marriage. They simply do not want to repeat such horrible situations. The willingness for man and woman to remarry shows how powerful the God-given physical and emotional set of desires shape people's lives.

[3] It is difficult to share of our failures. When we openly admit our failures to others, including our children, not only do we make ourselves accountable, but we are able to encourage others on how God has through His grace enabled us to conquer every little sin that mars our lives. This is the way to model repentance for our children and show them how to deal with failure.

[4] We recognize that many of Jesus' so-called followers had ill-motives. This reminds us of the great need for regeneration. More will be said about the need of our child's conversion at a later point.

[5] The phrase "caught not taught" is a phrase that means children learn more from what they see rather than from what they hear.

[6] This no doubt is one of the many roots to the acceptance of modern secularism.

[7] Parents convey poor values as well as the good values based on truths. If what they pass on is inconsistent, then the foundations laid for the lives of their children will be weak. We use 'truth' to describe the positive things they are learning which is consistent with how God describes it in the scriptures. God the Father reveals His Word. Jesus Christ modeled it and the Holy Spirit instructs us.

[8] The wife needs to submit to her husband 'in the Lord.' This means wherever the Lord has not clearly instructed otherwise in His Word, she must follow and support her husband's decisions.

[9] This love for the things of God makes a child very receptive to God Himself and His truths. This is the best thing a parent can do for his child. I recently asked my Dad if Grampy could have improved on things. Even though they lived in very difficult situations such as the Great Depression and he often had to be away from home, my Dad said that Grampy could not have done things better. "He was a good father." This kind of testimony is life-impacting.

[10] Instruction includes correction. This requires for the parent to insist on the obedience of their children. Sometimes parents must use more than words to enforce their instructions. Through correction children learn how important are the things which we believe and teach. Children interpret the absence of correction as confirmation that the issue at hand is of little or no real importance.

[11] Of course, man will at times and to different degrees fight his conscience. As parents strengthen the conscience by instruction and reminders, the conscience has more control over the child and by the Spirit of God helps lead the child to Christ.

[12] This is affirmed over and over again in the scriptures. Note how Ephesians 6:1-3 convincingly connects obedience with a child's well being. "Honor your father and mother (which is the first commandment with a promise), that it may be well with you, and that you may live long on the earth."

Chapter #2

ONE GREAT TEAM: DAD & MOM

Purpose: Build a scriptural perspective of the responsibility, need and ability for husbands and wives to work as teammates to produce godly children.

A. Great Teammates

When we hear the word 'team,' our minds tend to think of a sport's team. We rarely think of the husband and wife as teammates. And yet, God has designed the husband and wife to be the best teammates possible.

Let us think for a moment what makes a good team. A good team functions well together. They like being together. They work as one. They have a common goal. This sounds like a good marriage to me!

KINGDOM MATH
$$1 + 1 = 1$$

But you might be a bit distracted by wondering why we are discussing marriage in chapters about parenting. A young child's world is bound up in what he sees at home. They know of no other world. As an infant, they do not understand the implications of employment, neighbors or even church. They only recognize a few voices, that of Dad and Mom, siblings and maybe grandparents. They do not know the difference between good or bad, tall or short. They certainly do not appreciate all the pretty clothes they get dressed up in as a little baby! The parents are the child's world.

The parents have an enormous influence for good or bad on their children. In this chapter we will provide a detailed explanation of how the husband/wife relationship strongly influences the child. As your marriage improves, your family will get better. Because of this, we would like to make some suggestions for improving this teamwork between husband and wife especially as it impacts the family. Since the success of a child's training is dependent upon his parent's solid marriage, then we should expect that certain parenting problems will resolve themselves when the husband and wife work together in harmony.

My wife and I remember the first time we heard this. One of our sons was being startled awake each night by terrible nightmares. His loud screaming also awakened us. Of course, we would scramble down to his room to see what was wrong. We did not know how to resolve this. The couple giving us parenting advice at that time suggested that we as husband and wife should spend time with each other in front of our children.[1]

Linda and I typically spend about one hour together later on in the evening after the children go to bed reviewing our lives and praying. When we reviewed our situation, however, we discovered that our children rarely saw Linda and I sit down together in discussion mode. We deliberately met late in the evening to have an undisturbed time together! However, we saw wisdom in this couple's advice, took up this challenge and started spending ten minutes together (not long) in front of the children several evenings each week.

During this time, the children tried to divert our attention from each other to themselves, but we were forewarned of this possibility. We followed our instructor's advice and simply explained this was Daddy and Mommy's time. We would talk or play with them later. Within a week's time our boy's problem solved itself. One might wonder whether this was a coincidence, but we can assure you it was not. When the nightmares made a reappearance, we started wondering what was the problem. Guess what the problem was? Right! We stopped having Daddy and Mommy time in front of them. Right away we started meeting again in front of the children, and our boy's nightmares disappeared. It was wonderful to sleep through the night.

Why did our talking together in front of our children solve such an odd and peculiar situation? We will look at this more closely.

Think through your last week's schedule. How much time did you as husband and wife spend together talking in front of your children? Television time does not count.

B. Biblical Teaching on Marital Oneness

The husband and wife team spirit is based on the oneness God established in marriage. Many couples have been disappointed with marriage because they founded their marriage on romantic notions. Every couple, though, has the opportunity to focus on this oneness. Unfortunately very few do.

Oneness is a biblical teaching that strongly affects marriages and families. God revealed His plan to humanity. One will find distortions of this teaching in the world (and sometimes unfortunately in the church), but the clear teaching comes from God's Word. When speaking about the origin and nature of marriage, we must turn to the early chapters of Genesis to see what God said soon after He created man and woman.

> *For this cause a man shall leave his father and his mother, and shall cleave to his wife; and they shall become one flesh (Genesis 2:24).*

Genesis actually says, "They shall become one flesh." The word 'they' refers to Adam and Eve, the world's first two people, but it is true of any man taking a wife in marriage. Jesus' own reflections on this teaching help further emphasize the concept of oneness and teammates.

> *And He (Jesus) answered and said, "Have you not read, that He who created them from the beginning made them male and female, and said, 'For this cause a man shall leave his father and mother, and shall cleave to his wife; and the two shall become one flesh'? Consequently they are no longer two, but one flesh. What therefore God has joined together, let no man separate" (Matthew 19:4-6).*

Instead of 'they' Jesus describes them as 'two.' "The two shall become one flesh... They are no longer two, but one flesh. ...What therefore God has joined together, let no man separate." Marriage is the ultimate super glue where there is no longer any division of the original two objects. They have been fused together for life.

This 'oneness' concept is built into marriage, but we need to allow this fact (truth) to influence and shape how we think about each other and ourselves. For example, since the couple is one, they should stop thinking of themselves as two separate individuals with independent lives. In Christian tradition this has resulted in the practice of a wife giving up her family name to take on the husband's surname. I remember when we first got married. We delighted in giving up our own bank accounts and forming one joint account. I can still see the gleam in the eyes of my wife when she signed some checks using her new name.

Pause for Reflection:
Do you think of yourselves as one or two? What actual steps have you taken in your marriage that confirms this? Name one or two things.

Understanding Oneness
The changes, however, must go beyond this. This oneness concept must change how we perceive each other. For example, we must refuse to compete with each other. We are to live in cooperation with and support for each other. Have you ever heard one spouse saying to the other, "What about my time?" or "What about my ...?" This is the competitive perspective that counters the oneness spirit. The 'my' word reveals an incomplete belief in what God has stated about the couple's lives.

The Apostle Paul helps us understand this when he says that the husband and wife are like one body. When they care for each other, they are caring for their own selves.

> *So husbands ought also to love their own wives as their own bodies. He who loves his own wife loves himself; for no one ever hated his own flesh, but nourishes and cherishes it, just as Christ also does the church (Ephesians 5:28-29).*

Everything is fine
except when the body
doesn't cooperate!

Paul's idea of the body helps us think through different situations find ourselves in. He basically tells us what we all know: If something is part of your body, you will treat it well. If your finger hurts, you will take care of it. Because our spouses are considered to be part of our own body, we must actively conform all our thoughts, words and actions to building each other up. We purpose not to be competitive but complimentary.

34

This simple thought helps a lot when we think of the way we sometimes talk to our spouse.

C. Barriers to Marital Oneness

The world does not understand or accept this concept of oneness. They live as two independent units. Unfortunately, these thoughts and ways have crept into the church. Any thought, action or habit of dealing with oneself without regard to one's partner counters the design of marriage. Far too often conflict is accepted as normal; competition is common. Note how the signs of division contrast with the spirit of oneness.

- **Divided:** Marriage is a 50/50 arrangement. Each is responsible for his or her half.
  - ✤ **Oneness:** Marriage is 100/100 covenant.
- **Divided:** They live together for self-pleasure. No assurance of staying together.
  - ✤ **Oneness:** Built on commitment to each other's good.
- **Divided:** Each handles their own financial affairs.
  - ✤ **Oneness:** Joint accounts before God. "Our money."
- **Divided:** Argumentative. The louder and stronger one dominates.
  - ✤ **Oneness:** Each person graciously listens to the other.
- **Divided:** Struggle for leadership. There is no accepted leader.
  - ✤ **Oneness:** The husband leads under Christ's headship.
- **Divided:** The wife is treated as a servant rather than a teammate.
  - ✤ **Oneness:** The wife is a prized helpmate. The husband is convinced he cannot succeed without her.
- **Divided:** Disagreement on how to raise children.
  - ✤ **Oneness:** Discuss God's perspective with each other.
- **Divided:** Unresolved conflict causes distance between spouses.
  - ✤ **Oneness:** Confession, apologies and the restoration of affection and care is a common scene.
- **Divided:** Parents get a child involved in parental arguments.
  - ✤ **Oneness:** Parents calmly discuss issues apart from children.

Pause for Reflection:
Go through the above list and check which areas your marriage is divided or express oneness.

Expressions of Disunity:
Have you heard these thoughts expressed before?

"This is my money. I will do with it as I wish!"
"I do not care where you live."
"I'll do it my way; you do it yours."
"I need my own free time."
"I need a job to be fulfilled." (Wife)

When we have wrong concepts of marital 'oneness,' they will negatively affect the way we live, think and make decisions. Let us look at four of these distortions in more detail.

Distortion #1
❖ **(1) Oneness is equivalent to physical union.**
Some people have not clearly thought through this teaching on oneness and think that oneness only describes physical union. Jesus, however, clearly teaches that 'oneness' describes a couple's marital state rather than their joint activity. Even when a couple is apart from each other, one in Canton and the other in Pittsburgh, the two are still one flesh. They are not like a zipper that can be undone but like two welded pieces where the two items are forged into one.[2] A Christian marriage is fused together by God Himself, thus forming a 'triunity.'[3]

Distortion #2
❖ **(2) Oneness in marriage does not apply to unbelievers.**
Some Christians wonder whether this principle of oneness is applicable to the marriage of unbelievers. If marriage is a spiritual matter, does a couple's oneness depend upon their faith? No. God is involved in the affairs of everybody all the time. If two people marry, they are still bound by the spiritual laws God built into the world whether they acknowledge them or not. Unbelievers might have more difficulty carrying out this oneness, but they are still accountable to this standard as all are. To the degree that they live by it, they are blessed.

Distortion #3
❖ **(3) Marriage brings automatic blessings.**
Others have asked, "Why is it that some non-Christian marriages are better than Christian marriages?" We sadly concur that this sometimes

happens. Jesus explained this phenomenon in His closing words of the Sermon on the Mount.

> *Therefore everyone who hears these words of Mine, and acts upon them, may be compared to a wise man, who built his house upon the rock. And the rain descended, and the floods came, and the winds blew, and burst against that house; and yet it did not fall, for it had been founded upon the rock. And everyone who hears these words of Mine, and does not act upon them, will be like a foolish man, who built his house upon the sand. And the rain descended, and the floods came, and the winds blew, and burst against that house; and it fell, and great was its fall (Matthew 7:24-27).*

God is not mocked. Whatever a person sows, this he also reaps (also see Galatians 6:7). To the degree anyone builds his life, marriage and family upon biblical principles, they shall be strong and flourish. On the other hand, to the degree believers or unbelievers neglect applying biblical principles to their marriage, their marriage will be plagued with problems.

God has designed marriage for our good. As we observe marriage principles that follow His design then God's blessing and goodness pervade our lives. Once we better understand this connection between God and His truths, the more we are apt to practice them.

This truth is seen in reverse too. Any couple that insists on fighting and arguing for their own rights and preferences will suffer. Their marriage will turn ugly. Their children will greatly suffer. They are countering God's truth of oneness.

Distortion #4

❖ (4) **Living together is oneness.**

Increasingly, couples are living together without getting married. This wreaks havoc on the couple and any children. First, we need to realize they are not 'one.' They are not fused together. The two are still the two.

This becomes very apparent when we analyze these situations. Marriage works because of the commitment based on the fact of oneness. 'Living together' is immoral because it is based on meeting one's own needs rather than the other person's needs. This lifestyle brings harm to children living in such situations.

Summary

Other religions and philosophies have nothing like this Biblical truth to explain the state or character of marriage. Cultures might have traditions, but they cannot explain why these traditions are important except that they exist. Cultural teachings cannot survive the modern attack on marriage. The scriptures, however, explain how God has instituted oneness in marriage. This is a transcultural teaching. It affects every family in every nation. The oneness between the husband and wife then becomes a foundational truth for the family as it expands its influence by adding children.

D. Importance of Marital Oneness to Children

The parents' oneness lies at the foundation not only of your marriage but your family. The union is not to be broken or threatened. All the husband and wife's words and actions ought to confirm this fact. When this foundational truth is expressed in real life actions, the child can grow up in the confidence of love and security. The child should never need to wonder whether his parents hate each other or will separate from each other. Why is this oneness so important for the child?

The parents' life is the child's world. Any time the husband and wife start arguing, it is like two tectonic plates rubbing against each other in the world of the small child. An emotional earthquake happens. Fears arise.

In today's world, most small children know of other families who have experienced divorces. They link their parents' arguments with the possibility of divorce. So like little earth tremors, they sense something bigger is happening deep down that threatens their secure world.

When a child's father and mother are not acting in harmony, then the child's world begins to shake much like an earthquake.

After all, children's security does not come from the home or the world, but their parents' agreement to watch over them. They fear all that love and care will be gone. They do not know what to do when deserted and left on their own.

The child, who does not see the parents' commitment to oneness, can unconsciously develop certain odd behaviors in order to keep his parents from destroying his world. For the child, everything is at stake. They are willing to endure rather embarrassing situations like wetting the bed, screaming, stealing, etc., just to keep the parents together. It seems that they subconsciously think that if the parents focus on their own need (even though it is often extreme), then they will receive more attention from their parents.

Parents rarely connect their lack of oneness with the child's odd behavior. The solution in these cases is not to change the child but their own selves. The parents can make a big difference for good just by making a few changes toward having a harmonious home.

Pause for Reflection:
List one or two ways that you as a couple can improve your oneness. Include one way which enables your children to see that oneness.

E. Three Ways to Model Oneness

Instead of competitive living, God has designed husbands and wives to live in a complementary fashion. Good parenting comes through good marriages.[4] This is partly from the love and care given to the child but also because of the good training that is taking place. Chapter one has identified three general areas parents influence their children's lives through how they interrelate to others: positional, relational, and responsive. Below are three ways a good husband-wife relationship shows itself to be so vital to raising good and happy children.

(1) Opportunities for oneness in conversation
A couple has plenty of opportunities to express their oneness to their children through their words. Sometimes a husband or wife has a 'bad' day. The husband or wife becomes selfish, moody and thinking about his or her own wants and needs. Is there anything we can do during these times? Yes, there is!

We should be acutely aware of the temptation to become our mate's accuser. The word 'satan' actually means accuser. Once we have given into accusations, we are no longer supporting and building up our mate but tearing him or her down.

> *And the ... serpent of old who is called the devil and Satan, who deceives the whole world; he was thrown down to the earth...for the*

accuser of our brethren has been thrown down, who accuses them before our God day and night (Revelation 12:9-12).

Instead of turning against our spouses by focusing on our suspicions, we need to determine to stand for them. We must live by faith in the fact of oneness rather than giving into the spirit of division. Refuse to focus on your emotional response and instead deliberately focus on how God would want you to build up your spouse.

This does not mean that we cannot mention our concerns to our partner or share the pain that we are suffering because of them. Keeping those things hidden can be dishonest and unhelpful. The problem is that we often use prideful and selfish words that lead to arguments. Arguments compound the evil by adding maligning words. Paul reminds us, "To malign no one, to be uncontentious, gentle, showing every consideration for all men" (Titus 3:2).

Listen to the difference between these two responses.

"Are you up to that (problem) again? I knew you were not being honest with me!"

"I know you are going through this (problem) again. If you would like to talk to me about it, please let me know. I really care for you."

One approach fosters good communication; the other shuts it off. We need to remind ourselves often of our heart commitment to oneness. That way we can stay supportive and keep all our words and actions affirming our oneness.

Pause for Reflection:

Do you and your spouse act as one or two? How well do you respond when your spouse becomes inward and selfish?

Some of us have learned to quickly accuse people without knowing it. More likely than not, we have learned to accuse and be judgmental of our spouses from how our parents responded to each other. This includes the words we say, the intensity of voice, shouting, facial expressions and even actions like hitting.

Children will pick up this divisive spirit from us. After all, if we show them how to reject or shout at someone who has done something that displeases us, then they will tend to follow our pattern. We are in essence training them to respond this way.

Pause for Reflection:

During your last marital argument, did you say any words against your partner? If you have, did you apologize and seek forgiveness to restore what ground was lost?

(2) **Opportunities for the husband to love**

The child learns how to love through his parents' interaction with each other, especially in the way that his father cares for his mother. A close, warm, loving relationship expressed through Mom's tender touch enables the child to know of the nature of love and gentleness. This love stems from a special relationship depicted in Paul's following words.

> *But we proved to be gentle among you, as a nursing mother tenderly cares for her own children. Having thus a fond affection for you, ... you had become very dear to us (1 Thessalonians 2:7-8).*

The husband's constant show of love toward his wife, however, is the place where the child can see the real strength and power of love in a world of sin and selfishness. This love flows from a commitment to each other rather than through mutually happy feelings. This commitment to oneness starts shining when things get rough, just like rocks that get polished by tumbling over other rocks. God commands the husband to love his wife even when she is unlovely and unwelcoming. The husband's own model is Christ who died for a people who deserted Him when He needed help the most.

> *Husbands, love your wives, just as Christ also loved the church and gave Himself up for her (Ephesians 5:25).*

The wife needs extra encouragement and tenderness because her emotions get wrapped up in her thinking and through the changes her body goes through monthly. Peter says it this way. "You husbands likewise, live with your wives in an understanding way, as with a weaker vessel, since she is a woman; and grant her honor as a fellow heir of the grace of life, so that your prayers may not be hindered" (1 Peter 3:7). Husbands, your commitment to your wives is going to be tried, severely tested in some cases. You need God's faithfulness so that you can be kind even when your spouse is not being kind to you.

As a husband, I have found a little exercise that helps me a lot. I tell my wife that I love her no matter what. Those are words I say, sometimes to her but often to myself, but I affirm the commitment behind these words deep in my heart. "I am here for her, even through the 'down' days." After this, I take practical steps to love her and maintain that constant stream of love. By God's grace I do not get irritated with her. I speak graciously. I am kind. Deep in my heart, I have resolved to love my wife no matter how terrible the storm might get. My heart is at perfect peace when I do this. I deny the temptation to treat us as two. I live by the facts—we are one. My wife has always been grateful for this!

The husband should never underestimate how important his wife is to him. She is his valuable teammate. He needs her both as a companion as well as a helper to carry out his duties. His thrill of devotion to her is preserved by this concept that she is his invaluable asset. If lost, he just would not be the same.[5] He needs to keep her as a good team member.

We see this thought graphically portrayed in scripture. Adam is presented in a perfect world with everything going for him. God said that everything He made was 'good.' No flaws. In order not to be 'alone,' God created a helpmeet for him. "Then the LORD God said, 'It is not good for the man to be alone; I will make him a helper suitable for him'" (Genesis 2:18).

When the child sees this kind of love demonstrated in the home by his father, he is equipped with the faith necessary to love others in the world. A child's security is built on the devotion of the father to the mother and the mother to the father. This is the expression of oneness that should characterize every marriage. Children growing up in this atmosphere know that they can love others that are not nice or pleasant.

When the son is older, he will see the needs of others and go out of his way to help his brother or sister. Later on, he will go out of his way to help a neighbor or stranger. When married, he will use that same love to love his wife.

I remember seeing the love of a church elder for his wife. He was greatly gifted and will be remembered for his giftedness. His compassion and care for his discouraged and depressed wife, however, became a beautiful example for the church on how to prioritize the need of the wife even though he had many church and work responsibilities. I can imagine how his daughters will naturally look for a man with love like that when they are old enough to marry.

Jesus patiently treated and cared for those around them despite their many problems. Fathers have the privilege of training this love into their children.

Pause for Reflection:
Evaluate your devotion as a husband for your wife. Would you be happy for your daughter to marry a man like you? How can you grow in your love for your wife?

(3) **Opportunities for the wife to submit**

Parents teach their children to obey them, but the spirit of obedience is largely learned through watching how the mother subjects or yields herself to her husband. Does she do what her husband says with pleasure or does she have a resentful spirit? The scriptures specially command the wife to submit to her husband, "Wives, be subject to your husbands, as is fitting in the Lord" (Colossians 3:18).

The Greek word used here for 'subject' means to yield to or put oneself under the control of. The wife is to subject her preferences to what her husband wants. This is not easy to do! The husband can be quite selfish at times.

God has designed both male and female in His image. They both are of value, and as a result, they are always to be treated respectfully. To establish the oneness, however, the Lord appointed the man as a leader. The wife serves as his helpmate. Although many question the advantages of this yielding, Jesus clearly displayed how to humble oneself in order to serve a greater good. Jesus gave up His preferences so that He could serve His Father (see Philippians 2:4-11). Jesus regularly sought His Father's will rather than His own, "I glorified Thee on the earth, having accomplished the work which Thou hast given Me to do" (John 17:4).

When the wife like Jesus humbles herself, she is ready to help the family wherever needed. I just heard a father thanking God for his dedicated wife who sacrificially gave herself to care for their family when they went through a time of sickness. It was touching to hear this prayer. Unfortunately, sometimes we see abuses on both sides, but when the husband is loving and the wife follows her husband's lead, we see them operating as one wonderful team.[6]

Your best friend is your spouse!

What do children learn from observing how their Mom responds to their Dad? Children observe from their Mom's good example that obedience is proper and good. They know that Mom is tired but still goes on and prepares a nice meal without grumbling.

Through a faithful Mom children learn how to live for the preference of others. Mom, no doubt, has her own ideas about things, but knows how to trust God with these matters. Children watch how the Lord is able to work out all these circumstances that Mom has trusted to Him. She is at peace. She is, after all, not pursuing her own will but God's. She believes God will hear her prayer and in time carry these things to fulfillment.

Any child who has seen this kind of faith in his or her Mom will be able to work with anyone. They have learned that they can sacrifice their own preferences for the sake of others. This is exactly the training that a child needs. Jesus modeled this for us as He carried out His Father's will.

Moms have their challenges of course, but by denying their own desires, they display oneness. Complaining, fussing, or stubbornly refusing to subject herself to her husband models disunity and disobedience. Bad attitudes quickly descend into the hearts of our children and can be seen in their reluctance to obey when it interferes with their activities. It also shows up in a complaining and whining spirit.

Pause for Reflection:
How much respect do you as wife show to your husband? Do you complain when serving your husband or find honor in your service as you fulfill your calling to God? If your husband does something that you disagree with, how do you respond?

Biblical Principles of Unity
In each case the husband and wife are asked to make a sacrifice of his or her own preference to get what God wants done. They are not after their own will but God's. They work as a team. They are, after all, a team living to do God's good will together.

Children learn many things through their parents. We have focused on the most important things that will ready them for real life. We realize that without Jesus Christ, many of these sacrifices are impossible. As the parents keep growing to be more like Jesus, the hope is that their children will see enough of Christ that they would desire to know and serve Him. After all, there is no better life.

The church is composed of 'one' body much like a husband and wife are one in marriage. The unity principles are the same (Ephesians 5:32). Note the apostle's comments in Philippians 2:2

Make my joy complete by being of the same mind, maintaining the same love, united in spirit, intent on one purpose (NASB).

Do make my joy complete--live together in harmony, live together in love, as though you had only one mind and one spirit between you (Philips Translation).

> • **Same mind** Unity of thought
>
> • **Same love** Equally devoted to the other's good
>
> • **United in spirit** Hearts bound together after Christ
>
> • **One purpose** Common goals and drive

Summary

God has established marital oneness: the two have become one. The parents' expression of oneness accomplishes two significant things as far as the child is concerned.

1) Development of Security

When the world of the child is secure, he can tend to other needs in life. Many seemingly unresolvable problems are avoided. The child is content and happy, whether rich or poor.

2) Development of Moral Character

The child is learning how to properly respond to others in a humble, loving and kind way. Through the example of his parents, he gains faith (i.e. confidence) that he can get along with people even in difficult circumstances. He does not need to get his own way to be joyful.

The world might be at war. Neighbors might hate each other, but when a child sees this oneness lived out before him in the lives of his or her parents, that child will stand out as a bright light in a very, very dark world.

Parenting Principles & Practices

- God establishes 'oneness' at marriage.
- A marriage will only be as good as this 'oneness' is lived out in word and action.
- Disharmony between parents causes great problems in children. Harmony benefits them.
- God gives commands in His Word to help parents maintain their marital oneness.

Parenting Questions

1. Where does the concept of the husband and wife as teammates come from?
2. Explain one of the distortions people have of this marital oneness.
3. How are children affected by the oneness that is or is not expressed by their parents?
4. What should a spouse do when their mate becomes selfish?
5. How does a husband's love shape a child for the world?
6. How does a mother's submission to her husband help a child get along with others?

Notes from Chapter #2

[1] We owe many thanks to the Ezzos and others for stimulating us to rethink our parenting practices.

[2] This oneness is very evident in the life of their children. With advanced understanding of human cells, we now know every child's cell gene coding is equally composed by both a father and mother. The husband and wife literally are fused into the life of a new person.

[3] This word 'triunity' is used to describe the idea of a couple who marries in the Lord. We see this concept in Ephesians 5 where the husband functions under the umbrella of the Lord. The wife in turn submits 'in the Lord' to her husband. The husband is mandated to love his wife as Christ loved the church.

[4] Some families face great difficulties. A spouse might have died or separation has occurred. These situations make it much more difficult to raise children. God, however, shows His special concern by His volunteering to be there to help the widow in need (Psalm 146:9; Proverbs 15:25). The parent, in these cases, should draw closer to God for His special help. The way that the parent draws close to God then becomes a special modeling relationship from which the child can learn.

[5] At times, in God's wisdom, He takes away one's spouse. At those times we can trust God for extraordinary grace and through our close times with the Lord show a spirit of oneness.

[6] Children are confused when there is a reversal of roles between the husband and wife. It has been observed that parental role confusion is linked up with homosexual tendencies in children.

Chapter #3

PARENTAL AUTHORITY

Purpose: Develop a scriptural perspective of the parents' responsibility to properly govern and care for their children.

- Who is in charge of your home?
- Who should be?

The answer to these two questions is often different. The parents will often say they are in charge, but in fact they have allowed the child to rule the home. The biggest problem, however, is not that the child has grabbed control of the family and has his parents meeting his every desire. What is worse is that the parents continue to put up with this revolt or are unaware that it is happening!

In this chapter, we will learn God's perspective of authority in the home. We will not only observe some very practical reasons why parents need to take charge of their families but provide the practical steps and cautions needed when restoring families back to God's order. Parents cannot properly raise their children without rightly understanding and using their God-given parental authority.

A. God's Way of Order in the World

What is authority? Authority is the right to lead, govern or rule. Authority has been passed down by God's decree to carry out His good purposes upon earth. In particular, He has given parents the authority to rule in the home to care for the family. God uses authority to bring order and justice to this world. He uses at least three kinds of authorities to do this:

➤ Government/law (Romans 13)
➤ Judges
➤ Parents

1) **Many people tend to reject authority**

Many people disdain and/or mistrust authority because they have seen excess or abuse. They cannot appreciate how authorities can protect real love and care. There are several possible personal reasons which help create this overreaction.

• She was hurt by someone in authority.
• He saw corruption or misuse of authority.
• A person selfishly used his authority.
• A hypocritical person said one thing but did another.

Although many people are suspicious of authority, it does not mean that one should simply discard it. The Bible is very clear on the importance of authority. In fact, as one looks more closely at this issue, he will see how authority, when rightly lived out, protects love. This is most clearly seen in how God reveals Himself in the scriptures.

2) **God is good!**

We need to understand God's perspective of authority. Look at how God describes Himself here in Exodus 34:6-7.

Exodus 34:6	Exodus 34:7
Then the LORD passed by in front of him and proclaimed,	
God's Compassion	*God's Wrath*
"The LORD, the LORD God, compassionate and gracious, slow to anger, and abounding in lovingkindness and truth; keeps lovingkindness for thousands, who forgives iniquity, transgression and sin;	yet He will by no means leave the guilty unpunished, visiting the iniquity of fathers on the children and on the grandchildren to the third and fourth generations."

We see both the compassion and wrath of God together revealed in this one passage. Even if we do not understand how they blend together, we dare not separate them. This is how God revealed Himself. Distorted images of God create wrong perspectives of life such as in parenting.

God regularly uses His authority in both the actual creation of the world as well as in its maintenance. Sometimes we hear that the God of the Old Testament is so unloving. This is because people have not carefully read the Bible and do not see how God's great love and patience perfectly blend with His authority. Think for a moment. What was the world that God made like? Did it reflect His anger, severity and meanness or joy, love and abundance? The world that God made was absolutely wonderful but His full majestic authority was embedded in it!

Let us look at what happened when man disobeyed the mighty Creator in the early chapters of Genesis. Did God destroy this dust-made rebel named man right away? No. We find that God chose to work patiently with man and in the end gave His only Son Jesus Christ to die for him so that he might enjoy His love, goodness and joy forever.

We are not saying that God does not express wrath. He does. The verses above confirm this. He is the absolute Judge. God goes to extra lengths to keep us from that judgment. That is love. Distortions in society occur when people either disregard authority or compassion. The family was designed to preserve both of these characteristics and thus bring further blessing into the world. The closer we model ourselves after God, the greater the blessings will flow into a family.[1]

3) **God shows His goodness through His authority**

God used His great and absolute authority to postpone judgment and bring mercy and grace. This is just what we need in our marriages and families. God has placed the parents to be in authority over their children so that they might receive the greatest good. Let us summarize this in four points.

- God is the Creator and therefore has the right and responsibility to govern or lead all of His creation including the people He has made.
- We do not like to be ruled and neither do our children. This is because of our sinful inclination to self-rule. We want to satisfy our own personal desires (i.e. selfishness) without respect to what God wants for our lives.

- God therefore sees fit to preserve His care for people by giving authority to parents to govern their own children to restrain their evil words, thoughts and behaviors.
- Parents therefore must use their God-given authority, love and wisdom to protect and care for their children. This includes both the restraining of evil deeds as well as the positive modeling of what is good, lovely and right.

4) **Biblical teaching on parental authority**

The scriptures teach about this authority that parents have over their children from two perspectives: (a) from the parent's perspective and (b) from the child's point of view.

(a) Father's Responsibility

The father is responsible to rightly govern and care for his children. The scriptures speak clearly of this. "And, fathers, do not provoke your children to anger; but bring them up in the discipline and instruction of the Lord" (Ephesians 6:4).

> *Just as you know how we were exhorting and encouraging and imploring each one of you as a father would his own children, so that you may walk in a manner worthy of the God who calls you into His own kingdom and glory (1 Thessalonians 2:11-12).*

Note the three things that fathers are supposed to do: exhort encourage and implore their children. The rule is given to the father; the mother is to support the husband in his rule. A verse from Hebrews points out another important aspect of parenting.

> *Furthermore, we had earthly fathers to discipline us, and we respected them; shall we not much rather be to the Father of spirits, and live (Hebrews 12:9).*

Parents are to govern their sphere of responsibility (the family and home) as God would. They are not only to bring instruction and correction but also to be patient and kind. They are responsible to do all they can to raise up godly children. Godly children by definition live God's way and serve others. They grow up to be men and women that devote themselves to God and serving others.

(b) Children's Responsibility

The fourth command of the Ten Commandments instructs children to honor their fathers and mothers. "Honor your father and your mother, that your days may be prolonged in the land which the LORD your

God gives you" (Exodus 20:12). If we are in any doubt, the Lord repeats this injunction repeatedly throughout the Bible. "Children, obey your parents in the Lord, for this is right" (Ephesians 6:1).

> *Children, be obedient to your parents in all things, for this is well-pleasing to the Lord (Colossians 3:2).*

The word to 'honor' is the same Hebrew word that means 'to be heavy' or 'to glorify.' In other words, what the parents say is to be considered most weighty or important by the child. The command assumes the parents' authority over their children and so gives them the responsibility to provide, guide, chastise, protect and equip them for life. Practically this means that at times they need to compel the child to certain actions.

When societies are at their best, there is much respect from younger people for their parents and the elderly. An evil age, however, is marked by disobedience. A child's defiance and despising of his parents' words reveal that the society and the children have degraded to a very low state.

> *But realize this, that in the last days difficult times will come. For men will be lovers of self, lovers of money, boastful, arrogant, revilers, disobedient to parents, ungrateful, unholy (2 Timothy 3:1-2).*

The fact is that even though a society or set of parents might tolerate this disrespect, nobody likes it. The scornful child insults others, disregards the needs of others and is arrogant. For this reason God sends judgment on people with such attitudes including children. God says, "The eye that mocks a father, and scorns a mother, the ravens of the valley will pick it out, and the young eagles will eat it" (Proverbs 30:17). If parents do not do their job of creating respect in their children, then God will restrain those children through more extreme methods.

God establishes the parents' authority to carefully watch over their children so that this disrespectful attitude is not cultivated.

(c) Three summary points

- A child is responsible to obey his or her father and mother.
- A father is charged with exhorting, encouraging, imploring and disciplining his child.
- A mother also has authority over the child and assists her husband in carrying out his responsibilities.

Pause for Reflection:
Think through your child's words and facial expressions. Does he or she respect you? Do you expect compliance? Do you receive it?

B. God's Order for the Home

God's ways are always best. We might see misconceptions and abuses of authority, but this does not mean authority should be done away with.

Try this short experiment. Think through which families you admire and which ones you do not.

Those parents that exercise proper authority over their children always get the winning points! To the degree that parents do not act according to their authority and responsibilities, the children become reckless, defiant and arrogant. Truly the solution is not to give up parental authority but to secure and maintain it.[2]

1) The need for parental authority

The father and mother need to exercise their authority to shape their children. Because they gained wisdom and knowledge through their years of experience, they know what is best for the child.[3] Their influence, instruction and correction all work together to produce a contented child. They are responsible to pass this instruction on to their children.

Those parents that have rightly used their authority with a sense of compassion will raise up the world's greatest people. These children are the ones devoted to bettering others rather than themselves. They respect government and other authorities and fit into society as responsible citizens.

2) What are we training our children to be?

Perspectives on authority are shaped into a child very early in life. More often than not, the parents are not even aware of the training that goes on.

Let us look at an example of a father who calls his little child to come, but the child runs in the other direction. The father might laugh because his child acted in a cute way by running away, but if the father does not catch the child and make him obey, the child is actually being encouraged and trained to disobey. Indeed, this time the situation might be totally harmless, but the consequences of not dealing with the child's disobedience are multiplied. The father has taught the child that his word is not to be taken seriously. The child basically finds permission to reject his father's right to rule his little life.

Similar problems surface when a parent is inconsistent, that is, sometimes enforces his authority and at other times does not. This inconsistency causes more disobedience and confusion into the family. When the parents disagree on how to raise their child, for example, this usually allows for inconsistent care for the child. The child shelters himself under the shield of the agreeing parent. Disobedience is allowed to permanently stay in the home. This also happens when parents agree on what to do, but because of laziness or busyness with their own lives, they neglect to properly govern their children.

Pause for Reflection:

Do you agree with your spouse on how to raise your child? What do you do when you disagree? What should you do to solve the problem?

The earlier God's perspective is established, the easier it is for both the parent and the child. Parents need to agree on how they will handle certain situations. They need to work together and act as one authority. Otherwise, they will look like two authorities and the child will play one against the other to get his own way.

The parents must decide what is best and enforce what is to be done. However, we should remember that consistent pre-toddler training helps avert many of the challenging tests that the toddler brings. Consistent training of the child when he is young will help him conform to his parents' instruction even when he is older.

Please do remember, even when we do what is right, the child still does have a sinful nature that seeks to express its own desires. We cannot completely restrain that nature from expressing itself, but surely we can constrain it.

3) Changing is not easy

If the parents have been indulging the desires of their children and not been exercising their authority over them, then they ought to realize that there is going to be war when new standards are implemented. The conviction of the parents to live God's ways will be tested, severely at first. This is no time for the parents to give in.

Even little toddlers and infants will rebel–testing the very standards the parents have instituted. They will demand their supposed rights to tell Dad and Mom what they want and when they want it. The first days of regaining control can be really terrible. I remember one incident before we started to learn these principles about spoiling our child (I forget which child). Linda was up all different times at night caring for our crying baby. She was exhausted. And yet, she couldn't but help tend to the baby's cry.

I told Linda that this was not right and decided that we would have a 'cry out' night. I volunteered to take the baby into another part of the house, and the baby and I would both camp out there. I would make sure that the baby was well cared for and endure the baby's manipulative cries. The baby did not like it; neither did I (or Linda upstairs)! Finally, the baby succumbed to her or his tiredness and fell asleep. The baby would test me again the next night, but with each successive night the baby's cry was shorter and less intense. Finally, within a few days, the baby slept through the night. This serves as an example of how important it is to endure the initial protest to gain the long lasting peace of God's design.

Pause for Reflection:
Are there any things that you think you ought to change in your home but fear the repercussions? Write them down along with the reasons you fear the change.

4) The Parent's Part
Here are a few things to pay attention to when implementing changes with your children. Remember that these instructions are related to age.

- Speak directly to the child face to face.
- Make him repeat to you the instructions that you just gave him.
- Make sure you are really going to carry through what you say.
- Do not forget to check and see if you are setting a good example.

There are other parental modeling influences that greatly affect the children. They have already been partially introduced. We also need them to help us understand how to properly relate to each other.

C. God's Design for Relationships

Respect for authority will take us a long way in rightly raising our children, but equally important is maintaining a close relationship with

AUTHORITARIAN	God's Way	PERMISSIVE
• Harsh	• Discipline in love	· SOFT
• Strict rules	• Consistent	· LACK OF RULES
• Insensitive	• Sensitive	· SUPER SENSITIVE
• Shouts	• Instructs	· BARGAINS
• Rule focused	• Training focused	· FEELING FOCUSED

those in authority.

Perhaps it is easiest to explain if we show you two extreme parenting models that parents use when caring for their children: authoritarianism and permissiveness, the latter sometimes called bonding. We can see them on either side of the chart above.

 **The Barren**

Authoritarianism

Authoritarianism sounds excessive because it is. The authoritarian parent makes sure no one questions his or her authority. If his commands are not carried out exactly, the parent comes down hard on the child. We see very little traces of compassion, tenderness or understanding but usually harshness. The parent in this case looks more like a police officer or army sergeant.

These children obey their parents, but only out of fear. The problem is that the parents' ways do not instill a love for instruction in their children's hearts and foster good relationships.

In those situations barriers are built up between the child and the parent. This most often happens because of the father's unwillingness to bridle his anger. All he wants is everyone to listen to him. If his family members cross him, he explodes.

An authoritarian parent is interested in order more than relationship. The child as a result will sense that and react against it. He will not want to talk much with this kind of parent. Built-up resentment establishes a long-standing bitter relationship.

This is not what God wants. As the child grows up, this suppressed anger will express itself in several different ways, especially in the teen years. There is also another extreme kind of parenting.

 The Frustrated

Permissiveness

Permissive parenting provides excessive attention to the child's 'needs,' especially emotional. Permissiveness, even if thought of as love, will in a little time lead to chaos and produce a little 'emperor' in the home.

Bonding is a word that describes the way the parent strives to create an intimate relationship with the child by sharing the same experience and feelings. This goal is good, of course, but the parents are so focused on creating good memories that they avoid all forms of reproof and discipline. The parents are convinced that giving the child what he wants, making sure he is happy, and that he never cries produces the best child, but it allows a place for bad thoughts and habits to form. Unfortunately, they are convinced by secular philosophy that bonding equals love.[4]

These children, however, have no respect for their parents. The parents have no backbone. The parents might instinctively know what is best for the child but refrain from doing it. This 'soft' love develops a bitterness in the parent and child that creates a barrier between them. What was so greatly hoped for–a good relationship–often becomes, "I'm glad they are in school so I can have a break!" The spoiled child, on the other hand, begins treating others impolitely and rudely and in his arrogance expect that others will change their routine to satisfy their own desires.

 The Blend

God's Way

The Lord's way is infinitely better. Christ models and teaches a combination of the two important aspects of parenting: authority and love. We see this blend in Christ Jesus who was filled with both grace and truth.

And the Word became flesh, and dwelt among us, and we beheld His glory, glory as of the only begotten from the Father, full of grace and truth (John 1:14).

Grace is kindness in action. Grace is filled with goodness. Truth on the other hand is unbending and strong. Many people react against so-called Christianity because of its absolute truths. This is unfortunate because they have never seen the truth dressed in love and grace. They have not seen the glory of Jesus Christ.

God uses the family to bring us into a close warm relationship with those who are in authority over us. Just a while ago, my little three year-old boy came by and climbed up on me when I was lying on the couch. I became his big pillow. We then had a couple of minutes of fun tickling and tackling.

Although I might be considered a strict father by outside standards, my children know that they can hug me, kiss me, trick me and trust me. Many have never been able to experience this close relationship with anyone in authority. God wants every child to experience both this strong unbending sense of authority blended with kindness and love.

When one receives affection from a person in authority, fear departs leaving love and respect.

Our mighty God created the universe as described in Genesis chapter one. Starting in Genesis 2:4, God started using His personal name, Yahweh,[5] to describe Himself. He surprisingly cultivates a close relationship with man (literally Adam). This mighty God made man in His own image so that He might personally relate to him. The one who was able to speak the universe into existence is the same as the one who stoops over to talk and walk with man.

And they (Adam and Eve) heard the sound of the LORD God walking in the garden in the cool of the day... (Genesis 3:8).

If this is not enough to convince us of God's desire to relate to us personally, maybe we can just think for a moment about how God best likes to describe His relationship with His people. Christ is pictured as the bridegroom; the church is His bride.

Christ holds all power and authority, and yet He is the One who brought us close by dying on the cross for our sins. Colossians chapter 1 clearly shows us these two associated thoughts–authority and love. "And he is before all things, and in Him all things hold together ... to have first place in everything" (Colossians 1:17-18). "...Having made peace through the blood of His cross." (Colossians 1:20).

God designed love and care to blend with a parent's authority. For this reason, I believe, there is both male and female. The husband as head exercises authority, but the wife is designed to be sensitive to the needs of the child. God has safeguarded a husband's tendency to exercise authority without love by a wife's sense of compassion.

We are not suggesting that the husband should not be compassionate or that the wife should not act out her authority as a mother over her children. Both are needed. We are only suggesting that God has brought the couple together as one so that they can together better express the full character of God to their children, just as Jesus modeled these attributes in His life.

Parents need to use the power and strength of their authority to create a good relationship with those who are under their authority. Our perspectives of authority are soiled with stories of the abuse of power. We, however, must not allow such stained images to limit our ability to understand how glorious and wonderful it is to live under God's great power and love.

Pause for Reflection:

What rules your home? Authoritarianism or permissiveness? What are some of the consequences of that kind of parenting that exist in your home?

Many of us have experienced this love of God through Christ. Jesus and His death on the cross prove God's love for us and what is more important brings it right into our lives. "We love, because He first loved us" (1 John 4:19). We will speak more on the power of love in families later, but let us just quickly review how God has arranged the best modeling situation for our children.

A Balancing Act

A child will find what he needs most by a compassionate parent who exercises authority well. In this way the child gains both the needed wisdom and love he needs.

Trust blossoms under such conditions. If there is no love, then there is only fear. However, if there is only love, then there are no guidelines for living. Authoritarianism and permissiveness produce lopsided children. God design is to pass His ways on to children through the parents with the perfect balance of His love and authority. When God's love is rightly  expressed through the parents, it produces a kind spirit in the children expressing itself in a lovely trust in God, care for people and a firmness about what is right and their duty to do it. The elderly Apostle John clearly refers to this.

> *There is no fear in love; but perfect love casts out fear, because fear involves punishment, and the one who fears is not perfected in love. (1 John 4:18).* [6]

We must protect the family. Wherever the family structure is not supported, the children will suffer. Let us look briefly at two illustrations where this balance fails.

Government: When the government tries to take over the family role, it ultimately fails. Government organizations provide an authoritarian model. They know of law but not grace. It has no personal interest in a relationship with a child. Even if it did, it would be too distant and remote. Correction needs to be immediate.

Working mothers: The same kind of problem occurs when the mother goes off to work. The time to nurture a close relationship is not there. A babysitter or daycare worker can never provide that immediate attention of correction or tenderness of love. There is a great difference between a hired shepherd and the shepherd that owns the sheep. Jesus says it this way.

> *He who is a hireling, and not a shepherd, who is not the owner of the sheep, beholds the wolf coming, and leaves the sheep, and flees, and the wolf snatches them, and scatters them. He flees because he is a hireling, and is not concerned about the sheep. I am the good*

shepherd; and I know My own, and My own know Me (John 10:12-14).

Class instruction cannot replace the intimate relationship between a parent and a child at home. Provision for material things cannot substitute tender love. Love must be worked out in time and space.

God has designed the family to bring the most necessary things a child needs through the parents. The family as an institution should be highly protected. When the family began to be depreciated in value in the late 1960s, society began to unravel. Problems like spiraling hospital costs, increase of emotionally troubled people taking legalized drugs and an embarrassingly incompetent public school system (even though more money than ever is invested in it) bring the country closer to its grave.

Pause for Reflection:
What steps can you take to form a blended rule of authority with compassion for your home? Think about which way you tend to be. How can you become better balanced?

Not too late!

There are some matters that need to be tended to if we have not given authority the proper place in our homes. First, we should realize that it is never too late to help our children even when they have grown older.[7] Many parents reading this might think, "I have made so many mistakes. Is it too late?" It definitely is not too late if you change now. We will spend quite a bit of time in later chapters on how to retrain our children, even our older ones.

When we have failed, however, we need to humble ourselves before the Lord and repent. This means that we come to recognize and acknowledge that our past ways are not pleasing to Him and that we will now start doing what is right. We might not fully understand what the implications are, but we start by taking the first step and then the following ones, one by one.

Even though a parent might feel guilty about their failure, it is a terrible thing to bend the rules because they feel bad. What the child needs is consistency. They want to know we have changed. The only way to communicate this is for both the parent and child to live by God's standards. This produces the much-needed security in the lives of the children. Even if the child is older, the parents can begin being consistent. They need to be careful to explain their past sins and ask for forgiveness. That consistency will shake the child's old ways. This often happens when parents come to know the Lord at an older age.

Summary

In many cases parents have allowed too much wrong to continue on in their families. They need to take back control over the home and lovingly exert their authority. A parent must go by the principles and models provided in God's Word rather than by their feelings. This will be harder for Mom than for Dad, so Dad needs to lead the way. Make sure the husband first talks over what his plan is with his wife before he does it if at all possible! They need to communicate so they can work together. The wife usually has a way of making the husband's confrontation more gracious and acceptable. Remember to work as a team!

In future chapters we will discuss how to handle particular situations. We will do our best at outlining how to restore order and relationships to what they ought to be. Our confidence will be in God's Word and not in our experiences during these times.

We will not tackle everything at once. Just as our Father tenderly deals with us, training us step by step, so we will take steps to accept God's gift of authority and exercising it. The parents will need to pray for wisdom to understand God's ways for their children. Our hope is that the great goodness and love of God will be shown to our children through our lives.

Children will challenge parents who are exercising the authority that God has charged them with, but if they can combine this authority with love and compassion, then the child will really come to appreciate God's design.

Parenting Principles & Practices

- God gives authority to the parents so that they will in turn govern and care for their children, bringing them up in His ways.
- Without the parents exercising proper authority, the child's selfish tendency will grow, causing all sorts of conflict now and later.
- God brings the greatest good into this world by blending authority with compassion. Love needs to be draped all over our children's lives.
- The parents must follow Christ to bring the greatest good to their children. He alone can perfectly lead us to the blending of truth and grace.

Parenting Questions

1. Why do some parents think authority is bad?
2. Is authority bad? Why or why not?
3. How does God demonstrate authority's proper use?
4. Describe or define authoritarianism and permissiveness.
5. List at least two reasons a parent should not let the children rule the home.
6. Is it too late to catch up and restore things? Why or why not?

Notes from Chapter #3

[1] This is another way to describe the concept of holiness.

[2] Equalitarianism (egalitarianism) is unbiblical because it denies the inherent God-given authority in the parents. They mistakingly equivocate value with rights. With the lifting up a child's rights, they banish the authority that parents would have over their child.

[3] Of course, parents too make mistakes. However, if we would compare the wisdom of a parent against that of the child, the parent will always be the wiser.

[4] Bonding is strongly anti-authoritarian by the way it tries to play out egalitarianism (i.e. The child's opinion is equal to the parents). The parent spends most of her time making deals with the child. When the child's sin nature insists on undesirable 'deals,' the parents are greatly distraught, not knowing what to do. They usually give in and compromise.

[5] Yahweh is unfortunately called LORD in the English Bible. Yahweh (or Jehovah) is a transliteration of God's personal name. LORD is more of a title than a name.

[6] The love spoken of here in 1 John 4:18 is a mature and devoted love that brings people to a consistent life of obedience. This is our hope for ourselves and our children as they mature. Fear is needed to protect ourselves from wrong behavior and its evil consequences when that love is not fully developed.

[7] The rate of teen suicide is increasing fast. We need to bring hope to our children now before they completely give up hope.

Chapter #4

CULTIVATING SELF-CONTROL IN OUR CHILDREN

Purpose: Show the need for self-control and the means of cultivating it in our children from an early age so that they may live good and godly lives pleasing to God and focused on serving others.

Developing self-control in children is a challenging topic. There are numerous reasons for this.

1. We might not think self-control is very important.
2. We as parents lack self-control and wonder how a child could obtain it.
3. We are ignorant of how self-control is learned.
4. We do not want self-control. We enjoy the excesses in certain areas of our lives.

Our challenge, then, for this chapter is to show the importance self-control plays in our daily lives, how self-control is developed and the advantages of building self-control into our children.

A. The Important Role of Self-Control

Most parents do not think about the necessity of self-control until they get exasperated with their child's wild behavior. Even then, they may not realize that it is an issue with self-control. The typical parent thinks that they are supposed to put up with their out-of-control child, perhaps thinking, "That's just the way he is." They believe this 'putting up with' is part of what parents are supposed to do. They are right in a sense.

Parents are to exude great patience toward their children. This does not mean, however, that they are to neglect training their children to reach high standards. Remember, these high standards like being kind, gentle, helpful, etc., are not high in the Lord's sight but normal.

One main problem with tolerating disobedience is that the parents start panicking once they see how stubborn and selfish their children can be. When 'veteran' parents see a young married couple with their new little one, they smile and take joy in the parents' joy. Nevertheless, deep down, they also might be thinking about how that sweet little child will soon become his parents' terror. After all, this is what many parents have experienced. This is why terms like 'terrible twos' are commonly used.

Pause for Reflection:
Do you want your children to exercise self-control? Have you thought about what would happen to them if you did not train them to live by self-control? Do you know what self-control is? What does it looks like in a two year old?

Scripture and Self-control
The fact is self-control plays an important part in all of our lives. We cannot live without it. Quite a few Proverbs highlight the importance of having self-control. If we lack self-control, then we will run into all sorts of problems. Let us look at five areas of life that self-control are important for.

➢ The one who is not able to control his time will not be a diligent worker. "The way of the sluggard is as a hedge of thorns, but the path of the upright is a highway" (Proverbs 15:19). "He also who is slack in his work is brother to him who destroys" (Proverbs 18:9).

➢ The one who cannot control his words will ruin his own life. "A fool's mouth is his ruin, and his lips are the snare of his soul" (Proverbs 18:7).

➢ The one who lacks self-control often falls into terrible habits like drinking, gambling and gluttony. "For the heavy drinker and the glutton will come to poverty" (Proverbs 23:21).

➢ The foolish man does not control his anger. "A fool gives full vent to his anger, but a wise man keeps himself under control" (Proverbs 29:11).

➢ The one lacking discipline follows his desires rather than God's law of love. He lives by lusts rather than God's principles. "For the commandment is a lamp, and the teaching is light; and reproofs for discipline are the way of life, To keep you from the evil woman,

From the smooth tongue of the adulteress. Do not desire her beauty in your heart, Nor let her catch you with her eyelids. For on account of a harlot one is reduced to a loaf of bread, and an adulteress hunts for the precious life" (Proverbs. 6:23-26).

We do not need to read many of these proverbs to see how important self-control is in our lives and in the lives of our children. Self-control is easily developed when the child is small, but adults with their set ways and perspectives find it much harder to change.

What is self-control?

Self-control is the ability to control what we think and do, to keep our hands, mouths, eyes, ears, feet, and desires from activities that lead to sin and instead accomplish that which is good.

God has called each set of parents to teach self-control to their children so that they may carry out His commandments. Modeling this principle is very important.

> *My son, observe the commandment of your father, And do not forsake the teaching of your mother; Bind them continually on your heart; Tie them around your neck. When you walk about, they will guide you; When you sleep, they will watch over you; And when you awake, they will talk to you. For the commandment is a lamp, and the teaching is light; and reproofs for discipline are the way of life (Proverbs 6:20-23).*

Self-control is the tool by which people can be responsible to God, others and even themselves. This virtue describes the ability of a person to govern his desires in such a way that he will accomplish what he knows is good and right. Most of the character qualities that a society respects such as faithfulness, attentiveness, loyalty, generosity, diligence, and patience depend on rightly governing one's life. It is one of the fruit of the Holy Spirit generated in a Christian. "But the fruit of the Spirit is love, joy, peace, patience, kindness, goodness, self-control..." (Galatians 5:23).

The notion of self-control assumes that others are more important than one's self. They learn how to put off fulfilling their own interests so that they can serve others. A free and orderly society can only be built with this quality. Without it, man is unable to follow his conscience or the rules of a society. There is no freedom without self-control for an uncontrolled man is convinced his desires are more important than the needs of others and as a result oppresses others to fulfill those desires.

Do you know where all quarrels and conflicts come from in personal relationships? The Bible tells us they derive from our selfish desires. Again, we see that desires rule the person. "You lust and do not have; so you commit murder. And you are envious and cannot obtain; so you fight and quarrel. You do not have because you do not ask" (James 4:2).

Pause for Reflection:
Is your life known for self-control? In what areas are you the strongest? The weakest? Do you expect self-control in your children? Give an example.

What about self-expression?

Before moving on, let us think about those who espouse the popular idea of self-expression. They believe that self-expression is important because it lies at the source of creativity and happiness. This is an unbiblical belief system that generates distorted parenting techniques and approaches.

There is a place for self-expression, but it always should remain within the constraints of what is proper and right. Do we not think this way when we train our children to crayon within the lines? This is not what we find in our society, however. Those people who hold to the above beliefs question the value of self-control. They are greatly deceived. The opposite is true. The greatest writers, painters, sport figures, and speakers are highly disciplined. They pay very careful attention to how they use every moment of their time.

Let us look at three differences between self-expression and self-control. We will call the group that emphasizes the need for self-expression: A) 'The demanding child'[1] and the group which emphasizes self-control: B) 'The contented child.' Each is a result of the way the child is regularly treated.

1• The Child's Attitude toward Self

A) THE DEMANDING CHILD

He gets what he wants.

The demanding child learns that it is easy to get whatever he wants. If he wants to be picked, up, he gets picked up. If he wants to watch a program, he gets to watch it. The child only needs to cry or fuss, and those around him cave into his desires. He is trained to think that his opinion and needs are more important than the needs of those around him.

B) THE CONTENTED CHILD

He respects the needs of others

The child with self-control learns that he is just one of many people around. At times he needs to wait. This is okay. He will keep busy doing something else. He learns that those around him have not forgotten him. They love him, and in time they will come and satisfy his needs.

2• The Child's Attitude Toward Authority

A) THE DEMANDING CHILD

He has no respect for authority.

This demanding child is consumed with his own way. The child will think his own opinion is as important if not more important than his own parent's opinion and judgment. He disdains his parents' authority and is convinced that they are there to meet his every whim.

B) THE CONTENTED CHILD

He respects authority.

The child with self-control learns that there are many times when he will not get his own way. He is content with this even though he might not know why. He respects his parents' authority.[2] He stays under their protection and is better able to learn from others.

3 • The Child's Attitude toward the World

A) THE DEMANDING CHILD

The world revolves around him.

The demanding child becomes so intent on getting his way that the world becomes a place to serve his desires. The child becomes a manipulator of the things around him to get what he wants. He is willing to harm and pollute to obtain his desires. The child is not content unless he gets what he wants and is still not really content even after he has gotten it.

B) THE CONTENTED CHILD

The world is a place of exploration.

The child with self-control is content to be by himself and will naturally and curiously learn from his environment. He is able to concentrate. The child learns to be happy even when his wishes are not met.

Summary

Self-control, then, is the ability to constrain what one does so that he might accomplish some higher goal. Have you ever seen what is called modern art? Modern art is very undisciplined. One artist swung a paint bucket with holes in it over a canvas and called that art!

Real control, however, comes from training. Training calls for self-discipline and the resulting concentration, sacrifice, determination and perseverance. This results in wise and principled children filled with joy and love. God wants us to be able to obey Him so that we can serve Him and others.

The Garden of Safety

We can use a garden surrounded by four walls as an example of the importance of having self-control. The four walls stand for the parents' rules. As long as their children obey, then they stay within the garden walls. To protect their children, their parents must compel them to stay within those walls to protect them.

If at any time, whether because they are being sneaky or because the parents do not care, a bridge is established that leads out of the protected garden. The child gets to do things other than the parent desires resulting in many dangerous situations.

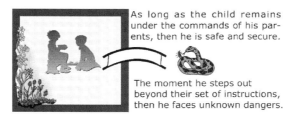

As long as the child remains under the commands of his parents, then he is safe and secure.

The moment he steps out beyond their set of instructions, then he faces unknown dangers.

Pause for Reflection:

Do you encourage or tolerate self-expression in your child even though it is not best for him or her? If so, repent. Confess your sin and ask God to train you to properly develop a child who seeks God's way rather than his own. God wants us to train our children in obedient because He cares for them. He wants the best for each of them.

B. The Development of Self-Control

We might be asking, "How does self-control develop in a person's life?" This is what we want to explain here especially in the context of training a child to have self-control.

Anyone who has unsuccessfully tried to break a bad habit will think that it is virtually impossible to develop self-control. This is not true, however. Everybody exercises some self-control. The problem is trying to get control over the areas that cause them trouble. Very likely, the trouble is because they did not have self-control in the first place.

We do admit certain areas are more difficult to exercise self-control than others. Different people have different weaknesses. Some live in circumstances which are hostile to the development of self-control such as when parents do not exercise self-control or having friends who do not exercise self-control. We, however, all desperately need self-control trained into us early on in our lives. The earlier the better. Let us note some aspects of the development of self-control.

The Problem

The need for self-control stems from two problems: 1) Sinful tendencies and 2) The lack of training.

Sinful tendencies

Since we are born with a sin nature, we all have a tendency to live by our own selfish desires. We have a moral bent toward evil just like a plant that turns its leaves toward the light. These desires tend to overrule us in one or more areas of our lives.

If a person is covetous, then he will be willing to use his words, actions and thoughts to obtain some object that he desires. He might steal or lie as a result. The desires pull him into situations where he compromises his convictions about what is right or wrong. The life of Samson shows us the consequences of not lining our desires up with God's purposes. He allowed his sensual desires to guide him rather than God's Word. The consequences were terrible.

All children have a sinful nature which produce sinful inclinations. The only difference is that these desires in little children are undeveloped. As he gets older, his sinful nature, his propensity to treat himself better than others, begins to express itself more and more cleverly. A young child cannot fully coordinate the parts of his body to get what he wants. He is less able to use his expressions, speech and environment to manipulate others. When he is older, his body becomes the vehicle to express these sinful inclinations. Parents, of course, as long as they are around, tend to interfere with their children's 'big' plans.

Lack of Training

Another problem with self-control is the lack of training. Parents need to be quicker to acknowledge that a child does not naturally acquire the

experience and knowledge needed to perform certain tasks. Training includes the passing on of confidence, knowledge, motivation and skills to another. In this case, we are instilling the necessary things in our children to have self-control.

For example, a child might not know how to pick up his clothing and fold them—a simple common task. He does not see the importance of it, nor does he know the way to do it. He perhaps has even tried to mimic Mom but just got frustrated. His hands and eyes have not been trained to move the clothes in certain ways that are considered folding. That skill has never been taught to him. As he gets older, he will have the physical capacity to fold the clothes but not the training.

What ramification does this have for training? With regard to folding clothes, on the good side the mother probably does it for him. She shows her care for him in that way. On the bad side, he probably will not ever make his bed. This would make him a messy and inconsiderate roommate.

Pause for Reflection:
What evidence do you find for your child's sin nature? Have you agreed in your heart to control the expression of that sin nature? Pray for yourself and your child so that your child might gain self-control.

The Motivation
I heard a speaker once say that the further away from home a child gets, the less the values and instructions of the home influence him.[3] Why is this so? How do we get our children to do what is best even when we are not with them? We will be looking into this process because it has everything to do with good parenting. Many parents have allowed bad, but convenient, short-term parenting techniques to interfere with reaching good long-term goals.

We govern ourselves according to what we think is best. Our decisions are influenced by many factors. It is these factors or motivational points that have much to say regarding our final decisions. Let us look into how parenting fits into this process. We will first examine outward and inward motivation or 'shapers' and then summarize how the whole process works together.

Outward motivation
Motivation from things outside our lives plays an important part in the decisions that we make. Outward forces like parents, friends and rules pressure a child to conform or not conform.

Police or supervisors help produce self-control. The presence of a policeman instantly slows traffic down to its proper speed. The driver fears that he will get a ticket. Therefore, he is able and willing to ease up on the gas pedal and drive more slowly. The speed limit sign does not sufficiently motivate some drivers to stay at the right speed.

A supervisor walking down the hall brings instant alertness to his workers. The colleagues are concerned about their job and pay. If the boss sees them as highly productive, then they might be able to get a raise. If, however, the supervisor sees them slothful or unproductive, then they might be fired. Their desire for higher pay and security causes them to put their hands and minds to work harder whenever the supervisor is near.

These shaping influences are considered 'outward' because the motivation comes from outside. In each case, there are outward forces that motivate the person to perform in a certain way. They cause a person to think a certain way which in the end shapes their decisions. They are properly seen as being 'other' controlled rather than 'self-controlled.' The extra force from outside causes the individual to exercise control over his body.

Parents are the greatest motivating factor for their children's decisions especially in the formative years. Parents rightly use all sorts of means to shape a child's decision. If a child refuses to go with his parents on the sidewalk, the parent can squeeze his hand until the child realizes that it is better to go his parent's way. Reward, pain, pleasure, delight, friendship are all used as outside influences to guide a child to better behavior.

The ability for a parent to control his child's circumstances decreases as the child gets older. It is at this point many parents are surprised when their child rebels against their instructions.[4] The child is simply unwilling to be shaped by the parent. This lack of control partly comes when the child is bigger, stronger or financially independent. In other words, the parent's 'presence' factor is no longer very applicable. These things, however, only cloud the real issues at stake.

If at any point a child begins to disrespect his parents, an avalanche of problems develop. The greater the disrespect, the more the disobedience. We see this illustrated in the prodigal son (Luke 15:11-32). In such cases a parent's constraining influence is no longer present. Those parents who find problems with their teens usually can trace this disrespect to unresolved conflict from the past. Without respect, parents lose their influence. The feeling of bitterness speaks louder than the respect or desire for a parent's acceptance. Discipline, love, instruction and humility are all integral to maintaining respect and will be discussed later.

The amount of outside influence a parent has over the child will decrease over time. The parent will no longer be with the child. Early on, the parent needs to be preparing the child for adulthood. Parents need to learn how to help the child internalize godly values and perspectives.

Inward motivation

Inward motivation speaks of the motivation that comes from within the person. The parents' greatest hope is that all the 'good' principles and values that they have taught their child are internalized and accepted in the child's life. In this case, even when the parent is far away or has passed on, the child is still affected by those principles. His inner thoughts and values strongly guide how he makes daily decisions. Sometimes this process is conscious and deliberate while for most people it is quite hidden and subtle. The parent's insight becomes the child's wisdom.

> *My son, do not forget my teaching, but let your heart keep my commandments; for length of days and years of life, and peace they will add to you. Do not let kindness and truth leave you; bind them around your neck, write them on the tablet of your heart. So you will find favor and good repute in the sight of God and man (Proverbs 3:1-4).*

If a person can appreciate and accept the reasons why something should be done, it can be said to be internalized or has become his own. His father might have told his young boy to be polite to women. As the boy got older, he came to respect this rule for himself. He now treats women in a special way on his own even when his father is not around. This internalizing of rules and values is the basis for self-control. A child acquires this cache of wisdom from his parents over a long time.

What does a person do when no one is watching? This is the day-to-day problem each of us meets in different ways. Some find pornography or gambling online difficult problems. Others have a problem with backbiting. A person is tempted to do things he would not do if a certain person was watching him.

The one that is motivated by his own thought-out principles will carry out what he believes is right even when no one is watching. He will drive within the speed limit all the time because he has agreed this is the proper way of driving. Otherwise, the pressure of other drivers would make him go faster. His internal rules and values help him maintain his course.

God desires children to acquire their parent's wisdom and values to protect them and lead them to Himself. This Christian aspect of parenting is often neglected. As we look deeper at this spiritual side of parenting, we will discover how the whole process is meant to work. Children are not just learning from their parents but from the Lord.

Inward and Outward

Although we have spoken of outward and inward shapers, we should realize that these two forces blend their work. This process becomes very special when the Lord's principles and values are taken into consideration. We have spoken of the 'fear of God' earlier in this book. The scriptures list many positive factors stemming from the fear of God. This is because it summarizes how God's values become part of our lives. We might think of God as our Father. Our great Heavenly Father has Himself entered this training process.

The fear of God combines both the outward and inward aspects of motivation. God is always present to a person who fears Him. No matter where he goes, God is there. God then is a constant external factor. The greater the fear of God, the more God shapes a person's decisions.[5]

Internally, we have God's voice speaking to us through our conscience and His Word that has been stored within us. These thoughts begin to regularly shape how we approach certain issues in our lives. In the end we call the decision to obey God our own but He, as our Heavenly Father, has fostered this thinking. His truths have become internalized in us. They have become so much part of our thinking that they are our own. It is in this way that we resemble our heavenly Father.

Some people look at the fear of God in a negative way, but it actually helps to properly shape a person's thinking. Knowing the negative consequences of disobedience help influence us to make the right choice.

If the Lord wanted to eradicate our evil deeds, He would simply eliminate us. That is simple enough for Him. He did not do that. Since the person that fears God always acknowledges His presence, God's laws are more easily accepted as his own. This facilitates the internalization of God's ways into our lives.

This is how it should work. A parent brings consistent training and modeling to the young child so that they learn to obey. As they get older, they begin to understand how their parents live in the 'fear of God.' At first they do what is right because of external pressure but later by the fear of God. They are guided along until their commitment to important values is fully matured.

When this happens, even when a child is far from his parents, he will still obey them. The process of developing this fear of the Lord is very important, and the scriptures give much instruction on it. The practical steps on how to do this will be discussed later on.

Summary

These inward and outward 'shapers' influence the very decisions that we make.

It is true, a boy might want something that belongs to another, but because of pain associated with taking a friend's toy in the past, he has a greater desire not to suffer the chastisement. He decides not to take it this time. Once trained, he realizes that having another person's toy is not the most important thing. He is not controlled by his desires (i.e. lusts) but by living in the 'fear of God.' He learns he can be content even without taking something from another.

Motivation plays a key role in how we make decisions. We are much more able and willing to refrain from bad behavior when we are aware of the negative consequences. When we learn to avoid certain bad behaviors, we discover the blessings of obedience. This blessing encourages us to obey again and again. The understanding of what is right or wrong has been so embedded in these individuals that they just 'naturally' make certain decisions. They no longer feel like decisions. That is the way they are.

The standards of God's Word are to guide the child not his feelings or desires. The child is expected to speak kindly, be truthful, humble and focus on others. Biblical standards are enforced on the outward until they are incorporated inwardly and provide the needed self-control leading to a godly life. Now we will discuss how we can develop self-control in our children.

C. Develop Self-Control in our Children

God's goal for young men and women is to have self-control. We see this clearly in the following verses.

> *Then they can **train the younger women** to love their husbands and children, **to be self-controlled** and pure, to be busy at home, to be kind, and to be subject to their husbands, so that no-one will malign the word of God. Similarly, encourage the **young men to be self-controlled** (Titus 2:4-6, NIV).*

The big question, then is, "How do I best teach self-control to my child?" Let us look at four ways.

#1 Honor parents: Help your children obey your words

The key to developing self-control in children is to cause them to honor and respect their parents' directions. It might seem counterintuitive to make our children do what we say, hoping that they will do it later on, but this is how we train self-control into our children. Listen to the scriptures. "Train up a child in the way he should go, even when he is old he will not depart from it (Proverbs 22:6)."

The things we train our sons and daughters to do now will be the things they tend to do later in life. This is what they become familiar with and are most comfortable with. The opposite is true too. If we train (i.e. model) them in some bad response—such as blowing up in anger, then this shapes how they respond.

To develop self-control in our children we need to keep them doing the right thing. They must do what we say. Let us again use the illustration of the protected garden. The child is safe playing in that protected area. Outside the walls, there are unknown dangers. The parents' rules form the walls or boundaries to that garden. The parents do all they can to keep their children in the garden. Maybe the child will fuss and cry to go outside the walls, but the wise parent cares enough not to cave in to their child's foolish requests or demands.

We help the child stay within our rules and guidelines. We need to take two kinds of actions to accomplish this: positive and negative. Remember the goal is to protect the child. We are not living for the rules; this is authoritarianism. Neither are we living for 'freedom' of choice for that leads to those dangers that lie outside the garden. The children do not know what is good for them. Instead, we keep them within the confines of parental instruction until they have internalized the rules of life.[6] This will be discussed more later on.

#2 Chastisement: Associate pain with things you do not want

A parent must consistently compel a child to stay within the boundaries. They must use all their resources and energy to make it unpleasant for the child to disobey. We dare not reward their disobedience or bargain with them (which is still giving them a reward). We simply make it unpleasant so that they choose what we think is right. This instruction and guidance is the major purpose for chastisement. Much more about this will be discussed in a later chapter.

Our goal is to help the child associate his disobedience with pain and grief. Whenever they choose to disobey, then it will not go well with them.[7] Later on they will internalize the concept that whenever they disobey God then they will suffer bad consequences. Make it very unpleasant to disobey. Make it so that they do not want to repeat that experience. Children are fast learners when parents consistently train them!

#3 Proactive: Instruct what you <u>do</u> want

Parents must think ahead what they want their child to do. Do not wait until the child does something wrong and needs correction. Teach him the right thing to do, and he won't need as much correction.

Parents must also train their children to stay within the perimeter of their rules. Show them how to specifically do different tasks. Parents must be clear about what they do want. They should reward their children's obedience with ample encouraging remarks and smiles.[8]

#4 No choice: Do not give them a choice

Our goal is to be clear and concise. Language that encourages 'choice' or 'suggestion' confuses the child. Did you ever hear a parent ask a child, "Let us go…, okay?" That is suggestive language. If the parent really desires that something is to be done, they should just tell their child of the fact and not give them a choice in the matter. They are the authority.

Let us explain why this choice method does not work. The parent hopes to shape a child's desire to conform to theirs. They carefully supply information on the importance or pleasure of doing something. The parents hope the child will agree with them and like to do what they want. This most often does not work because the child's self-will is at stake. When parents give him a choice or make a suggestion, they are giving him the right to say no. The child sees it as an opportunity to have his or her own way. Even though the child might see its benefits, he often goes contrary to the wishes of the parents! The parents are in authority and should use their position to make important decisions.

Our goal is not that our children stay in the safe confines of the 'parental garden' forever. Some parents have done this; the child is never released into his or her own maturity. These children do not develop properly. The parents' goal must be to cultivate God's good standards within them. If a parent rightly does this early on, then the child will mature very quickly and the parent can expand the area in which the child can function. We give children limited choices within the guidelines of what we think is right, sensible and proper. More will be said about this in the chapter on freedom and boundaries.

Pause for Reflection:

Some parents are known for being negative and critical. Their negative words damage their relationship with their child. If you are this way, repent from it and ask God to do a special work in your own heart so that you can learn to encourage your child.[9]

D. Developing Self-control

Self-control or self-discipline is developed from much repetitive training. The most important area to tackle first is obedience. The child honors his parent's word only when he obeys it. When the parent speaks, the child should obey. If we start when our babies are little infants, they will know of no other alternative. This resolves much of the parents and child's frustrations. In any case, the training takes time and repetition.

Some parents fight against the idea that a child always needs to obey the parents. Perhaps they believe this pressure will somehow hurt the child. In fact, the opposite is true. Let us assume most parents attempt to instruct their child in one or more ways. Most parents are held back by not always carrying through on each instruction or command that they give. They might give a command but at times allow the child to disobey.

Every time the parents are inconsistent, they send mixed messages to their children. Inconsistency in training communicates a message to the child that the parent is sometimes willing to bend the rules. As a result, the child disobeys more. This in turn causes more disobedience, more chastisement and a longer time to train the child. The caring parent can avoid this by being consistent. It might help the parent to view this form of child training as 'training to disobey' and results in further struggles with their children.

The earlier a parent starts training the child, the better. We should think of training as something that is always going on. From our child's earliest days, we are always training them in some area. If we establish routines early on, then we can have a relatively peaceful and quiet home where parents have a wonderful relationship with their child.

Christ's Example

How did Christ show the quality of self-control? Jesus exemplified this quality of self-control. He only spoke what His Father wanted. Everything He did was according to the will of His heavenly Father. He spoke some truths only to some people. To others He spoke in parables. He did not get carried away with miracles nor did He let the crowd name Him king.

He did not take revenge for people's mistreatment of Him. He was willing to sleep little and work hard for good purposes. He stayed up late praying. Jesus was willing to go without comforts in order to better discern His Father's will and minister to the people. On the cross Christ most clearly showed self-control when the pressure was at its highest. He persisted in doing what was right when it was very difficult to do so. Jesus successfully resisted calling the angels to deliver Him. As an excellent teacher, Jesus did not compromise the truth.

Self-control leads to strong and wonderful men and women. Each has their own desires and make-up, but they have learned how to suppress them so that they can do what is right and proper. It is our job as parents to make sure our children get this training. We dare not trust others do it. We first constrain our wills to do the will of our Father in heaven. Each thought, word, deed and attitude needs to match what our God wants. Our child will follow on in this glorious path!

Pause for Reflection:
Do you desire to be like Jesus and have children that are like Him?

Summary

Self-control is an essential building block to the creation of great men and women. To the degree that we as parents lack self-control, we model unrighteousness. We must train our children to do what we do and what we tell them. We will use many affirming words when they do what is right. When our authority is tested, we must use physical discipline to enforce our words.

As children get older, they will internalize these rules. The fear of God will keep them even when far from home. This training also more deeply prepares children of their need for a Savior because of their sins. Start early. Be consistent. Follow Christ. The rest just works out as God says in His Word.

Parenting Principles & Practices

- Developing self-control in our children is an essential part of caring for them.
- Training is necessary to develop self-control.
- Self-control is necessary because of the sinful nature and a lack of know-how.
- Self-control is quickly learned when parents consistently combine a good example with positive encouragement and chastisement.
- The earlier parents start training their children, the better it will be for all concerned.

Parenting Questions

1. Why is it so important to develop self-control?
2. Describe a child that lacks self-control. What are some problems the parents of these children face?
3. What is self-control? Please define it one or two ways.
4. Explain the difference between the demanding child's attitude toward the world and the contented child's attitude.
5. How does the sinful nature create a need for self-control training?
6. Why should a parent want to transfer the motivation for self-control to be inward rather than outward?
7. What two things can parents regularly do to develop self-control in their children?
8. Why is a walled garden a good illustration of the need for self-control?
9. Why is much chastisement avoided when training of the child starts very early on?

Notes from Chapter #4

[1] The title 'demanding child' derives from the demands the child puts on others. It is the 'permissive parent' who breeds these demanding and unpleasant children. See more in Chapter #3.

[2] We are not saying that the contented child perfectly submits to authority. Generally speaking, however, he fits in with authority. He tends to comply with those in authority.

[3] This is the reason that urbanization faces problems that would never touch small villages. They are away from family and friends' pressure and influence.

[4] When a parent gives up his authority to govern his child, the child's rebellious nature can arise alarmingly very early in life.

[5] We must keep in mind that though the Lord's presence is always there, it is not always equally felt or sensed. His presence is brought alive by our faith. This is the reason the enemy attacks our faith.

[6] We do not mean that parents have forever to accomplish their task. They have a set time of about 18 to 21 years to do their job. God has wisely made a child's body to grow slowly so that they spend plenty of time with their parents before they are to live on their own. Children have lots to learn.

[7] At the same time, they are learning the rewards of obedience. Things go better for them when they obey. This is just what the scriptures say!

[8] Rewards are not bribes. Bribes manipulate people. Bribes work because they utilize the person's greedy desires. We do not encourage this godless response. Rewards are given afterwards, not by force but by freewill. We should avoid using rewards for regular tasks. We want to train them to do what is right without material reward. Obedience is demanded by God. Material rewards should be special. Use them when a child has learned a new skill or passed some special skill-related event like learning to swim.

[9] Negative remarks often reflect a person's own failure to obey God in that area of one's life.

Chapter #5

CHILD TRAINING & ROUTINES

Purpose: Enable parents to construct and maintain effective routines for their children.

Once there was a world famous king. He had everything he could ever have asked for. He had power; he even had peace. On top of all that, he was a profound philosopher known for his writings and wise sayings. People from around the world took tours just to see how great his kingdom was. There was just one problem. Although he excelled in just about everything, there was one area he did not master. The downfall of his kingdom came in a short time just because he did not exercise self-control in that one area of life.

A. Effective Training

Self-control is all-important. If a person lacks self-control in only one area of his life, it can bring his marriage or family to ruin. Whether it is gambling, immorality, anger or stealing, any area that is out of control will control him. Destruction follows. King Solomon's willingness to disobey God in the one area of sensuality caused his kingdom to be torn in two. Two verses in scripture remind us of how essential self-control is.

> *A city that is broken into and without walls*
> *is a man who has no control over his spirit (Proverbs 25:28).*

He who is slow to anger is better than the mighty,
And he who rules his spirit, than he who captures a city
(Proverbs 16:32).

The heart of the issue is "Who is leading whom?" Either we will train our children to rule their desires or we will allow their desires to rule them. In the latter case, they will become self-centered and demanding. We can ask a different set of questions to help us see this more clearly. Does the child set the schedule and demand his own way? Or does the parent, who is appointed by God to raise the child, set the daily routine? Do you require that your child conform to your desires? Or do you allow him to rule your time and money according to his desires?

To effectively cultivate self-control in children, parents must set up good routines and develop a flexible schedule. They must take the time and initiative to train them to comply with the routine. A flexible routine goes a long way toward building up confidence, experience and acceptance of what needs to be done in life. The patterns that become familiar to them will naturally be adopted for their own, as they get older.

In the last chapter, we looked at several important general principles on how to train our children. In this chapter, we will look at specific training steps and illustrations for how to do this. We will also develop routines and schedules and show how they all support and reinforce one another.

Self-control or self-discipline is established by repetitive training. The most important area to tackle first is the child's response to his parent's word or instruction. When the parent speaks, the child should obey.

If parents inwardly believe that children do not always need to obey, then they will be at best inconsistent in their training. Parents need to deal with their doubts about the necessity of obeying God's Word. Otherwise, they will train their child to disobey. God is not pleased with this.

Parents, for example, might tell their child to do something, "Come here" but allow the child to run the other way. They might even laugh and say how 'cute' he is. Disobedience is never cute. Every time the parents are inconsistent, they send a mixed message to their child. Inconsistency in making them obey communicates that obedience is not important. So the child disobeys more. This, in turn, causes more disobedience, more chastisement and a longer time (if ever) to train the child. The caring parent can avoid this by being absolutely consistent. Be true to your word. Mean what you say and say what you mean.

Wrong training early in life induces behavioral problems. Some consequences will be obvious right away, while others will not be seen until much later on. We will show how this is so in one area of life as we trace the pattern of early baby cries through to the toddler stage and later.

From Crying to Complaining

All would agree that a baby should be loved and cared for. The wise mother learns early on that some cries are for legitimate needs while others are used to control and manipulate. At only a few weeks old, the baby will already assert his or her will by crying. Making loud noises with tears is the only ability the baby really has control of and even this is learned. The tendency to control the environment through crying, to 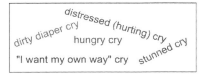 please their own desires, is often the first expression of a child's sinful nature.

My wife says that a baby has several kinds of cries: a hungry cry, a distressed (hurting) cry, a dirty diaper cry, a stunned cry and then the "I want my own way" cry.

If the parent is not careful to discern these cries, the child is able to learn to manipulate his or her parents. The baby, for example, likes the warmth of his mother. If he cries, then he is rewarded by being picked up and held close to his warm, soft Mom—maybe he will even get an extra snack! He might not really be hungry, but he likes the extra attention.

Of course, it is not wrong to be snuggled up next to his mother. This picture is recognized the world over as one of the most tender scenes of life. When the baby, however, insists on getting up through the night for Mom's company, the mother will not get her rest. The mother sometimes hands the baby over to the father. They both start losing sleep and irritability sets in.

The pattern, then, goes like this. Baby cries and the Mom comes running. The baby soon discovers that with each cry, he or she is comforted and held.

New parents especially need to be aware of the child's tendency to use his cries to manipulate them. If Mom immediately responds to every cry of the baby, the baby's cries will turn into whining and then later into complaining as the child grows. If allowed to go on, complaining turns to demands and rants. Excessive unmet demands are called temper tantrums. Notice what bad habits are formed when a child is not properly trained to use his or her voice. Parents must start training their children early because they learn to manipulate their parents at a very young age!

To avoid confrontation, for convenience, or out of just plain ignorance, some parents resort to taking the baby to bed with them. This leads to other problems. When problems are avoided instead of resolved, greater troubles are created. Because these avoidance routines become regular and expected, they are difficult to break out of. They are not impossible to change but require more perseverance. The parent must think down the road and see that at some time the baby will need to break out of this habit. Meanwhile, it is not very conducive to the parents' sleep and interferes with the husband and wife relationship.

With a regular 'feed, awake and sleep' routine,[1] the parent is more easily able to discern the precious baby's cries and to appropriately respond to them. What should we do, then, when the baby is fine–not sick, not hungry, no dirty diaper, etc., but still cries?

We need to allow the baby to cry.[2] By allowing the baby to cry, the baby learns that his demands are not the most important matter in the world. The child can learn to wait. What are the results?

➤ The child gets a wonderful lesson on self-control.
➤ The baby learns to fall asleep on his or her own.
➤ Tired Mom and Dad get their needed rest.

As we deal with older children, we should recognize that crying, complaining and whining are fruits from the same seed of discontent, the seed of self-centeredness. Their demands should not be rewarded. They should never get what they demand. If the child fusses when asking for something, he should never get that item. If we give it to the whining, demanding child, we just taught him that whining gets results, and he will use whining more. We must never reward self-centeredness.

A child might declare, "I want to watch that program." The parent responds, "Not today." The child protests, "But I want to watch it!" The parent calmly reminds the child, "You know that anytime you shout at Daddy or Mommy, you will not get what you want. If you ask again, then you will not be able to watch it tomorrow either." If the television is on, the parent quietly goes over and shuts it off. If possible, the parent in a natural voice can suggest to the child another activity. Some children need time to themselves so that the lesson can sink in, that is, "I am not going to get my way by fussing."

The child can show respect to his parents by honoring their schedule and purposes. Naturally, the schedule should be made with the child's needs in mind. At the same time parents must help their children obey God by training them to honor their parents. Consistency by the parents will make it easier for the children (and for the parents too). Do not make exceptions. Every exception exponentially increases the difficulty in training the child.

Summary

Parents are always training their children! Whenever we do not deliberately train our child to do good, bad and frustrating habits always occur. It is like a neglected garden where little weeds become large plants that choke out the good plants.

> *I passed by the field of the sluggard, and by the vineyard of the man lacking sense; and behold, it was completely overgrown with thistles, its surface was covered with nettles, and its stone wall was broken down (Proverbs 24:30-34).*

If the parent does not train the child, then the child effectively trains the parent to meet his every wish and desire!

Pause for Reflection:

Does your child whine or complain? First, examine your own life for a complaining spirit. Plead with God that He would bring joy to your heart! Then ask, "Am I rewarding my child by giving him what he wants when he makes complaints or demands." "Do I reward his whining, crying or screaming?" If yes, give an example. Pay attention to your response to his whining and demands.

B. Expectations for Our Children

What can we expect from our toddlers? Let us mention a few things. You can expand your own list or make one for an older child. These suggestions will help get you started.

• *Plays happily by himself*

Our young children should know how to play contentedly by themselves. This does not happen automatically. They have to be trained that way.

So many people have come up to us after observing our children playing by themselves and said, "Your children are naturally quiet." They think it is just the way our family is. They do not understand all the hard work to get them to be that way!

Dad and Mom have become so used to entertaining their child that they have never even thought there could be another way. Parents who focus all their energy on a selfish child often allow their marriage to decay. Moms have responsibilities other than entertaining the child. They need to train their children to quietly amuse themselves in a safe place.

Pause for Reflection:
Does your child exhibit the self-control necessary to play contentedly by himself?

• *Sits quietly in the high chair*

Our little children should sit quietly in their high chair. They can learn to eat neatly, first with help from the parent but later on by themselves.[3]

When you put your child in the high chair, do he cry and fuss until you have to take him out and hold him? Or even worse. You do not even attempt to put him in the chair any more. Perhaps you have allowed his demand to sway your decision about putting him in his chair for meals (he does not like it). You are avoiding the scene that occurred when you last put him in his chair.

Pause for Reflection:
Does your child sit calmly in his high chair?

• *Does not persistently demand to get out*

Our children should be content wherever we put them. Yes, they do go through certain testing times, but on the whole, they can learn to be satisfied with wherever their parents put them, whether it be the playpen, potty, room or car seat. There might be an initial fuss, but it should diminish in less than two minutes after the parent walks away.

Pause for Reflection:
When we put our children in the playpen or some contained area, do they fuss and fuss until they are taken out?

• *Inside: Do not touch 'valuables'*

Children must learn early in life to respect the property of others. We should not need to child proof our homes by removing our valuables.

When parents start putting away every special or delicate item to keep them away from their children, they should know something is wrong. They should see that their children do not have the necessary self-control to keep from pulling over the plant or breaking the beautiful vase. They are not yet trained to refrain from touching certain things.[4]

Pause for Reflection:
Have you removed things from your living room because you did not want your child to break them?

• *Outside: Remains where told*

When we send our child outside, we need to know that he will do what we will tell him. We have a front porch, a walk by our house in our yard, a sidewalk and then the street. Depending upon the age, we train our child to obey us to stay within one of those certain boundaries. When older, children can go far away out of sight of his parents, but they must first learn to ask permission and follow the parents' rules.

When a child does not obey us, then we have not quite reached the point of training that is possible and that the Lord expects of us.

Pause for Reflection:
Do you find that you need to accompany your child everywhere to keep him or her safe?

An Illustration

Let me give you an example. When my little Rebekah was about 15 months she came to play in my office/ study. She sees many interesting things going on in the hallway: siblings playing, lots of comings and goings, etc. She wants to chase after them into the hallway, but she stays in the study

playing. She will stay by the door and watch but will not go beyond the boundary into the hallway.

I let her open and close the door. I do not need to keep it shut to keep her in. Neither do we use a gate. I can still get work done because she has built in rules (self-control) that govern her. I do not need to be her police force by keeping an eye on her. How does it work?

Two simple things are functioning when a child has self-control.

- **(1) She is content to play by herself.**

She is willing to amuse herself. We have a supply of toys in the study for her to play with. She likes the mundane little container or a pencil and a piece of paper. Experienced parents know that children do not need or like expensive toys!

She will play with these things for a long time. Not only for five minutes but until it is dinnertime. She has been playing for an hour in my study while I write this article on self-control. She plays around with the different toys and books (not mine of course!) in my study. I do not have to entertain her. She entertains herself.

- **(2) She governs herself according to the rules.**

She constrains herself to go by the rules. She is only 15 months old, but she will not go through that door unless I give permission or someone comes to get her. She knows the rules. What are the rules? The most important one is not to go out the doorway, but there are many others. I need to clarify some of them.

Sometimes she will come by and touch my computer mouse or something on my desk. I have not set rules for some of these things. If it is there temporarily, I just move it out of reach. But if it is one of my many books or keyboard, I instruct her, "No, no." Sometimes to emphasize my command, I need only to clap my hands two times. She does often pout and cry for about 15 seconds when she cannot get what she wants but then goes and happily plays with other things. You might think she is a super-passive child. This would be a very wrong conclusion!

She is our child, and we think she is special as all parents would think of their own sweet child. Our point, however, is not to 'show off' her abilities but to show you how you can train your child so that he or she can do these same things. Our children are not worse or better, just trained. Every child can be trained. Let us look at the specific steps for how to establish these built-in controls in all of our children.

C. *Specific Steps for Training*

Let us start with a certain scenario. Upon reaching the crawler stage, a child is newly mobile and instantly introduced to new places to go. Our situation might be different in some ways, but is no doubt very similar in many respects. All our homes have valuables (e.g. a picture) and dangerous places for the child to go.

For example, we have a living room wood stove that heats the house and runs very hot 24 hours a day on cold days. This is not a simple fireplace that is constructed in the wall. It protrudes into the living room by about four feet including the hearth.

Your child is just starting to crawl. What would you do? You foresee the danger. I gave this scenario to a group of parents, and they had all sorts of suggestions. Some would put up gates to divide off their living room. (We would need to get a fifteen-foot gate!) Another suggestion was to stop using the wood stove altogether. This would be safe but not to our liking. After all, how long will it be before the child learns not to touch the wood stove especially with multiple children?

Other suggestions were equally impractical or ineffective. A child only needs to pull over a vase or touch a wood stove once to make much damage. We will tell you how to resolve this problem that eventually confronts every family. The wood stove is only an example. Substitute your own precious thing for the wood stove. Interestingly, the parents never made one suggestion: train the child not to touch the wood stove.

Linda was clever. The wood stove is a dangerous thing to small hands. The boundary had to be broader for safety's sake. We hardly wanted her to face dire consequences during training. Training includes the correction of failure. We, however, needed a more neutral boundary.

She chose to have our baby stay off the small rug in front of the hearth. She pointed out the curve of the rug to our child and then instructed her not to go on the rug or even touch it. She pointed and said, "No." She had a tiny stick and would tap her on her hand if she even touched the rug. She then would remove the baby's hand from the rug. Do notice that she needed to stay near the child for the first couple days of training.

You can probably guess what our little one did once Mom turned her head? Our cute little Rebekah would look at that rug and crawl back over toward it. At that point, Linda would repeat the command "No, do not touch". Sometimes Rebekah would stop and crawl away. Sometimes she got a sting on her hand for touching it. When Mom consistently treated the child, the child soon learned that it always is a bad idea to touch that rug. After that, she did not touch the rug. Our stove was red hot, but she would not go near the rug. Those were her crawling days.

What about when she started walking? What happened? In the same way, she carefully avoided the hearthrug and the whole wood stove area. She applied the same lesson of self-control on crawling to when she started walking. She simply avoided the hearth rug.

Since she was trained from early on, she knew what 'No' meant. Words were not enough, however, to always counter her desires. We only needed to connect the most gentle swat from a tiny switch (branch) on her hand with the word, "No." After which, we would without hesitation remove her hand to where it should be.[5]

She would fuss and cry not because it hurt but because she was prevented from carrying out her will. In this way, the word 'no' was associated with the slight discomfort of the switch. After doing this in a number of settings, we would no longer need to use the switch but simply say, 'No.' She would still have the same, "I do not like this!" kind of cry, but she would quickly humble herself and do what she was supposed to do.

Let us summarize these points with a chart. We are asking, "What should you do when your young child starts crawling and then walking?" We will list five steps of training and comment on each of them.

Anticipate	What potential problems will you face?
Decide	What boundaries need to be set to accomplish what we desire?
Train	What is the best way to drill these guidelines into them?
Repeat	What things keep you from being consistent?
Enforce	How can we make resistance counterproductive?

1) Anticipate: What potential problems will you face?

We need to be proactive rather than reactive. Proactive parenting allows us to calmly strategize and plan. Reactive parenting usually implies shouting, yelling or even screaming. "No, don't do that!" "Didn't I tell you that before!"

Once the child can crawl, evaluate the whole room. What will be off limits? Notice those things that might be dangerous or could easily break. The parent needs to decide and then make rules for those areas. The child will need to be instructed for each rule. With the switch in hand, clearly state 'No' and show them what they are not to touch. Once the pattern of training is done several times, it is easier to train in other situations. By that time, you merely need to say, "No." The child wants to avoid any confrontation where he will lose.

This proactive approach will be repeatedly used when visiting a friend's home, going to the store or to church. Children will learn at home and apply it elsewhere. When we take our child to a new place, we need to remind them that the boundaries are similar to the boundaries at home and clarify new rules. We might note, for example, that our friends' steps are not carpeted, so we do not allow our child to climb those steps.

2) Decide: What boundaries need to be set to accomplish what we desire?

In the above scenario, we chose to make the rug off limits rather than just the hearth. This is where we first trained her when she became mobile. We knew she would test us. The older children know that the rug is okay if one is careful. That is fine with us. (Everyone likes to get up close to a nice warm fire!)

If there is a vase on a tall table, we should make the table off limits, perhaps even the area. The child is not permitted to touch electrical cords. If the table is broad and stable, it is possible just to make the vase off limits. It might be okay for the child to read a book or do a puzzle on the table. We just need to make sure the child can understand what is wrong and right.

In my study, the boundary is quite obvious, a different carpet separates the study from the hall. We can make this border more obvious by using masking tape or even by temporarily laying a rod on the carpet at the boundary line. If we are going to make boundaries, then we are also deciding to enforce them. Inconsistency on the parent's part of enforcing the rule will be interpreted by the child to mean that the boundary is only a boundary some of the time.

> ### The problem is not strong-willed children but weak-willed parents!

Due to the parent's inconsistency, the child will regularly attempt to cross the boundary and cause much consternation for the parent. In these cases we see parents making excuses for their strong-willed child. Instead they should confess that they have been inconsistent and straighten out their way. Yes, there are strong-willed children, but God has prepared even stronger-willed parents for them!

3) Train: What is the best way to instill these guidelines?

Training essentially is a set of repetitive procedures that informs, shows, warns, praises and chastises. We need to rehearse our instructions to the child not only so that the child is clear but also that the parents (themselves) are clear too. It is easy for parents to forget what rules they set.

If the parent has any doubt about whether he has sufficiently explained the rules and consequences to the child, then he should refrain from any needed correction. Instead he should sit down and clearly discuss the rules with the child. If the child often makes excuses, it is essential to have the child repeat the instructions and consequences back to you. In this way, we avoid excuses like, "You are not fair" or "I didn't hear you." The parent is fair and has let the child know what will happen if he persists in some kind of unacceptable behavior or attitude.

Both the parents and the children should know what is expected. If something is not permissible, then everyone should know of the consequences. Teaching comes before chastisement.

4) Repeat: What things keep you from being consistent?

We need to consistently train our children. If we keep doing the right thing ninety percent of the time, it is not enough. Children will then be caught in a struggle with their parents. They will regularly test the parent so that they can get their way as much as possible, even if it is only ten percent of the time. Our goal is to destroy any hope in the children that they can get their own way. Their arguments, fussing or acts of self-pity must not be successful. Only when their hope of changing the parent's mind is taken away will they stop aggressively testing their parents.

Since inconsistency produces much more trouble and testing, we need to identify those things that keep us from being consistent. Do we just not want to get up and deal with them? Do we feel bad that we need to hold back the child's freedom? Perhaps it is a certain time of day when you are just worn out. Figure out a solution and the children will behave much better.

5) Enforce: How can we make resistance counterproductive?

Never give what a child fusses for. Always make it counterproductive. Think of some extra negative consequence for undesirable behavior. This means that they lose out from any whining, rebelling or just having 'an attitude' about some rule. We often tell the child that they cannot have or do what they inappropriately asked for, not only for that day but also for the next day.

D. General Training Principles

There are a number of general training principles that we need to keep in mind.

✤ Have a good routine and schedule

A good routine is essential. The child and parent alike get used to what is expected. Once a good routine is functioning then the parent can more quickly discover what is wrong and learn how to fix it. We will discuss this more.

✤ Start very early in life

When a baby begins to stay awake a little longer, start to give him a little awake time to be by himself, not entertained or held by grandma. This goes for sleeping too. Do not allow the baby to sleep in bed with you. Taking the baby into your bed looks like the perfect solution for a crying baby. Do not set up bad habits.

Once the baby is older, these habits will be much harder to break. After checking and making sure nothing is wrong with the baby, one might need to let the baby cry a bit by himself in his bed. Sometimes they are overtired and need to cry a bit. The longer they have been used to getting their way, the more they will cry. Don't worry. They will settle down and get used to the new routine.

The earlier we start setting up the right habits, the easier it will be for the child and us. A tap with a little switch (i.e. branch) will help enforce the authority of your words. Every child is different, but each needs to be trained to obedience. Some will be easier to train; others will be quite difficult.

If we have a stubborn child, it is very likely that the parent also has that stubborn spirit. God knows what He is doing when we receive a certain child. The parent does not need to be frustrated and feel like giving up. He can parent in the confidence that God will give him or her the extra grace to care for that child (see Ephesians 2:10).

✤ Join in family activities (e.g. pray)

Have the baby and young child join in a daily prayer time with the family if he is awake. One of us usually holds the baby in our lap and holds his hands during prayer time. He begins learning how to hold his hands still during prayer very early. If the child is not yet sitting by himself, we simply hold the baby or have him nearby. This kind of training makes it so that our two year-old can quietly attend our joint homeschool session.

✤ Train what not to touch, do or go

As the baby grows, there are things that he should not bite, hold or touch. We do our best not to tempt the child. Sometimes, however, a rule is in order. When the child is taking some inappropriate action, we usually highlight the action (point to it) and gently say, "No, no." As we take it away, the child knows this action is impermissible.

The child learns that there are things they desire but cannot have. There are places they would like to go but are not allowed. They learn these important lessons of life. This is where patience and self-control is developed.

✤ Say "No, no."

This sets up a special verbal clue what they cannot do. They will associate the tap of the rod (or other appropriate flexible object) with the words they hear from us. Eventually, they will quickly respond just to our verbal clue. The slight tap refers to taking a little straight branch off the tree, making it smooth and gently tapping our child's hand when reaching for objects that are off limits.

If he is reaching for things that he is not supposed to touch, we tap his hand and say, 'No, no.' If he goes where he should not, we tap his foot. If he sits where he should not (like on his brother's hand), then we tap his bottom.[6]

✤ Return an object to its original spot

If a child takes something, he should know he is responsible to put it back. If we teach him early on, this can be like a game. "Where does it go?" the parent teasingly asks the child. The child puts the book back and the parent praises the child's right response.

✤ Other consequences

The parents must make sure that the negative consequence for doing something wrong outweighs the pleasure of getting what he wants. If the child learns that it will not be profitable, then they will give up.

However, if the parent gives a child a piece of candy at the store, then you can be sure that he will continue to fuss when the candy is gone. The more consistent parents are in their training, the quicker their children will live contently under their parents' rules.

Let us give a few real life examples.

Getting in a High Chair

A little girl gave her Mom trouble about getting in her high chair for supper. She fussed and squirmed when Mom tried to sit her down. She wanted to sit in a big chair. It would have been easier to allow her to sit in the big chair, but there would be a lost opportunity for training. Furthermore, that action would mean the end of the highchair.

Instead, her Mom reached for her little stick. When the young daughter saw it, she quietly sat down as if nothing unusual had happened. (She had already been trained by the little stick.) Mom did not need to use it on her. Once the daughter saw the stick, she, without doubt, knew Mom was serious and gave up her 'testy' spirit. In this case, she only needed to be reminded of Mom's authority.[7]

Putting on a Pretty Hat

Once, we tried to put a fancy coat and hat that someone had given us on our daughter. We wanted to put the cute clothes on her. Our child thought otherwise. She wanted to wear her own jacket. She fussed about putting the coat on but was willing. Her siblings were saying how nice the coat and hat looked. This did not change her mind. She did not want to wear the hat. She would not accept it. She pulled it off (this happened on the way out the door to church).[8]

I did not really care about the hat. In my heart, however, I knew that if we gave in to her wishes, we would have problems from here on. We paused before going out the door. We went to get the switch, and she quickly complied not only to wearing the hat but also leaving it on. Even what is more important, her testy rebellious spirit instantly changed into a compliant and cheerful spirit.

We need to be careful about telling our children to do something like wearing the hat. If we want to give them a choice, then we should do that. If we ask them to do it, then they need to learn to comply. We must be ready to enforce our words.

Summary

Rules and limits are demonstrations of love. If we do not teach our children self-control, then we are creating a child who will constantly run into conflict with authority. There will be times when the child challenges the rules. This often happens when they become aware that there are other ways of doing things. They become conscious of their own wills (two year-olds) or see a friend get away with something are two examples.

Those who have not properly trained their children often end up calling them 'terrible twos.' (We do not allow name calling in our home.) Although it might seem that the children have the major problem, the opposite is true. The parents have failed. The good news is that they can change and begin to rightly train their children. They only need to carefully affirm their rules, properly correct them (more on this later) and endure a bit more crying and fussing. The child should, in time, gain a compliant attitude. He will apologize, and we will forgive. All is restored. We have blended truth with grace. Obedience has been honored. The child is happy again!

Pause for Reflection:

We are humbled by our many parenting failures. We wish we knew to train them from the beginning–when it does not hurt so much. "Please God, forgive us. But now please help us become consistent so that we can minimize 'extra' grief to our children. Amen." The earlier we start, the easier it is for everyone involved.

A Big Problem

There are parents who are so focused on their own lives that they want obedience only so that there will be no inconvenience to their lifestyle choices. These children will react to the lack of genuine love and attention. We all need unconditional love. All the discipline in the world will not give these children what they need the most.

Remember that discipline restrains evil, but we still must love them. We must treasure and nurture (not spoil) our children. This is done through simple acts of taking walks together, reading a book together, wrestling on the floor or working around the home together. Don't get so conscious of the training process that you forget the goal of the training: the cultivation of a beautiful relationship.

E. Establishing Childhood Routines

Self-control is cultivated by having a good routine from the very earliest baby days. A routine sets the stage for good habits to be formed and is the context in which self-control can flourish.

> *A routine is a group of regularly performed related activities. Children need to be trained to do each of these behaviors.*

If there is no routine, the baby or child will not know what to expect. He will then see this as an opportunity to get his way and indulge his desires. Having a routine is essential to training.

What do we mean by routine? Routines occur when we carry out a certain set of activities in the same and timely manner. For instance, from the very first time you sit your child in the high chair, you always say, "Time to eat. Let us get in your chair." This is instruction. Then cheerfully sit him down and always buckle him in even if he fusses, squirms or you think he does not like it. <u>Do it anyway</u>. Ignore his every dislike and focus on being cheerful about the whole routine.

If you always do the same thing in the same order, he will know no difference and will accept this as the way things are done.

God has routines in nature too. The sun, night, stars and moon all perform their duties. They change at times, but the process is the same. During the winter, the sun goes down earlier. The sun, however, still goes down. Darkness creeps in. People and animals go to sleep. The process just starts earlier. Seasons include a variety of events. One comes; the other goes.

There will be times when the child will balk–do not ever give him what he wants. If he fusses, balks, cries or whines, still do what the routine demands. If he knows you will always be consistent, he will get past his fussing. Do not change the routine. He is trying to get his own way. Parents must decide what is right. Once we make an exception, we have just made things much more difficult. Be consistent.

Routine is established with the child's needs in mind. Routines change as a baby and child grows. Always introduce the next routine with pleasant words and a nice tone of voice. A tired child will be glad for a nap if it is associated with pleasant words and calm routine. A pleasant and somewhat expectant voice trains the child to look forward to an event.

There are a myriad of routines that form part of a child's daily life. Some of them are listed below.

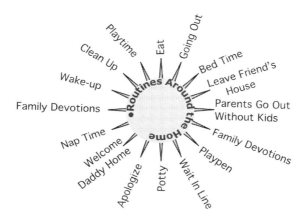

If you have neglected a certain routine, and the baby or child has been dictating what you do at feeding time, sleep time, play time, etc., you need to take back the authority you gave away. Decide what you want and with his needs in mind, take steps to get into a routine. Here are some areas that need routine:

- Potty training is perfected by routine.
- Good eating habits
- Proper sleeping habits
- Obedience is assisted by routines

The above chart highlights the many routines that are necessary to help the child know what his role is. If routines are initiated when the baby is tiny, they do not know any differently and the absence of struggle is noticeable. They accept "This is the way we do it in our family." They do not know there could be another way!

Breakdown of Routines

We need to remember that every routine is made up of a number of individual components. Below is an example of the 'Rise and Shine' or waking routine.

- Wake up   (How does one wake up? Self, alarm, be called?)
- Get up   (How much time to get out of bed?)

105

- Make Bed   (Make the bed to Mom's satisfaction).
- Dress   (Putting on the right clothes the right way).
- Put away clothes (Putting away bed clothes and dirty laundry).
- Hygiene   (Toilet (mini-routine), brush teeth, hair, wash).

Each of the routines can be broken into their specific tasks. A routine will go smoothly when the child is trained in each specific set of tasks. Young children typically get so used to routines that they dislike doing things another way. Dad quickly finds this out when Mom is sick, and he tries helping the children with something. The children know the right way to do things! Our children, for example, get upset if they do not brush their teeth just the right way. Train them right, and they will do it right (most of the time).

Sometimes the training process takes a while. Brushing the teeth routine includes: going to the bathroom when told, reaching the brush, getting a small cup of water, wetting the brush, putting a tiny bit of toothpaste on the brush, putting the tube back covered, brushing correctly, spitting out the toothpaste, taking a little drink of water, rinsing off the toothbrush, putting the toothbrush away in its proper place, putting cup back and leave the room for what is next.

The parent shows the child how to properly carry out the routine by explaining the different parts and monitoring the child's capability. The parent will do it for the child for a while until the child seems to be able to do part of it on his own. The child then takes over the parts that he can do while being supervised. Self-control is fully implemented when the child does the specific task, and later, the whole routine without any parental observation.

Points of Frustration

When a parent feels frustrated over something that his child has or has not done, he probably has discovered a task within a routine that is not being rightly done or even the complete absence of a certain routine. Training is required. For example, what happens to coats, boots and hats when your child arrives home? If you find yourself upset about where they end up, then you need to train them more effectively.

It would be helpful to review the whole routine (coming home routine) and each task that you want completed. This will help you more clearly see what tasks are needed and the overall purpose of the 'coming home' routine.

Remember, a parental attitude of joy and patience along with firmness is important to gaining a child's cooperation. No one wants to be around a grouch, including your child.

Pause for Reflection:
What are your children doing that frustrate you? Identify what you would like done, think about what your child can do and go over with the child the routine you would like.

Routines are tools, not masters

It is easy to see our routines as our end goal to happy parenting. This approach will cause difficulty. God has placed the parents in charge rather than a set of routines. Routines serve parents and children. God sets parents in charge because they have the wisdom to discern God's goals and make the necessary adjustments.

We have discovered good routines enable parents to have more flexibility when needed. This Friday, we have an evening Thanksgiving service. Because our children go to bed at regular times, does this mean we should not go to the service? Not at all.

We might add a nap to their day or plan to let them sleep a little later the next day, but it is important to be with God's people celebrating God's goodness. That is more important. So we adjust to God's schedule. There will be times that it is impossible for them to attend (because of sickness, conflict, etc.), but it should not be because we want to strictly keep some routine. Add a 'go to church' routine!

We need to allow God's will to govern our lives. We make adjustments and the children see that we make the Lord's way a priority. They learn that they also should make Him a priority.

F. Children's Daily Schedule

A mother can easily get overwhelmed with the many things to do during a day. Having a good schedule greatly clarifies her goals and helps her keep attentive when interruptions occur.

A daily schedule includes a combination of routines. We might have nine regular routines such as getting up, eating lunch, etc. throughout each day and several irregular ones depending on what day of the week it is. Saturday morning is the time when our children clean the house (do chores). We might want to include going shopping or visiting a friend. The schedule helps put things in order so that parent and child know what is expected.

This schedule is an example of one we use for our home-school children. It is not exact. As children get older, their school days extend well into the afternoon. Our older children keep their own schedules. At times, we need to make sure we are working with each other such as in giving rides or having family devotions. They, however, have their own routine.

> 7:00 Rise & shine: Wake Up (Get up, make bed, dress, put away clothes, hygiene)
> 7:30 Family devotions at breakfast table: Devotions
>   (Assemble, pray, sing, scripture)
> 7:45-8:30 Breakfast (Eat, do assigned jobs)
> 8:45-12:00 School (joint and separate)
>   Noon Lunch (arrive, eat, do assigned jobs)
> 1:00 Nap routine
> 1-3 Back to school
> 3-5 Friends/library/play/computer time (half hour)
> 5:00 Pick up designated areas/PBS television or video
> 5:30 Set table (assigned)
> 6:00 Supper (arrive, eat, do assigned jobs)
> 7:30 Bed routine (Dress, hygiene, pick up)
> 7:45 Family Devotions (Assemble, sing, scripture, pray)
> 8:15-9:30 Go to bed: 8:15 Rebekah; 8:30 Isaac; 8:45
>   Kathryn, Benjamin; 9:00 Daniel; 9:30 Allison

Build in flexibility. We remind our children that just because we regularly do a certain activity, it does not mean that we will always do it this way. Children will try to insist on the authority of the schedule rather than the parent. We need to make clear that the parents are always in charge and can change things if they so desire.

Job Routines

My wife keeps a small white-board at the kitchen entrance where daily jobs are added on to the above schedule.[9] This is the "Who does what board." This way she does not need to hear the famous, "But I did not hear you 'excuse.'" She does not have to tell anyone. She simply has trained them to read the board several times a day.

The above is the semi-fixed homeschool day schedule. There are many other things not mentioned in it. Dad and Mom also have schedules. Parents do not rotate around the child's schedule, but the child around the parents. This helps simplify life. Of course, as the children grow older, they will have more activities, and these can seem to dominate things. We have purposed to keep life simple.

Sports and entertainment

Some parents feel compelled to give their child every opportunity that presents itself. Soon, sports, classes, entertainment and other activities (seeing movies, parties) have almost suffocated family life. The family ends up never being together except to escort the child to the next activity. Our suggestion is to purposely build a home-based family.

Our children can get their exercise riding a bike around the neighborhood. A sports team is too demanding. As a pastor, I am humbled at the many parents who involve themselves and their children in regular sports activities on the Lord's Day. "Yea, my son has a match. I cannot make it to church."

I wonder if they know that they are training their child in a secular mindset, "We only listen to God when it fits into my schedule." The child learns that it is more important to please the coach than to worship God. The father needs to decide what is appropriate for his family. He is accountable to the Lord Almighty. May God help us make godly decisions rather than follow the pathway of the world.

Summary

God has given us the tools we need to train our children to do the right thing even when we are not around. We do not need to accompany our children everywhere. (It's a good thing with eight children!) By training, routines and schedules they pretty much operate as we wish without much fuss. Like a technician, we identify the routine and the different elements that we want accomplished. We spot the problem, add training and get the routine up and running. This enables our children to accomplish what we see is best.

This kind of training, along with time scheduling provides us with plenty of time to do what we need to do at work and at home. We also allocate time to be with our children and just enjoy them. Dad might take them to the park. Mom might bake a special desert. We focus on developing a relationship with them rather than 'always' criticizing them for things that they are not doing right.

Dad, for instance, reads a chapter out loud after a meal from "The Chronicles of Narnia." They love to listen to the story. We have a nice meal, then together we listen to the story and enjoy our special family time. Spice up life by playing games together and doing things together. This might include visiting faraway grandparents or cutting the bushes and cleaning up the yard. Have fun together! Work together! Enjoy each other and the time God has given you.

Parenting Principles & Practices

- Parents are always training their children, either for good or bad.
- We should expect crawlers and toddlers to do what we tell them.
- Carefully thought-out routines are a prerequisite to training.
- Training consists of instructing and enforcing specific behaviors and attitudes.
- A routine is a set of repeated tasks that the parent has trained the child to perform.
- Parents need to keep schedules flexible to accomplish God's will.

Parenting Questions

1. What happens if the parent does not deliberately cultivate self-control?
2. List what happens when a parent does not train the child to rightly use his or her voice and words.
3. Explain how the spirit of complaining typically originates.
4. Write down two things we can expect toddlers to do.
5. What are the five steps to training your child?
6. We know a child has self-control when he exhibits what two things?
7. What is a routine?
8. How is a schedule different from a routine?
9. What should a parent do if something interrupts their child's schedule?
10. What should a parent do when he or she feels frustrated about something their child is or is not doing?
11. What is the danger to family life if there are too many activities?

Notes from Chapter #5

---

[1] Read our training manual on getting ready for birth and caring for infants in "Godly Beginnings for the Family" (www.foundationsforfreedom.net).

[2] Remember children and adults go through cycles. It seems that once the child is trained, he or she either tests you or grows out of that schedule! Parents need ample gentleness, understanding, love and firmness. When the child is being adamant about resisting his nap, perhaps you can just keep your hand on the little one long enough to help him withstand the urge to stand up until he falls asleep. Meanwhile one can gently sing a song. When the child sleeps, quietly leave the room.

[3] High chairs are hardly required. They are common in our culture so I use them as an example. The point is that the child learns to patiently wait for his or her food.

[4] Although our children are trained, not all children are. If you have other families to your home, you perhaps need to think about putting away your nice vases or just trust them in the Lord's hands. Hospitality is a command of the Lord. Preserving our trinkets does not come near in importance to practicing hospitality. Once you know the parents, see if you can help train them!

[5] Some people are shocked at 'hitting' a small child. They might even call it abuse. We look at this quite differently. We view the danger of allowing the child to go near dangerous objects and not to listen to instruction as irresponsible. Think a moment. Do you not give your child an immunization to protect him? Or would you not, like I had to, bring your son with a broken leg in to the hospital where they would increase the pain until it was properly set? We need to look long term rather than focus on our immediate feelings. More discussion on God's perspective of physical discipline is given in a later chapter.

[6] This is not the same as spanking. The amount of discomfort and the emphasis on training distinguishes it from spanking.

[7] If the child fussed every time she was placed in the highchair, then we would have to change our strategy. In that case, we would use the rod every time she fussed about getting into the chair. What is the difference? In the first case, she was just feeling out whether we were still in charge. Once seeing that we were serious, she conformed. This happens once in a while. Easily solved. But when there is a bad habit associated with a poor attitude that is accompanied by standing in the high chair and trying to climb out, then we need to retrain her by use of the rod.

[8] So many bad things happen on the way to church! The evil one tries to get us upset so that we do not hear the Word of God. Some things can be prepared the night before: picking out clothes, filling the diaper bag, but there is often that one incident that still occurs. Make corrections as needed and then focus your mind back on the Lord. If this happens regularly, pray together as a family for this problem. Point out to everyone what is happening.

[9] We have since bought a bigger white board (big family) with magnetic strips and have put it on our refrigerator.

Chapter #6

CORRECTING OUR CHILDREN

Purpose: Provide a scriptural perspective of properly dealing with disobedient children so that they might become joyful family members.

A. Cultivating an Excellent Parent-Child Relationship

Parents must keep the goals for their children right in front of them. Not only must they pray for their children's godly development, but they also should praise and encourage them in the many small steps that they take to get there.

As we learn to deal with disobedient children, it is easy for us to lose sight of our goals. Because of the long-term nature of training children, a parent's eyes might never be lifted above the problems that are so obvious. Please remember, as we discuss correction, that it is only one of a variety of means to reach our goals. Throughout this lesson, we will discuss two kinds of disobedient children: the trained and the untrained.

First, we will focus on general guidelines for parents to correct their children. These parents have made a start to training, but no matter how well a child is trained, he will sometimes disobey his parents. There are times when the child is legitimately forgetful, but this is not often and is easily corrected with a word of reproof. When a child is willfully disobedient, he is to be handled differently. We will discuss chastisement (physical correction) in the next lesson, but in this chapter, we want to focus on general principles that work hand in hand with chastisement.

Second, we will learn how to deal with children that have not been trained. They have very little self-control and despise authority while seeking to fulfill their own desires. One boy explained that when other people ask him to do something, he is quite willing. If his parents ask him to do even a small thing, however, he gets upset and treats it as a very big thing. Parents can get quite desperate for help in this kind of situation.

The parent is in authority. The child will challenge that authority. When we attempt to bring our child back to where he ought to be, we will face opposition, crying, rude remarks, stubbornness, etc. Parents must be confident that they are leading the child along God's way. Otherwise, they will tend to drift into compromise and, in the end, give up. Before they know it, they are back to where they started, maybe even worse off. Dad and Mom must work as a team to endure the resistance that will come from correcting their children. They need each other's support.

Pause for Reflection:
What kind of challenges to your parental authority has your child given you? How did you respond?

The Goal of Parenting
The goal for parenting should be to have an excellent relationship with our grown children, who are full of God's love and principles. So, let us look at the stages of training to reach those goals. At any time, we should know which stage our child is at and how we generally need to relate to him.

The surgeon, for example, knows that his goal goes far beyond having an operation. He could, if he so desired, perform five different operations on one person. He must strictly limit his operative procedures so that he may obtain the greater goal of his patient's good health and overall well being. His goal for a good recovery shapes the timing of his surgeries.

The parents' purpose must also be greater than just correcting the child or making him obey. We are accountable to God to bring up children that respect authority, have mastered self-control and are able to express their love for God and man. Self-control will be seen in their attitudes, thoughts and behavior. Modeling and teaching God's love and righteousness and training them to limit their desires to serve God and others accomplish this goal. As a child learns to respect his parents and siblings at home, this will enable him to easily transfer this attitude to relationships with God and other people. Notice the following illustration.

THE PARENT'S GOAL FOR THEIR CHILDREN

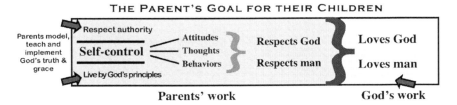

Our two goals are summarized by Christ's commands to love God and love others.

> *And you shall love the LORD your God with all your heart, and with all your soul, and with all your mind, and with all your strength. The second is this, you shall love your neighbor as yourself (Mark 12:30-31).*

Here are five principles gathered from this discussion.

- God has given everything parents need for good parenting.
- Parents learn how to care for their children from God the Father.
- Our greatest goals are not wealth, wit, skill or position but to love God and others.
- We can train our children only to the point of respecting God and others. God alone by His Spirit can change our children's hearts. Our duty is to persistently pray for our children.
- Children need to become Christians to really love God and mankind as Christ did.

Parents can model a love for God and others but cannot change child's heart. We must pray for them, coax them and even plead with them to love God. In the end, we must leave this work with God's Holy Spirit.

At the same time as we focus on these goals, we will nurture a good relationship with our children. The real test of their respect for God and others is seen in whether they respect the parents' authority and can have a close relationship with them. Good parent and child relationships are the results of proper training.

Let us take a look at the way the parent and child should relate to each other. We have marked off five different stages of relationship that the child should pass through as he grows. Please remember that the given ages are **only suggested as** a guideline and not meant to be the rule. We use them to emphasize the stages of the relationship between the parent and the child. Unfortunately, many parents never take their child beyond the first stage and end up having no real relationship with their child. Please carefully read the chart below.

THE GROWTH OF PARENT–CHILD RELATIONSHIPS				
Pre-birth ~ 5 m.	6 m. ~ 2 1/2 y.	Ages 3 ~ 11	Ages 12 ~ 19	Ages 20+
#1 CARETAKER	#2 TRAINER	#3 TEACHER	#4 COACH	#5 FRIEND
The parent gives tender love and care to the child building trust and security.	The parent orders the child's day and insures compliance while teaching boundaries.	The parent teaches how biblical principles relate to the instructions they are to keep.	The parent guides his child as to how to apply God's principles to different areas of life.	The parent shares as a good friend, listening to her child rehearse aloud different life situations.
Loving	Learning	Valuing	Discerning	Sharing

The ultimate goal for our children for him or her to be one of our best friends on earth. Is this not the essence of the family? The way our grown children relate to us is the final test of how we did.

Pause for Reflection:
What kind of relationship would you like to have with your children at each of these stages? Is it possible? How do you obtain that goal?

Good Relationships

What does it mean to have good relationships with your older children? In our house, at about 10 or 10:30 p.m., all a sudden my wife and I, who are usually getting ready to pray, hear an increasingly loud sound coming from upstairs. The sound is our two oldest daughters running down the stairs to join us and make some good conversation among us. One of them usually teases Dad. Sometimes both do! We all laugh and have some fun talking. Sometimes we even talk about matters that are more serious. We are so glad to be together as a family.

The scriptures promise that God will bring blessings into our family through the lives of our children. Children do not only create a community of joy and love (Psalm 127:3-5) but also extend the mission that God has given to the family (Psalm 103:17).

> *Behold, children are a gift of the LORD; The fruit of the womb is a reward. Like arrows in the hand of a warrior, So are the children of one's youth. How blessed is the man whose quiver is full of them; They shall not be ashamed, when they speak with their enemies in the gate (Psalm 127:3-5).*

> *But the lovingkindness of the LORD is from everlasting to everlasting on those who fear Him, and His righteousness to children's children (Psalm 103:17).*

God's design is to bring blessings into our lives through our children, and it is not only for the first six months of life when they are still cute. Our pursuit as parents, then, is to train up children in a way that they are joy to our souls. They are the ones through whom our love, joy and work are sent into the world. Through them, God's praises go out to the world.

> *For He established a testimony in Jacob, and appointed a law in Israel, which He commanded our fathers, that they should teach them to their children (Psalm 78:5).*

All the important concepts that help us reach that kind of relationship fit into this general framework. Stage #1, the caretaker, is the most obvious. Stages #2 and #3, the trainer and teacher, are the most crucial. The last two stages will develop rather naturally if stages #1-3 are in place. Stage two helps associate correction with instruction. Stage three uses biblical principles to assist the child in affirming the worth of his parents' instruction and values. As children understand the principles, they then adopt them as guideposts for their own lives.

The scriptures repeatedly state without reservation that children are a blessing. Few people nowadays think this way.

- They want a child
    - but then start fearing the toddler stage and
        - dread teenage rebellion and do not know ....

This does not sound like a blessing! Parents are raising their children in fear rather than faith. Unfortunately, parents often give in to these fears at critical times by questioning their parenting practices and becoming inconsistent in the treatment of their children. Blessing means to share in a happy family that loves to be together. We need to keep our eyes on our goals and follow through with determination to rightly train our children and correct their disobedience.

Now that we have a whole picture, we need to look at what practical steps need to be taken to get to that point. We will speak very specifically about chastisement and physical discipline in the next lesson. First we have to touch on other issues that are just as important but are often neglected.

B. Going Beneath the Surface: Touching the Heart

Children are not naturally compliant. Some might be more compliant, but they all struggle with obedience. Obedience does not come naturally. Disobedience does!

The fact is that all of our children, in a lesser or greater way, at some point will display a rebellious spirit. They have inherited a rebellious nature from their parents! They do not carry out what we wish or do it in the way that we desire. Some parents might think their children are an exception to this. They reason that their children are not so bad. The truth is, they are not looking carefully.

Comparison and pride blind many parents. They default to inferior standards. One might say, "I know my Joey would never … ." It might be true, but some parents are not very aware of what their children really do or to what standard God holds them accountable. We must examine our children by God's Word.

Other parents are relativistic and emphasize self-expression. They have no real standards. They think their child is great, no matter what he does. This harms the child more than helps him to reach God's goals. The child really begins to believe his parents. Watch out for this child!

Pause for Reflection:
How good are your children? The real test is what God thinks of them. Since this is harder to judge, we need to ask the next reliable test: What do your neighbors think of your children?[1]

Dealing with Bad Attitudes
Some parents are convinced their children are not that bad because they only focus on a certain set of actions. They never think of examining their child's attitudes. For this reason, many parents have a

rebel in their house. War has set in; there is no peace. Here are a few examples.

• After a reprimand or chastisement, the child shrugs a shoulder and walks away showing he does not really care what the parent just said.

• The daughter says, "Please let me through," but with such a sassy voice, she generates a horrible nasty feeling.

• The child is warned to pick up the room quickly but just keeps on playing with the toys as if he did not hear a thing his parent said.

• Mom told her son not to watch any more television but to get to his homework. He marches off to do his homework, but stomps on the steps leading to his room.

Rebellion is revealed in the actions but seeded in the attitude (heart). Just like a plant. The roots are hidden underground. Although we cannot see them, we know the presence of a plant indicates that there are also plant roots. The scriptures say that the true nature of a person (what's in the heart) is revealed by what he says and does.

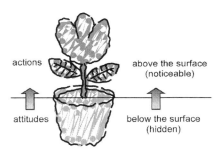

When we train our children, we often only focus on their behaviors and ignore their attitudes. We can see bad attitudes expressed in the haughty tone of a voice, the sour facial expression, or in the slowness to respond. Attitudes, as well as behaviors, can be evil and need to be removed to have a peaceful home.

Does a fountain send out from the same opening both fresh and bitter water? Can a fig tree, my brethren, produce olives, or a vine produce figs? Neither can salt water produce fresh (James 3:11-12).

The good man out of the good treasure of his heart brings forth what is good; and the evil man out of the evil treasure brings forth what is evil; for his mouth speaks from that which fills his heart (Luke 6:45).

The fountain's water will be characterized by what is down below the ground. Either it will be bitter or it will be sweet. It cannot be both. Only good can produce good; evil produces evil.

Did you ever have a child that obeyed what you asked, and yet something was still surely wrong? You had a hard time identifying it. It is likely to be the bad attitude that you noticed. They use their attitudes as well as other responses to express their rebellion.

rebellious actions

rebellious attitude

If we tolerate these subtle challenges to our authority, then our children will continue to act in this way. If we want sweet, nice and gentle responses, then we need to train them to respond that way.

Even if we correct their actions, as long as we tolerate these rebellious attitudes, we will never be able to train the child's heart. As a parent, we want heart loyalty. We cannot accept those attitudes that are hostile because God does not like them. Furthermore, they will jeopardize building a good relationship between us.

Most parents focus on actions, but for our purposes, we must go down and reach the heart. If a parent wants loyalty and closeness, they must not allow things to keep them apart. Bitterness is an oft-warned against problem in the scriptures.

See to it that no one comes short of the grace of God that no root of bitterness springing up causes trouble, and by it many be defiled (Hebrews 12:15).

We need to identify the problem and set some general rules to rightly deal with bad attitudes. We need to judge which actions along with which attitudes are disrespectful and not acceptable. The standards and consequences must be clearly made known to the child. Every culture has different manifestations of disrespectful attitudes.

One of the most sour experiences of life is to face a child that complies on the outside but not on the inside.

For example, the child can say, "Thank you" with a bad intonation and a curled lip. They did say, "Thank you," but the **attitude** was bad. As parents, we might need to imitate them to show them how they look and sound. Then we can politely show them

the right way to say, "Thank you," and have them repeat it. We use a warm and expressive face to say, "Thank you" to show them how to properly respond.

Pause for Reflection:
Can you identify some of these bad attitudes in your children? Write them down. At a proper time, share your observations with your child.

How do we implement changes?
There are four ways a parent can properly deal with their children and prevent building barriers (4 'H's): Honesty, Humility, Hearing and Heart.

1) Honesty: The parent does not lie. The child knows there are no ulterior motives for the parent's actions. Honesty chases away superficial relationships.

2) Humility: The parent's ability to acknowledge mistakes. This does not make the wrong right, but it does enable the child to respect and love their imperfect parents.

3) Hearing: The parent's desire to listen to the child goes a long way in developing a good relationship. Malachi 4:5 says that restoring the father's heart to his child must occur before the child can be restored. In other words, restoration takes place when the father really begins to care for his child.

> *And he will restore the hearts of the fathers to their children, and the hearts of the children to their fathers, lest I come and smite the land with a curse (Malachi 4:6).*

4) Heart: The parents must secure the heart and affection of the child. This is done by dealing with the child's wrong actions and attitudes. Parents often ignore attitudes perhaps because they are more subtle. But as long as the child can express these rebellious attitudes, the child's heart will still be out of the parent's reach.

We need to start by apologizing for tolerating unacceptable behaviors and attitudes. Specify which attitudes are unacceptable. Tell them how tolerating these things has hurt your relationship with them and that you would now like to restore that, if possible. The children are now quite used to saying and doing things in certain ways. They do not even know how terrible those things are that they say and do. The children's bad habits formed in the first place because Dad and Mom neglected to discipline and train them.

Let them know things are changing. They need to know that you are no longer tolerating such behaviors, sounds and expressions. Tell them the consequences for such things.

Help them identify the problem. They might not be aware of what they do either. So maybe for the first or second time, do not chastise them. After they have made the face or 'attitude,' show them what it looks like or what their voice sounded like. Remind them that correction will start next week or whenever you decide. Be specific about what day and what the consequences will be.

Summary

Corrections must go beyond the typical focus on behavior or actions but must include the attitudes. By doing this, we eliminate the subtle but sure rejection of our authority. This does not change the heart, but it does curb it in such a way that healthy relationships can grow between the parent and the child. This is, after all, our goal!

Now we will look at an important key to developing good relationships even as the parents are curbing their children's improper behavior. Some parents fear that if they begin to restrain their child's bad behavior, their relationship with the child will be damaged. Concluding that correction would increase the hostility between them, they hold back what is so desperately needed. They could not be more wrong.

C. Principles of Trust & Freedom

Our God-given goals will help keep before us what needs to be done. When we see our child varying from what is expected, we need to make a judgment as to what is wrong and correct it. We must deal with every form of disobedience. Disobedience is like yeast that permeates the whole. We see this analogy given by Paul. "A little yeast leavens the whole loaf." When I make bread, only two tablespoons of yeast raise four whole loaves of bread. It is the nature of yeast to grow and spread. In the same way, one act of disobedience will influence him until dealt with.

The following principle has helped us discern and correct our children in many situations from the youngest to the oldest. Let us first discuss the principle and then discuss why it works so well. Freedom is built on trust and established by obedience.

If we cannot trust them in our sight, then we cannot trust them out of our sight.

Obedience earns trust. Repeated obedience produces more trust leading to more freedom. Disobedience creates mistrust and takes away the freedoms that have been gained.

The child is expected to carry out parental instruction at home before he is allowed (trusted) to carry them out where the parent is not present. If the child does not carry out his parent's commands in the parent's presence, he or she certainly will not consistently carry them out at a neighbor's house or at the park.

Children can understand the logic of this argument. If the child is disobeying at home, then he certainly cannot be trusted to obey at someone else's house. We can get even more specific. The applications are boundless. If the boys cannot play nicely in their bedroom, then they will need to play within our sight. What this means practically is that they will need to stay by our side for the afternoon, or however long we judge necessary, to see if they have corrected their attitudes and actions.

The scriptures describe this process of development. At first the children are led by law; this is a temporary stage. The laws are external stimuli and standards that they are held accountable to. The laws are the four walls of the protected garden where they are kept safe.

> *But before faith came, we were kept in custody under the law, being shut up to the faith which was later to be revealed. Therefore the Law has become our tutor to lead us to Christ, that we may be justified by faith (Galatians 3:23-24).*

Our goal is to help them to internalize these 'laws' so that whether they are far away or near, the laws will govern and keep them. These laws are superseded when a greater law (the law of love) rules their hearts. This is what Christ refers to when He instructed us to love one another.

The advantage of this process is that it puts the burden of the solution on the child. They desperately want the freedom of playing by themselves in their bedroom or when older with their friends outside. They know how the rule works. Because they have done something wrong, they have lost their freedom for a time. No one likes losing his or her once-gained freedoms. They cannot blame Dad or Mom. They were warned, but they also know the solution. If they are to regain their freedom, they will need to make corrections.

The solution focuses on the renewing of their commitment to do what is right. They are motivated to do what is right. Do you see the bargaining chips? Obedience for freedom.[2] If we are consistent in pulling back their freedoms when they disobey, then they will be less likely to disobey. Their desires then focus them on the worth and reward of obedience.

Responsibility and Freedom

The funnel does a good job illustrating this principle. We are thankful for Gary Ezzo's illustration. Children are responsible to live within the boundaries (their parents' instructions) wherever they are in the funnel (life), even though they are no longer in the parents' presence.[3] Once the parent understands this process, it is useful throughout the parenting years. This helps the child, young or old, to know what is expected. We will discuss how to form these boundaries for different stages of life later on in the series.

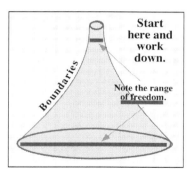

Let us first better understand the funnel. Freedom is represented by the width of the funnel and increases narrow to wide. This is somewhat related to age, but it has more to do with maturity. Maturity means he shows responsibility and is obedient. When a child is immature, there are few freedoms. When he is more mature, the child's freedoms are extended. Freedoms might include going further away to play, having an mp3 player, having more activities to do or associating with others after dinner. Freedom never means or implies the ability to do things that their parents or God would not accept.[4]

The sides of the funnel represent the boundaries, laws, rules or parental expectations. These boundaries should be clearly identified.

When a child gets close to the edge, remind them of your expectation and the consequence. When a child is small, the boundaries are very narrow and few. As a child matures, the boundaries will expand because the child can be trusted to obey his parents. For example, when a child is small, he cannot go outside the yard by himself. The rule is fixed, "Stay in the yard." When a child is older, he might be allowed to travel on a bus by himself and come back at night around nine o'clock. The 'laws' have been greatly broadened.

As freedoms increase, responsibilities also increase. Although the child's loyalty to his parents' instruction will not change, the principles need to be consistently applied to a greater number of circumstances. The parents will help define how the principles will apply in different circumstances. The child will need to learn to obey and apply the principles to new circumstances which his parents did not specifically apply for him. As children grow older, they face a greater number of new circumstances than the parent could ever imagine. This is the reason trust, training and prayer are so important.

For example, the child has been trained what is permissible to say and not to say. They have learned that at home. Parents expect them to maintain the same standards at the park with their friends or on the phone upstairs. We recently had to clarify our expectations. We got the children together and explained what swear words are. A friend of our son used one of the words. It is true that the children did not think it was a swear word. I decided that it was a swear word, even though it is now commonly used even by people in the church.[5] I simply told them if their friends say such words around them, then they will not be able to play together. Our children pressured their friend so that the friend no longer says it when around our children.

This parental model's premise is based upon the idea that a disobedient child has too much freedom and needs to be restricted. This highlights one of the biggest mistakes parents make. Children are given too much freedom before they show they are responsible. The child is too far down on the lower and wider circles of the funnel away from the source of truth (the parents).

The solution is to bring him back closer to the head of the funnel until he shows that he can obey at this level. This will mean restrictions and loss of freedom in one way or another. Fortunately, we can encourage the child to focus on what needs to be done to regain his former freedoms.

This highlights one of the biggest mistakes parents make. Children are given too much freedom much too early.

The scriptures acknowledge our innate desire to be free. The reason the child wants to grow up is to have greater freedoms. Freedom, however, is tied to our responsibility to live for others rather than for ourselves. If we cannot care for others when exerting our freedoms, then we cannot have that freedom.

> *For you were called to freedom, brethren; only do not turn your freedom into an opportunity for the flesh, but through love serve one another (Galatians 5:13).*

This freedom-boundary principle can guide children of any age, even before they can talk. Since it touches their longing for freedom, children quickly get the message.[6]

Parental instruction forms a child's basic set of rules for life. As the child grows, parental instructions alter slightly. Boundaries are extended.

What if the child is not held accountable? This breeds irresponsibility in the child. The child will be burdened with guilt because his sin has not been dealt with. The child will grow hardened and bitter toward both God and his parents. He will avoid them.

Sometimes, we notice that when a child has been with friends, he comes home rather rebellious, not as ready to carry out our instructions as formerly. It reveals some immaturity in handling freedom, or they are too easily influenced by friends with a bad attitude. He might be harboring a guilty conscience. We demand a change of heart (attitude) before they are allowed to play with their friends again. Since we do not know what the 'sin' is, we cannot chastise them. This is where this principle powerfully comes to play. They hate loosing their freedoms and are motivated to obey even if it means humbling their attitudes on their own. This approach works wonderful with all our children. This also helps reinforce the message that disobedience <u>never</u> pays off.[7]

Pause for Reflection:
Can you trust your child when he is out of your sight? If not, what areas of self-control does your child still need to work on?

Examples for a Young Child

A toddler has just learned to walk. He loves walking. However, he has to have boundaries set for him. He should be limited to certain play areas (limit the freedom to roam). We might use doors or gates as physical barriers or draw an imaginary line and associate the crossing of it with our word, "No."

The child will get used to staying in that one place during a certain time. As he gets older, it would be appropriate to extend the boundaries. In the new area, the child must first be taught what they can or cannot do. If they disobey a clear rule, then they should be chastised and placed back in the more restricted area.

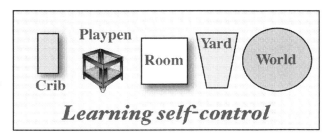

Learning self-control

A playpen is a good training place for a crawler. It is safe and small. The child can always be returned to the playpen to reinforce the connection of freedom with responsibility. This method can also be applied to toys. If they do not put away their play things, then they cannot play with them for a day or two.

Examples for an Older Child

An older child might be mastering boundaries like staying in the yard or staying away from certain cable television stations. How do we train them to obey in new circumstances such as on the sidewalk or track field near your home?

We tell them what boundaries we do or do not want in the new sphere of activity. We might observe them for a while to see what else we might add to what we have already said or to modify our instructions. We remind them that only 'big and responsible' children can play on the sidewalk near the street (make sure they have given safety instructions). This means that he has to carefully obey his parents. We warn him of the consequences of disobedience: chastisement and the loss of the freedom until we see obedience.

Guidelines with Older Children

We often use this 'freedom' principle with watching television, computer games, eating, talking on the phone, going to bed on time, etc. There is no limit. In each area, the parents have rules, rules for when the younger ones and modification of these rules for the older ones. No child wants to return to the old boundaries!

If they disobey in one area, make sure the consequence matches 'the crime.' If they got to bed late, then they will need to go to bed early for a set number of nights. If they disobey again, then it is obvious that they need further training. Going to bed earlier for a longer number of nights would be appropriate.

Use discernment to determine why the child got to bed late. Check his routine. Is there enough time to do what is expected? Why did he get to bed late? Was there an emergency? Did he need to use the bathroom again? Did he forget to do something?

If they used bad words while talking to a friend, then they cannot see their friend for a set time. If an offense is repeated, lengthen the restriction. If they sneak a snack, then make them go without that kind of snack for a set time (maybe two days).

God as our Father does such things regularly. He disciplines His children in the same area that they have disobeyed. Abraham compromised his wife. What he wanted so desperately (a son) did not come until much later. Because of Jacob's deceitful behavior, he paid fourteen years of service to Laban, his father-in-law, who was even more crooked than he.

Summary

There simply is no end to life circumstances in which we can implement this freedom-boundary model. When the children are very small, we just restrict their freedom. We do not explain anything. When the children are older, we need to explain more how the offense is related to the consequence. We are strengthening their self-control. One day they will not have us around at all. The funnel keeps expanding but hopefully all the important rules have been internalized by then, making it easy for them to obey the Lord.

Pause for Reflection:
Have you been able to put this freedom principle into practice yet? How have you restricted your child's freedoms because of disobedience? Have you slowly expanded their freedoms based on

obedience and show of responsibility? Have you explained your expectations for their behavior in the new situation?

D. Confession is Cleansing to the Soul

Confession of sin enables our child to maintain a healthy, cheerful life. As long as guilt has not been properly dealt with, children will feel burdened down. Guilty people, whether young or old, overreact rather than respond humbly to confrontation. This makes it much more difficult to solve problems. Regular confession accompanied by chastisement enables the relationship to be restored in a moment. The child loves this and so does the parent. Restoration is sweet to the soul.

Sin is like a wall that comes between people. Guilt causes us to hide and defend ourselves. We avoid those that we have wronged. We see this principle very clearly illustrated in the garden of Eden. Adam and Eve avoided meeting with God. John 3:20 tells us that sin separates us from God because the 'light' threatens the 'darkness.' "For everyone who does evil hates the light, and does not come to the light, lest his deeds should be exposed."

Did you ever wonder where deep animosity and hate is found? It is in families that have not straightened out many wrongs and offenses. Bitterness increases to high levels when we are in close, regular contact with someone that has offended us. Just talk to some parents with teenagers, and the point will be quickly proven.

Pause for Reflection:
Do people in your home apologize for their wrongs? What is the result of your policy?

Handling Troubled Relationships

This is where God's love shines so marvelously. Through Jesus Christ, we are able to get God's forgiveness for our own sin. Then we can pass forgiveness on to others by being gracious and merciful to them.[8]

One of the great tasks of parenting is to model and train the children to straighten out offenses. Preserving relationships with others is more important than holding onto our pride (love one another). By modeling humility, we are preparing our children to seek Christ for their sins.

The mission of a Christian according to scripture is to be a reconciler (2 Corinthians 5:17-21).

*Namely, that God was in Christ reconciling the world to Himself, not counting their trespasses against them, and He has **committed to us the word of reconciliation**. Therefore, we are ambassadors for Christ, as though God were entreating through us; we beg you on behalf of Christ, be reconciled to God (2 Corinthians 5:19-20).*

*If therefore you are presenting your offering at the altar, and there remember that your brother has something against you, leave your offering there before the altar, and go your way; **first be reconciled to your brother**, and then come and present your offering (Matthew 5:23-24).*

Parents show children how to humble themselves by modeling the attitude and actions of confession. The child should see his parents apologizing not only to each other but also to others outside the home. Parental confession should be made to the children when they have been wronged. With this foundation, children will not feel awkward apologizing but will take it as part of life.

If, however, the parents hold bitterness toward others, then, this process of fostering a spirit of forgiveness in our child will backfire. Such children often get very bitter towards this kind of parent. Their 'walls of sin' have not been taken down. Remember, if this wall of hostility continues, then your children will misinterpret your attempts to correct them. Emotion prevails over logic.

So let us rehearse what needs to be done when we hear two siblings starting to cry or yell at each other. Many of these principles are also applicable to the relationships parents have with their children or children with their friends.

We will now walk through the steps of restoration.

1) Call to Conference

All the possible guilty parties must be brought before the parent. Sometimes, witnesses are needed. At first, if one is not careful, all sorts of accusations will be brought forward. "He did it!" We ask them to be quiet unless spoken to. If they insist on speaking, then they would be chastised (see next chapter for more). After they quiet down, then we start the meeting by lining up those involved by age (this is sometimes necessary with a large family).

2) Raising the Hand

I usually start this conference by asking, "Who has done something wrong? Raise your hand."

Usually more than one child quickly look at each other and raise their hands. It is rare that all of them are not guilty of something. They usually know one or two 'big' things that they have done wrong.

3) Confession Time

I ask each of them that raised their hand what they have done wrong. I am firm at this point not to allow the others to 'leak' information. If needed, I will come back to them later.

I want to cultivate in the children both the attitude and ability to admit what they did wrong. At the same time, they can see that though they have something against the other person(s), they themselves also have done wrong. Another advantage for this is to prepare them for the gospel. By admitting their wrongs, they get to see their need for Christ.

If someone has been accused of something wrong but did not previously raise his hand, I ask him if he did that one thing. If so, I ask him if he thinks it is wrong. If not, I give my perspective on the issue. Usually it is wrong. I then ask him why he did not raise his hand.

4) A Deeper Look

I usually start by talking to the youngest one, the most vulnerable. He has usually already partially stated what he has done wrong. I now need to find out the full story so that justice is done and closure is brought to the incident. This is usually done by asking the youngest why they did something wrong to the other. I stay focused. I ask each one (from smallest to biggest) why they did something wrong so that they all can voice their chief complaints and appropriate defenses.

5) Correction

Sometimes, they have sufficiently banged up each other so that I do not need to do anything as a parent. They already were corrected! We are not dealing out revenge. We are disciplining them. More often than not, the switch (see next chapter) is needed to chastise them for disobeying their parents.

If it is not serious, it is okay for each of them to apologize to each other for the specific wrong action they did or wrong attitude they expressed. Sometimes, a toy has to be taken away (i.e. freedom restricted to play with a toy). At other times, a mere misunderstanding has to be cleared up. We get a lot of practice on this!

6) *Most Importantly*

Our goal for our children is to have clean consciences and good relationships. We cannot save them, but we can make them feel like they want to be saved. Confession and apologies cannot cleanse their souls, but they can cleanse their consciences. They no longer need to pretend they are right when they know they are wrong.

When they confess their sin and get their needed chastisement, they have a whole new attitude. (If they do not, something was missed.) If you have not witnessed the complete change that chastisement accompanied by apology brings, then you and your child have missed out on one of the most wonderful experiences in life. A hateful and despising countenance has been immediately transformed into a loving and humble heart.

Each offender needs to apologize to the one he has wronged, starting with the oldest. The parent does not do this, but sometimes the parent needs to prompt the child. If the child is just learning to talk or is confused what to say, the parent has the child repeat after him phrase by phrase, or for the littlest one, word by word. What do they say?

> ➤ "I'm sorry for ..... (hitting, hurting, acting selfishly)."

Be specific. List all the crimes, whether embarrassing or not.

> ➤ "Please forgive me."

Do not forget this important step. Do not let the other person say it is not important. It is very important. If they were guilty, then they should apologize too.

> ➤ Wait for an answer. Usually one hears an "I forgive you."

> ➤ Hug. Our American culture shows itself here. The point is that something should be done to show mutual acceptance.

Scripture might not mandate the hug[9], but it is a good way to enter back into the friendship stage. We sometimes see (5% of time) a half hug. This lack of enthusiasm probably means that some sin was not mentioned or that he is holding a little grudge. They see no justice. It is important to go back and see what might have been missed.

> *Reconciliation allows siblings,*
> *friends, parents and children to*
> *maintain good relationships.*

We train them in this process while they are young, and they do it fairly automatically after we have confronted them about some sin. I often ask them (ages 6-12) to straighten it out on their own. They usually can.

Pause for Reflection:

What steps do you need to take to set up this habit of confession and apology in your own home? What will be the hardest part? Do you apologize when needed?

E. Training the Untrained Child

If a trained child disobeys, we have the above means to deal with him. What about those who are not trained? More particularly, what about those parents who are beginning to sense that they ought to train their children in obedience?

Pause for Reflection:

Have you trained your child according to God's standards? If not, are you ready to take the steps necessary to get started? Why or why not?

If the child has not been brought up under godly training, then the child will need some serious confrontation. We suggest the parents take these steps.

(1) Agreeing on the Plan

Parents need to agree on a common policy of what needs to be done. What is God teaching you that you are now trying to implement in your home? Clarify God's goals for your family.

(2) Setting an Example

Consistently model each of these policies as parents. Remember each policy will have its practical aspects. For example, humbly apologizing to your spouse for being gruff helps show children the humble heart each of us should have. If we wrong our child, we should, though difficult, confess our sins to them.

(3) Confessing Your Mistakes

Parents need to explain the reason they are making changes in the way they deal with their child. Start by confession and apology for not rightly training them earlier. This explanation will differ depending on how old the children are. This discussion is important because it helps your child know you are serious. Again, <u>your</u> willingness to change encourages them to be open to change.

(4) Being Sensitive to Your Child

Make allowance for the child to confess and apologize for their wrongs, but do not demand it. Why? We think of it like this. We took so long to come to understand these things. We should give God time to work in their hearts. They will need to apply certain behaviors immediately, but some areas will come a bit slower. Be full of mercy and grace.

Meanwhile, they can have certain freedoms taken away until things are fully straightened out.

(5) Explaining the Biblical Principles

Explain the principles that you will consistently apply from that time onward. Include both unacceptable behaviors/words/attitudes along with the consequences.

(a) **State biblical standards.** If the child is older, make sure you clearly state the biblical purpose for making these changes. You should explain God's command requiring you to implement them as well as your desire to have a close relationship with your child. By referring to the chart, you can remind yourself of the stages of your relationship with your child. You, as a parent, are always in authority but might carry it out differently in various contexts.

(b) **Catch the bad attitudes.** Remember that God wants right hearts as well as right actions. Explain that we want right actions and attitudes. Be specific. Illustrate. For example, if we want them to ask politely for food to be passed at the table, then we do not only tell them to say, "Please, pass...." We also tell them to ask with a humble and grateful attitude.

(c) **Each principle is important.** If we do not see them patiently carry out these parental requests, then they will be restrained from certain freedoms until they faithfully learn to carry them out.

(d) **Apologize**. When they have neglected to do what is right, they will need to confess and apologize to the offended party. It should be done as we have stated above, from the oldest to youngest, yes, including the parents.

This might sound hard, but it will begin to make a big difference in the attitude of your children because they will see your sincerity and want to better their relationship with you. They might test you to see if you are serious. Be serious.

Parenting Principles & Practices

- Our end goal of parenting is to produce children who love God and others.
- The fruit of good parenting fosters a great relationship between the parent and their child.
- Parents must act according to the child's stage of growth.
- Parents must effectively deal with a child's rebellious attitudes and behaviors to maintain a good relationship.
- Parental trust in the child is built on a child's obedience.
- Freedoms are given to a child only when he can be trusted to obey in a given circumstance.
- Restrictions of those kinds of freedoms is necessary to make the child's desires work toward obedience.
- Confession and apology are important parts of preparing the child for their relationship with God as well as maintaining a good parent-child relationship.

Parenting Questions

1. What is the end goal of our relationship with our child?

2. List the five stages of the parent-child relationship. Which stages are your children in?

3. Why is it important to deal with the attitudes as well as the words and behaviors of a child?

4. How is a parent's trust in a child related to the freedom they give him?

5. How does this freedom concept help motivate the child to obey?

6. Explain the funnel concept. Describe what the sides stand for. What happens as one goes away from the mouth of the funnel?

7. Why is cleansing of the conscience so important?

8. How does a parent make sure that bitterness does not arise in their relationship with their child?

9. List at least two steps on how to start training a child that has not been trained.

Notes from Chapter #6

[1] Gary Ezzo emphasizes this perspective.

[2] Gary Ezzo uses this funnel concept in a slightly different way. We are grateful for his insights in this area.

[3] One should note that this expansion of freedom parallels the development of self-control where exterior laws become laws of the heart. We dare not grant freedoms to our children when they have not proven their ability to exercise the needed self-control for that situation.

[4] The Lord has told us that such 'freedom' is really slavery.

[5] Swear (cuss, curse) words are rude words used beyond their original meaning, usually from a haughty spirit and with mean intentions .

[6] Parents often exasperate themselves trying to explain things to young children who cannot understand. We just set and enforce the rules. (see stage #3).

[7] To be truthful, more often than not when this happens, the child will continue to act naughty at home until they are chastised and their consciences cleansed.

[8] Forgiving one another does not remove God's anger upon a person for a certain wrongdoing. God still holds them accountable. Repentance from our sin and belief in Jesus Christ as Lord and Savior, however, does thoroughly cleanse us from every sin. "If we confess our sins, He is faithful and just to forgive us our sins and cleanse us from all unrighteousness" (1 John 1:9).

[9] Different cultures have different ways to express restoration. Some kind of physical expression is good to complement the word of forgiveness.

Chapter #7

DISCIPLINE AND THE LOVING USE OF THE ROD

Priority

Purpose: Establish a scriptural perspective of discipline and describe ways to properly administer the rod to our children (chastisement).

Society used to consider the parent who did not spank or chastise his child unfit. Today, modern philosophy has so influenced our society and mindset that those who spank their children are portrayed as unloving, mean, unfit and abusive parents. Indeed, things have greatly changed! Is there still a place for chastisement? And if so, why?

A. The Understanding of Discipline

God's Word very clearly addresses the importance of consistent loving discipline. The Bible has much to say! Our main job will be to condense its many teachings into one lesson. Seventeen verses in Proverbs alone use the word discipline.[1] Spanking is crucial to raising a wise child. Hebrews 12 also has a comprehensive section on the discipline process.

The previous chapter on correction provided several key ideas basic to correcting our children. Those concepts gave us the right guidelines to know how to wisely use chastisement. Remember our end goal is to raise children that love and respect God and others. We accomplish these goals by teaching our children to respect us as parents. Even though we have God-given authority to command, we intentionally build close relationships with our children. We need to remove the many things that are barriers in order to imitate our heavenly Father. He exercises both His authority and His love. Using the rod is essential in obtaining these goals.

The rod (flexible stick) is just one part of the correction process. It is not the whole process. We will first look at what the scriptures say about this topic and then answer some practical questions about child discipline.

Chastisement is the proof of a parent's love for his or her child.

Definitions

As we begin, let us first define some important parenting terms. Part of the confusion comes from the different understandings people have of the same terms. The terms overlap in meaning.

- **Instruction**: Instruction is the verbal and sometimes physical persuasion used to urge a child to follow some course of action.
- **Discipline**: Discipline is the whole training process by which a child is brought to obedient action. Some use the term to refer only to the physical correction process known by 'chastisement,' 'spanking,' or 'smacking.'
- **Chastisement**: Chastisement (or use of the rod) refers to the physical pain or discomfort that is inflicted on the child to cause an acceptable standard of behavior. Spanking and switching are some common words used to describe this process. Unfortunately, the term 'chastisement' is no longer in common usage.
- **Disciplines**: Disciplines as a noun describe a structure of behavior such as controlling time, eating or other good habits. "He has good life disciplines."

The context in which a person speaks helps us better understand what another person is trying to communicate. For the sake of clarity the word 'chastisement' will be used when we mean to inflict physical pain upon a child during the correction process. The word 'discipline' will be used to refer to the whole training process.[2]

Ephesians 6:4 is one key Bible passage which helps parents get a better grasp of what God is saying to them. The apostle could have told the fathers many things regarding bringing up their children. He points out one negative and two positive commands.

> *And, fathers, do not provoke your children to anger; but bring them up in the discipline and instruction of the Lord (Ephesians 6:4).*

The father should responsibly care for (literally nurture) his child in two ways: through the discipline and instruction of the Lord. We might picture these two things as guardrails, which keep a car from falling off a narrow mountain road.

Our family was traveling by bus on the famous Cross Island Highway over the beautiful mountains in central Taiwan. At some spots the roads are so narrow that the buses cannot pass each other. Sometimes, they wait for the other to pass, but, at other times, they squeeze by because there is no way to back up.

We were in the bus that was on the cliff side. As we inched along, we scraped against the guardrail that was at the edge of the road. The metal made loud screeching noises. Even worse, when we looked out the window, we could not see the bottom. Everyone on the bus naturally leaned away from the cliff (putting more weight on the road side). We did not like scraping against the guardrail, but it was much better than not having it there! It made it difficult for us to go beyond its boundary. This is what discipline and instruction does for the child. They help keep the child on the right pathway.

Installing the guardrail on the edge of a mountain cliff took much

work. Several men lost their lives building that important highway. Is it worth having the guardrails? Of course it is. There is no sense having a mountain road without a barrier. Nor does it make any sense to have children if we are not going to put up barriers to protect them. The father needs to establish the two 'guardrails:' discipline and instruction.

The Discipline and Instruction of the Lord

The two Greek words used here are very instructive. 'Discipline' (*paideia*) refers to the whole process of training a child. That includes chastisement as well as education.[3] This Greek word for discipline is similar to the English word 'training' if we added the idea of chastisement to it. 'Instruction' (*nouthesia*) means to counsel, advise and warn. Parents must use words to build up, direct and encourage their children.

To restrain from bad behavior

Both of the Greek words imply the child's lack of ability to order his own way. Without these guards implemented by the father, the child will go off the road and down the steep cliff. We see children falling off all the time. Why do children need this help? Let us mention two problems.

➢ Children have a natural resistance to obedience.

The first guardrail is discipline. Parents are responsible to restrain a child from rebellious and selfish behavior.

All parents have faced resistance to their boundaries. The sinful nature is rebellious toward authority and intent on fulfilling its own desires without consideration for other people. No one would complain about a person's desire to eat, but it would be intolerable if a hungry man entered a restaurant, sat down, grabbed another person's plate and started to eat. A child must be trained to think about the needs of others and be willing to deprive his desires (often foolish ones) for the sake of doing what is right.

➢ Children simply lack knowledge.

The second guardrail is instruction or direction. The parent is charged with teaching what is right and wrong. The parents are also responsible to instruct the children on what kind of attitudes they should have.

For example, we should teach our children how to speak kindly to others. We help them understand the compassion we are to have toward others by pointing them to speak like Jesus. This helps clarify the loving attitude that we need to have. This instruction, though, does not always work! There seems to be something else that holds back or twists the learning process. This is the reason for the other guardrail.

Guidelines for different situations will be worked out more clearly in the following chapters. Boundaries are derived from general principles that are specifically applied to various situations.

Discipline and instruction in the Lord are needed to provide the training that the child needs to have to be 'other-focused.' They need to know how to suppress the urge to satisfy their own desires. The rod works wonders by using pain to cause the child to restrain himself from expressing the desires that might offend another, i.e., taking a toy that belongs to his friend. The instruction not only guides the child but also, as he gets older, helps him to adopt these principles for himself. This is an essential means for instilling self-control in the child.

We used to have a child in our neighborhood who would take whatever toy he wanted. He would come in our yard and take our child's wagon and walk down the street with it. The neighbors were unhappy with this child including us! He seemed oblivious to the inconvenience and consternation of others. Correction helps a child to understand the importance of a parent's instruction.

To implant the right behavior

Discipline (training) and instruction have a common purpose. They guide the child to right behavior. Just as the guardrail keeps the cars safely on the road, so discipline and instruction are crucial to building godly and respected adults.

Improper use of spanking occurs when the parent only uses it to restrain the child rather than positively focusing on the development of the child. In these cases, a parent only spanks a child when his child makes a neighbor angry or when he greatly disturbs the parent. Chastisement in these cases fall far short of our training purposes.

The child in these cases will be confused about what is acceptable behavior. He might regularly play loudly with his friends. One day his father spanks him for playing loudly as is his regular habit. The only difference that day was that the father had a bad headache and could not rest with his noisy child around. The child was not sure where the 'guardrail' is. These responses exasperate a child and push him into anger and bitterness.

Training's real goal is to enable, guide, confirm and help. The motivation behind the use of the rod should be love rather than the protection of a parent's selfish interests.

The proper use of chastisement encourages respect for authority and self-control enabling the children to reach their full potential as human beings. Without spanking, the child's poor attitudes toward life and his inability to control his body will cause him to be a victim to his own evil tendencies.

Pause for Reflection:

How did your father and mother do in training you? Did they carry out both chastisement and instruction? Are you doing better than your father? Explain.

B. A Scriptural Perspective of Discipline from Hebrews 12

Our wise Creator obviously knew that parents must have a clear understanding of the various aspects of discipline. The Bible is full of clear instruction and many examples of discipline as well as the consequences of withholding chastisement. Hebrews 12 summarizes much of what has been said in the other passages. Please remember that the Greek word (*paideia*) for discipline includes the ideas of training, instruction, spanking and reproof.

Let us draw some principles from the text and see how it applies to chastising our child. Although it might seem that we have overemphasized this topic of chastisement, you must remember that we must correct the many wrong notions put out by our godless society.

The author of Hebrews compares the way our Heavenly Father disciplines His children with the way our earthly father should carry out chastisement on his child. He taught from what was familiar (chastisement in the home) with what was more difficult to understand (God's ways). To be honest, due to difficult family backgrounds today, many of us have had to learn God's ways from His Word on our own and apply it to our hearts and homes. Our societies are in such great decay that there are very few good examples to observe and follow.

* Love's Creation (12:5-6)

Love is the motivation of true discipline.

> *And you have forgotten the exhortation which is addressed to you as sons, 'My son, do not regard lightly the discipline of the Lord, nor faint when you are reproved by Him; for those whom the Lord loves He disciplines' (Hebrews 12:5-6).*

God does not let His children wander away. He provides special care to keep them on the right track. Just as God disciplines His children, so a father is expected to chastise his children. God uses correction to properly care for His people. "For whom the Lord loves he disciplines." "Thy rod and They staff, they comfort me" (Psalm 23:4).[4]

The love of a father compels him to use the rod on his child. Chastisement is rigorous work. We need to stay on top of things, be alert and attentive to what the child is doing. The faithful father does this because of his love for his child. It is very sad to see a child without discipline.

Pause for Reflection:
What comes to mind when you hear the word discipline? How do your thoughts agree with the Bible's teaching?

* Pain's Reward (12:6)

If it does not hurt, it not effective.

And He (God) scourges every son whom He receives (Hebrews 12:6).

Temporary pain is an essential part to correction. The word used here, 'scourge,' is very strong and indicates that, at times, chastisement needs to be very painful to accomplish its goals.

> *Do not hold back* **discipline** *from the child, although you beat him with the rod, he will not die (Proverbs 23:13).*

Although parents **might feel** that they are 'damaging' their child, chastisement causes a greater good that could not otherwise be accomplished. The scriptures do not deny that the child will suffer pain from chastisement, but the pain is only temporary; he will not die (Proverbs 23:13). The scriptures repeatedly acknowledge that the child without chastisement will suffer far worse. Proverbs describes this undisciplined person as a fool which is a result of so-called 'modern' parenting. Parents weaken their children by neglecting the whole aspect of chastisement.

Some people avoid pain and conflict at all costs.[5] These people will not be able to properly raise their children. The child must experience the pain associated with chastisement to be properly trained. Parents need to view this training with more balance.

Perhaps we need to look at an illustration from daily life to better appreciate the use of this brief pain. Those who train for the marathon severely discipline their bodies. Their bodies ache and groan. All this is only for a race or competition! This modern generation does not object to this training. Nor should they object to the training of our little ones so that they might become better people. Training our children is so much more important than any marathon! Besides, as we saw in the scriptures, chastisement is a critical aspect of discipline and the parent's God-given responsibility.

Pause for Reflection:

Do you chastise your child? Why or why not? What are the consequences of your actions?

* A Special Belonging (12:7)

God chastises only His children.

It is for discipline that you endure; God deals with you as with sons; for what son is there whom his father does not discipline? (Hebrews 12:7).

Notice how the father is expected to discipline his child. Every father disciplines his children. This includes chastisement. The father in New Testament times that neglected this duty would show that something was tragically wrong.

Fathers have often left child training in the mother's hand. This is a shame. Fathers need to oversee the whole process. Fathers should unquestionably be involved in the discipline of their children. The father sets the way and overall direction of the home and the mother assists him.

Pause for Reflection:

Are you fathers involved in the training of your child?

* Abandoned & Lonely (12:8)

Children desperately need their parents' discipline.

But if you are without discipline, of which all have become partakers, then you are illegitimate children and not sons (Hebrews 12:8).

If a child is not disciplined, then it shows that his parents do not really care enough to correct him. Belonging brings a sense of accountability. The lack of discipline proves a lack of belonging. We understand that there are parents that do not discipline their children. The family that withholds correction when needed becomes dysfunctional.

This special treatment of discipline forms the basis of security and belonging. Without it, the child senses he is unimportant. He believes his parents do not think he is important enough to pay attention to. The child might think, "Is something wrong?" "Don't they care for me?"

Perhaps this is the basis of the self-esteem crisis today. When parents withhold discipline from their children, their children do not feel valued or treasured. God designed parents to give that extra love, security and care to their children. Without it, children develop all sorts of emotional and relational problems.

Many modern parents make it more difficult for themselves and their children by believing that spanking the child cause low self-esteem. The scriptures state the opposite. A child cannot grow with a healthy appreciation of self if he does not rightly think of others. Receiving chastisement in love helps them learn how to appreciate others over themselves.[6]

Pause for Reflection:
Do you worry about your child's self-esteem? Does it keep you back from chastisement? Allow this truth to encourage you to institute proper discipline in your home.

* Fatherly Respect (12:9)

Here is the clear connection between discipline and respect.

Furthermore, we had earthly fathers to discipline us, and we respected them; shall we not much rather be subject to the Father of spirits, and live? (Hebrews 12:9).

When earthly fathers discipline their children, those children come to respect them. God, the Father disciplines His children to create that same respect for Himself. God knows how important obedience is. He does not withhold discipline. The need for a child to respect his father is very important. The means of obtaining this respect is also clear–the rod. Why then, do so many people despise chastisement an important part of discipline?

Pause for Reflection:
Do your children respect you? Why or why not?

* A Higher Purpose (12:10)

God's higher purpose for us makes correction ethical and necessary.

For they disciplined us for a short time as seemed best to them, but He disciplines us for our good, that we may share His holiness (Hebrews 12:10).

> *For bodily discipline is only of little profit, but godliness is profitable for all things, since it holds promise for the present life and also for the life to come (1 Timothy 4:8).*

Fathers discipline their children. God the Father disciplines His children. They do it for a greater purpose. They look beyond the present scene to the future.

The long-term results from proper training makes everything worthwhile. The athlete anticipates winning and so endures all those stressful workouts. So must the parent. The parent desires to produce godly children.

** Good Results (12:11)*

Discipline is hard work. Is it really worth it?

> *All discipline for the moment seems not to be joyful, but sorrowful; yet to those who have been trained by it, afterwards it yields the peaceful fruit of righteousness (Hebrews 12:11).*

Yes. Both parent and child know the suffering moments after the use of a rod. No one likes it. However, when we see the result in a well-trained child, everyone is delightfully surprised. The scriptures describe it as "peaceful fruit of righteousness." This is our goal. This justifies the pain.[7] Without it we are producing problematic children. Is that love? Certainly not.

** Steady Forward (12:12)*

We need to understand the purpose of discipline and thus be encouraged.

> *Therefore, strengthen the hands that are weak and the knees that are feeble... (Hebrews 12:12).*

Bitterness dwells in the heart of the child that is spanked at random. These children know through other life situations that the parents really do not care for them. Parents are not thinking of the child's well-being but only of their own peace or convenience. The parent has no greater goal for the child but to keep him out of trouble. In some cases, the parent does the same thing for which the child is spanked!

We should share our higher purposes with our children. Put the goal out in front of them so that they will know that this stage will pass. Keep the children going. Encourage them to act responsibly so chastisement is only needed on rare occasions.

* Clear Boundaries (12:13)

Only by staying on the right path can the child be protected.

And make straight paths for your feet, so that the limb which is lame may not be put out of joint, but rather be healed (Hebrews 12:13).

Keep the pathway very clear in front of them. This is the instruction side of Paul's teaching in Ephesians. Talk over with your child what is expected. If they are being inattentive, make them look directly at your face. If they claim they forget, then have them repeat the instructions back to you. When teaching a new skill, repeat the process with him a few times.

Summary

Hebrews 12 captures the importance and responsibility of the father to carry out discipline in his home. This discipline has to include chastisement when necessary.

Let us turn now to some practical considerations for parents when implementing what the scriptures command.

C. Questions and Answers

Below are a number of common questions parents have about chastisement, spanking and the general use of the rod.

Is chastisement child abuse?

Chastisement is part of the training program and is not at all abusive when properly carried out. Chastisement can, of course, turn into abuse but this is only true when certain restrictions are not adhered to. It typically happens when parents have no positive goals for their family. They are only trying to keep the kids out of their way. This approach has no resemblance to the full training process that the scriptures call discipline or training.

Surprisingly, abuse often occurs when chastisement is altogether neglected. The parents slowly store up anger until they lash out at their child. Those who have been wounded by such scenes can still recall painful pictures from the past. The parent gets angrier and angrier. Then, when fully irritated with his child, he blows up and recklessly hits him.

A parent's personal imperfections often reveal themselves in the rough treatment of his child. For example, parents under the influence of drugs like alcohol or under certain financial pressures become less focused on the needs of their children and more on other matters. The children just get in the way. These parents are not at all thinking of training their children. They just want them out of the way.[8]

Disobedience should be dealt with by chastisement as one goes along. Do not to put chastisement off but use it to keep children from doing more wrong. In this way, disobedience does not turn into great emotional outbursts. Even if the parent does get upset, he or she should first calm down before going on with chastisement.

What can I do about worried neighbors?

Chastisement can be noisy! Neighbors sometimes get concerned when they hear your child crying. They do not see your caring love or understand your long-term plan.

It is essential that you start training your child when he is a baby. This will enable you to gain the child's respect for your 'no' very early on. This will not eliminate the need for chastisement but will reduce its necessity.

We have trained our children, especially the loud criers, to cover their mouths when they cry. It works![9] We also do not tolerate extreme crying or yelling. Yelling is an expression of rebellion. The child must be warned of this unacceptable reaction and if necessary be further chastised for that disobedience. Listen carefully to your child's cries to discern the differences.

Choose to discipline in private places that absorb sound. If you live in an apartment, flat or condo, choose the room away from the halls and with more insulation like a rug. You might cover an air vent for the brief moment. Walk-in closets are great.

When a parent disciplines his children in anger, he creates hostile children. The parent shouts, and the child shouts back. The parent hits; the child yells back. This is not desirable. God can help parents overcome their anger. Remember from our previous lesson about restricting boundaries. Using the rod is important, but it should be combined with restriction of freedoms to attain the goals.

What should I do about my anger?

The parent will sometimes get angry at a child's behavior. This anger will produce in the parent an urge to hit the child. The problem is that if the parent himself does not have self-control, he will tend to yell and hit harder than he should. He will also miss out on other important parts of discipline including training, instruction and restoration.

If you get angry, first quiet yourself down.[10] While quieting down, have your child wait in the other room. Explain that you are angry but need to properly chastise him. He will appreciate it!

Should we discipline our child in public?

No. It is inappropriate. Tell your child that he will be spanked when he gets home. If you are returning to an apartment at night or it is a long way home, discipline him in the car. Straighten everything out so that he can have a pleasant bedtime routine.

Sometimes, the child's attitude is bad. Without correction, you realize more trouble is coming. Take him to a private place[11] and spank him. Sometimes, it is helpful to take the child for a walk and hold his hand tightly so that it hurts. If we are at public worship, we first warn and then begin to lift fingers one by one. One finger means one strike with the rod upon returning home.[12] If the parent is consistent, this finger approach is quite effective. The more fingers, the more strokes he will get at home.

Are we doing anything illegal?

In most societies spanking or smacking (British) is still allowed. However, it is becoming more common for the legal authorities to make spanking illegal. They do not understand the issues at stake. They feel these laws help avoid the abuse that takes place. They are accelerating abuse by restricting proper physical correction. These laws steal parental responsibility to govern their children. Parents feel like they cannot handle the children. The government certainly cannot do anything about defiance in the home. As a result, we have impolite children that terrorize others in schools and on the streets. Bullies will grow into incompetent parents who will in turn greatly increase turmoil in society at large.

Behind the scenes, people with modern mindsets are spreading their reckless modern philosophy to others. The governments even pay them money to do it. Even if the nation has not made spanking illegal, it often has forces in place to regulate what they call abuse.

However, this is a moral issue. A biblical principle is at stake. This is one issue I would go to jail for, if necessary.[13] If chastisement is a clear sign of love, then I must love my children. I can take precautions and respect the government's ultimate goal of not hurting my child, but in the end I must obey the Lord. My children's welfare is at stake. The trend to make physical correction illegal should be a compelling reason for parents to start training their children when very young. This makes them much more compliant at later ages with little need for physical correction.

If the authorities invade your privacy, explain your overall purposes. People should be able to discern the difference between parental training methods and beatings. The authorities are overwhelmed with real situations where parents indeed do beat their children. They do not even have time and personnel to deal with these genuinely abusive cases. They hardly want to bother with the situations in which the children are being loved and cared for![14]

Beatings differ from chastisement like night differs from day. Chastisement is not punishment or revenge, but a way of inculcating right judgment and respect. If you live near a neighbor who likes reporting people, you might consider moving. People hear the crying and cannot discern the difference. Or even better, invite the person over for a meal and let them see how kind your child is.

What should I tell my child when chastising him?

Before the correction is needed, the parents should have already told the child what the rules (boundaries) are and the consequences for breaking them. With this instruction in place, chastisement can follow. If the parent has neglected to properly instruct the child, then he should not chastise. First instruct him clearly. Be sure he knows the rules and boundaries.

Having placed the rule before him, the child is better able to focus on whether he wants to cross the boundary. He knows the consequences. We want him to think, "I do not want to do this again!" The parent is the enforcer. The parent might say, "I do not like doing this but to help you be a better person. You know what happens when you...." Make the <u>child</u> responsible for his actions and attitudes. Chastisement enables him to clearly observe what happens when he acts irresponsibly. Usually the child can see that he has broken something, hurt somebody or that one of his siblings is crying.

Certify what the child has done wrong before chastising him. We should encourage the child first to state what he has done wrong, even if you witnessed it. We want to encourage confession. Have him clearly speak out what he did wrong. If he needs help, you might say, "Didn't you agree that you were not to...? Now I have to use the rod." At times, this conversation is best held until the period of restoration. At times he is too preoccupied or upset to profit from discussion prior to the use of the rod.

If needed, physical correction can be combined or substituted with restriction of some freedom. For example, our child was running around the church building during mealtime against our rules. We made him sit down next to us for the whole mealtime the following Sunday. We explained what we were doing and why. The next Sunday he sat with us during the whole mealtime. In that case, as he was older we thought he could learn more this way. If he is unwilling to comply or his attitude is bad, then it is obvious that chastisement is also needed.

What about time-out?

The parent has many different ways of correcting his child. Rebuke, restriction of freedom and use of the rod are three common means of correction. In most cases, talking to our children simply does not change their attitudes. In cases where the parent's word is being openly challenged (rebellion), nothing should replace the biblical injunction to use a rod. Chastisement is not the only way to correct a child who has done wrong, but it is the only way to gain respect. This will keep the child from making a whole chain of unwholesome choices.

Proper use of the rod cleanses the guilt of wrongdoing and restores his respect for the parent. Along with formal restoration comes immediate and full reconciliation—just like it never happened.

Other methods like time-out are ineffective. Many methods fail completely because they do not restore the relationship with the parent or cleanse the guilt. The child can sense that the parent is avoiding the application of the rod. When this happens, the child basically has free reign and can do and say some very nasty things. Chastisement is necessary to contain the foolish and rebellious heart of the child.

We can use other methods like restricting liberty, rebuke, and distraction. Remember, however, the rod is their backbone. They have no true effect without physical chastisement.

What is a rod?

The rod is a little branch of a tree, sometimes called a switch. Rulers break. Chopsticks or wooden spoons are not flexible and can do damage. A switch can be used softly with a slight sting or rather strongly, depending on the age, spirit and offense of the child. Get a little branch that is flexible rather than an old hard or heavy branch. Different sizes for different situations and individuals are good to have on hand. A leather strap like a belt is also useful.

What is proper use of the rod?

The rod is used for training. Chastisement is a form of training not revenge. The amount of pain inflicted is quite different for each child depending on age, temper, mood or level of stubbornness.

When used for training, the switch encourages the child to respond to the parent's requests. Once the child makes the connection, the child will need much less switching. The initial fear is instilled in the child and attached to the word 'no'. In initial training, the rod is used immediately, but ever so softly (a tap) with the small child. At ten months old, our daughter would consistently obey our 'no' (if she was not distracted).[15]

The most effective training takes place immediately following the offense.

As children get older, they can get defiant. Chastisement describes how the rod is used to inflict pain upon the child because he has clearly been willfully disobedient. Remember the purpose is to train. We are instilling in them a proper respect for authority. In the older child, it is primarily used for rebellion and defiance.

There are two kinds of rebellion. Open rebellion is seen in a willful disobedience accompanied by a bad attitude. "I won't ...." Silent rebellion reveals itself through sullenness, rolling the eyes, slow to obey, own time table, stomping feet, talking back, complaining and questioning why. Others have appropriately called these states active and passive rebellion.

Do children sometimes forget? Yes, but often, their excuse, "I forgot" is a cover up for rebellion. Children do sometimes forget or are distracted, etc. We do not switch them for this. Instead, we should warn them and call attention to their excuse. When we know they have clearly disobeyed us, though, we must use the rod.

The rod can be applied like this. Instruct the child. Slap his hands a certain number of times with a switch (small tree branch). Depending upon the age and offense, you can switch his bare legs. He can also be instructed to bend over and receive switches on his bottom.

Remember, before using the rod for the first time, make sure you try it out on yourself. Then you can better judge the amount of pain you will inflict. Do not be overbearing. The pain from a rod will sting but not last long. The pain afflicted on a child acts as a deterrent to future transgressions.

Can we warn them first?

In some situations where the command is unclear, warnings are quite appropriate. For example, we instruct our child not to go into the neighbor's yard. Since the children have been visiting that neighbor's yard for over a year, then first warn and remind them (i.e. instruction) about the new rule for a day or two.

In many cases, we only warn our child with our words when he has clearly gone against his conscience and our rules. Words are quickly tuned out. Only the rod will restore him to a proper relationship with his parents. The rod resolves the child's guilt from wrongdoing. It is so easy for parents to slide back into reproving their children when they need to be properly chastised. There is much more tension in the house when this happens.

What is first-time obedience?

First-time obedience is insisting that the child obey the first time the parent requests something. In many cases, the parents repeatedly warn their child. They actually fool themselves by thinking that they are helping the child by extending grace. This is not a situation in which to extend grace. Instead, they are confusing the child and will end up fostering more disobedience than they would have with first-time obedience.

Certainly, we should strive for first-time obedience. First-time obedience is obedience. Second-time obedience is disobedience. Let us think about this a bit more.

The parent that tells the child to do something over and over is causing the child to tune them out. The child has learned that the parent will not take action until he starts raising his voice–probably after the third or fourth time or more. The parent gets angry and frustrated; the child responds with the same. Why go through this process? It causes great friction in the relationship with the child. God judged Adam and Eve after the first offense. Your word should be very important to your child. He must know that you mean what you say the first time you say it.

How do I train my child to first-time obedience?

First, if they are old enough to understand the change that you are going to make, you should explain the new process to the children. Tell them what you were doing (being inconsistent in your training) was not right or fair to them. Certainly not best. Accept responsibility. Apologize and tell them the new plan.

It is always best to start off right by training when they are young. When they have been trained wrongly, they have to be retrained. Set up some practice situations where they can learn first-time obedience. Make it like a game (if they are young). Tell them, for example, to stand across the room. When you say, "Come," they are to come right away. Do it in a fun way. You can set up a number of practice situations. Since this is retraining, do not take their disobedience to be rebellion, at least at first. Remind them. Set a time when the switch will start being used for not coming or doing what is expected upon the parent's first request.

Remind them early in the morning of the new way of doing things. Remind them at noon. Congratulate them for success. Explain how much better things are. For example, Mommy does not get upset and yell. The parent will need to keep a small switch with them to be able to instantly correct any disobedience. The retraining is difficult but necessary. If you are consistent, retraining should take a few days to a week.

Why is it that many publications discourage physical discipline?

Modern thinking holds to the belief that the person who can freely express himself is the happiest. Therefore that mindset opposes all laws and rules that inhibit freedom. They believe these rules enslave and strip away freedoms and happiness. These assumptions are quite unbiblical.

This modern mindset does not believe in the use of physical correction as a tool to shape the child.[16] They resist setting boundaries and instead will try to use persuasion. They do not want to interfere (except in their power to persuade) with the child's freedom of choice. Modernists believe the child can choose what is best for himself.

The modernist parents start out in good faith in their system but run amuck very early on. Children are not as good as they thought they were (mild understatement). A rude awakening awaits them. Because of the terrible times of conflict these parents have with their child, they often do not want more than one! They cannot stand their one child and are confused about how to get them to do what they should. They miss the whole point of discipline. Instead of sharing in blessing, they suffer from the curse of an untrained child.

The Biblical perspective is the opposite. The Bible affirms that only by restraining one's desires to please self can a person reach the full potential he was designed for: loving God and others. The Bible clearly affirms that the child without chastisement grows up to be a fool. The 'fool' lives according to his desires rather than by principles and wisdom. He chooses what is easiest rather than what is best for him or others. He usually will be a slave to an outstanding sin such as stealing, laziness, gluttony, lust, etc.

> *"In the last time there shall be mockers, following after their own ungodly lusts" (Jude 1:18).*

It is these permissive perspectives that have shaped many modern societies and is leading them into chaos. The government is cultivating a disrespect for authority that will in the end lead to rejection of the government itself. Democracies will collapse and be replaced by totalitarian governments.

Summary Comparison Chart:
Modern Mindset versus Biblical Instruction

MODERN UNDISCIPLINE	BIBLICAL CHASTISEMENT
No Rules	Rules
No 'rod'	Rod
Human nature is good	Human nature is evil
Expression is freedom	Obedience is freedom
Undiscipline promises shame	Discipline develops potential
Persuade (talk a lot)	Command (talk little)
Parent is equal	Parent is authority
Modern parenting leads to spoiled, proud and inconsiderate children.	Biblical parenting leads to humble and considerate children with self-control.

Pause for Reflection:
Do you share any of the modern beliefs that need to be challenged by God's Word? Look at the above list one by one.

What about spanking with the hand?

Some are very opposed to any use of the hand. They suggest that our hand should be associated with our warmth rather than chastisement. This makes sense if not carried out to extreme.

God, however, does discipline us. It is not accidental. God does it because He loves us. We suggest that you chastise with the rod. The hand, however, was made to be 'handy.' In other words, sometimes you will not find a switch. (Maybe the children have hidden them! This has happened with us. We recently renewed our supply during the pruning of our apple trees.) We always have a hand, however. Immediacy of treatment is more important at times than consistency in process.

Who is responsible to chastise the child, Dad or Mom?

God clearly sets the father in charge over the family. Fathers need to be responsible for the overall disciplining of their children. God, however, has called mothers to be Dad's top assistant. She must carry out discipline throughout the day to be constant and effective. Again, if the child has been well-trained from when they were small, then maybe a child will need only to be corrected with the rod once a week depending on the child and the consistency with which the parents discipline their children (i.e. the more consistent the less correction is needed).

At times, mothers get too emotionally involved in the child's feelings. If a father sees this, he should step in and finish carrying out the chastisement. Or if any child is getting too 'out of hand,' the mother should wait for the father to come home. In these cases, it is very important that the child is more severely chastised. He is not to challenge Mom's authority.

Conclusion

Many parents today have a very poor understanding of how to parent their children. The rules are easy to learn, but it is much more difficult to convince the heart. Many parents unintentionally have submitted themselves and their children to the destructive modern mentality. Even though every situation around you confirms the foolishness of the modern approach, parents keep on enduring the poor relationships resulting from modern parenting techniques.

God's close relationship with His people requires Him to chastise them. This displays His interest in our well-being.

> *Thus you are to know in your heart that the LORD your God was disciplining you just as a man disciplines his son. Therefore, you shall keep the commandments of the LORD your God, to walk in His ways and to fear Him (Deuteronomy 8:5-6).*

As parents, we need to learn from God our Father on how to discipline. These verses assume that the father chastises his children. If our children mean anything to us, then we need to consistently follow through. Start early with training. Train your children to respect you as their parents. The child, then, will do as they are told the first time they are told to do something. Chastise them as necessary. Keep in mind the overall plan of producing children that will love God and others.

If you are faithful, God is faithful. You will have children that not only you love but others love too. You will want to be near them. They will want to be near you. After all, this is the reward of our training—a wonderful relationship with our children.

Parenting Principles & Practices

- Chastisement is the use of pain to bring a child to compliance.
- The father is responsible for the overall process of training the child. Correction is part of it.
- The mother is the father's assistant in carrying out discipline.
- Using the rod is a crucial part to bringing up godly children.
- We need to make sure that the boundaries (rules) and consequences are clear before chastising.
- We should not chastise in public.
- Reconciliation and discussion should follow chastisement.

Parenting Questions

1. What is chastisement?
2. How does chastisement differ from discipline?
3. What two positive things do Ephesians 6:4 tell a father to do?
4. Why is chastisement necessary?
5. What are we to do if our children need correction in public?
6. What might you say to someone who thinks chastising one's child is like beating him?
7. What is the difference between using the rod for training and discipline rather than things like 'time-out'?
8. Where is the best example found of how a father should rightly discipline his child? Explain.

Notes from Chapter #7

---

[1] Proverbs 3:11; 6:23; 7:22; 12:1; 13:1,18, 24; 15:5, 10, 32; 16:22; 19:18, 20, 27; 22:15; 23:12-13. Do a word study. Memorize some with your children! They will quickly learn that the use of the rod was not made up by parents but by a loving Creator.

[2] Physical correction is so deeply ingrained in the word 'to discipline' that it cannot be separated. The key is to remember that the one aspect of physical correction cannot be separated from the larger training process.

[3] We see this Greek root in the English word 'pedagogy' meaning the things related to teaching.

[4] Some people are offended by the way that we supposedly project our ideas of correction upon God. They do not believe that God would ever 'beat' His children. The scriptures, however, are more than clear about how God disciplines His children and expects parents to do the same.

[5] Many parents who avoid pain and physical discipline have had bad experiences. They need to realize that these problems stem from abuse of chastisement rather than its proper use. Training begins by forgiving their parents, meditating on these verses, and step-by-step careful training of their children. One excessive response does not justify another. Our children are more important than our 'hang-ups.' Proper discipline, in the end, requires far less chastisement.

[6] The lack of chastisement is only one source of the problem commonly known as low self-esteem. Physical discipline helps awaken a child to the importance of others. The child learns that they cannot just hit or hurt others as they feel like it. A child feels good about himself when he treats others well. Without chastisement, down deep the child feels bad about himself.

[7] We should note that the pain from living an undisciplined life is much greater than the pain of the switch. Note the difference, "A fool rejects his father's discipline, but he who regards reproof is prudent" (Proverbs 15:5).

[8] Abortion is the ultimate act of child abuse. It is amazing that those who believe one should not spank a child are sometimes the same ones who vote for the right to have an abortion.

[9] If they do not obey us, we will strike their hand with the rod to help them understand the importance of obedience. Thankfully, this does not often need to be repeated.

[10] Please refer to www.foundationsforfreedom.net/Topics/Anger/Anger00.html for training materials on dealing with anger.

[11] Church bathrooms tend to echo a lot of sound. Try outside the church building. Inside a private vehicle is good if it is semi-private.

[12] One author suggests five spankings for each lifted finger. Let each father decide.

[13] In America, one can still use the defense that it is his religious belief. We are not sure how long this defense will be allowed.

[14] Be careful and polite with these seemingly self-appointed children protectors. Some act as crusaders for their modern philosophical tenets. They can, at times, care more about their beliefs than the children or even the law.

[15] Michael Pearl at www.nogreaterjoy.org writes clearly on this important area of training. We have not seen this teaching elsewhere.

[16] One almost wonders if those who so strongly object to physical correction only use the so-called 'abuse' problem to cover up their real objection to exerting influence over another person's life.

Chapter #8

SETTING BOUNDARIES

Purpose: Enable parents to understand how to set up, implement and maintain proper and effective boundaries for their children.

Boundaries has become a popular word in the last decade or so. The idea, however, is not new. The word boundary is related to rules and the standards from which they come. Without standards, there will be no rules. Anything goes. The best rules come from high righteous standards. Rules must be enforced, though, if the standards will be valued and kept. The question for us in this chapter is, "How do I set and enforce proper boundaries so that I can reach the goals for my family?"

A. *Importance of High Standards*

Many parents have a struggle trying to close the gap between their hopes for their children's behavior and what their children do. This is more easily solved than the parents think. There are three key elements to doing this.

(1) God-given authority enables parents to shape their family according to their goals. Without acceptance and expression of their God-given authority, parents will be reluctant to compel their children to obey. They will try various ways of persuasion and have great love, but they will feel powerless to lead their family.

(2) Family standards represent those things that parents aspire to for their children. They love their children and want the best for them. Training along with its accompanying chastisement ensures that their desire for their children comes

to fruition. Previous lessons have discussed these matters in detail.[1]

(3) The subject of this lesson focuses on the third point: the setting, communication and implementation of boundaries for the children. In other words, what are we going to tell our children to do and how are we to get them to do what we tell them?

Parents have many wishes for their children. Some of these wishes are long-term achievement goals for when they are grown up. We are not speaking about these kinds of desires. Our discussion will center on the building blocks of the character of an individual.[2] These will enable the child to do a 'good' job in whatever he does. Character is based on who a person is while achievement is based on what he does.

Because we are primarily discussing young children, we need to start with training our little ones in our homes. Many regular activities are training grounds: picking up after themselves, caring for their toys, folding their clothes, etc.... In many cases the parents do not know what to ask the children to do, or how to get them to do it. Often, the parent becomes distraught over these issues. Here are a few examples of this kind of stress.

➢ Sometimes parents have thought up different jobs for their children but have not been able to get their children to carry them out. They hear their child say, "I don't want to."
➢ Sometimes the child might start off well but because of lack of encouragement or direction, the child just stops doing it.
➢ Sometimes, the parent assigns something but never trains the child how to do it. The child gets discouraged. The parent gets upset because the child does not obey, but the parent was not careful to teach the child how to do it.
➢ Sometimes, the child gets distracted. They end up with a half-done job.

In the end, both the parent and the child need to be self-disciplined to carry out their parts. The parent must patiently work alongside the child until the task is understood and able to be accomplished on their own.

The Place for Boundaries

The rules and boundaries that parents set up enable the child to reach his full potential. Many think that this potential can be accomplished apart from God's truth and work. It cannot be. Let us see the reason for this.

Proper discipline has two benefits: 1) It enables the child to suppress his natural inclination to serve his selfish desires, and 2) makes him sensitive to the needs of others. The areas that are not properly constrained will become the untamed trouble areas of his life.

The parallel teaching in the scriptures is the exhortation to drive out all the enemies in the land (of Canaan). Any nation that was not eliminated became a 'prick' and a 'thorn' to the Israelites. God says, "They shall trouble you in the land in which you live" (Numbers 33:55).

> "BUT IF YOU DO NOT DRIVE OUT THE INHABITANTS OF THE LAND FROM BEFORE YOU, THEN IT SHALL COME ABOUT THAT THOSE WHOM YOU LET REMAIN OF THEM WILL BECOME AS PRICKS IN YOUR EYES AND AS THORNS IN YOUR SIDES, AND THEY SHALL TROUBLE YOU IN THE LAND IN WHICH YOU LIVE. AND IT SHALL COME ABOUT THAT AS I PLAN TO DO TO THEM, SO I WILL DO TO YOU."
> (NUMBERS 33:55-56)

The training that parents give to their children enables them to tame those desires that would otherwise get out of hand. The more thoroughly the parent implements training, the better it is for the child.

The heart is the seed. All sorts of evil expressions grow from man's selfish nature. Early sprouts from a child's evil heart are essentially choked out when parents spank him. Let us look at what happens if parents are not careful to 'weed' out these sprouts and they grow. They will need to be pulled.

◆ **Lack of respect for authority (arrogance)**

〰 **Lack of control of one's emotions (anger)**

✖ **Lack of control of one's desires (lust)**

 Lack of sensitivity to the needs of others (selfishness)

◈ **Lack of ability to relate to others (competitiveness)**

✚ **Lack of contentment (greed)**

Each sprout represents an evil aspect of our hearts. When small, they hardly have an impact on the child. Our children are so cute! Jesus, however, saw the things that were in our hearts.

> *For from within, out of the heart of men, proceed the evil thoughts, fornications, thefts, murders, adulteries, of coveting and wickedness, as well as deceit, sensuality, envy, slander, pride and foolishness. All these evil things proceed from within and defile the man (Mark 7:21-23).*

This list is not meant to be complete but representative. Notice the labels that Jesus put on the sprouts that grow from the heart. If left unrestrained, these seeds will grow and multiply like weeds.

Seeds of 'evil' are small in a baby.

Self-control describes the process where the child is trained to set aside these desires and live by God's principles. This is a process that happens over time from crawler to teen. One or more 'thorns' will dominate those children that are not able to choose the right behavior over their self-preferences and thus face increased problems in life.

Seeds of 'evil' can grow and impact even a child's life.

The diagram shows how two growing influences (^, +) will negatively affect a child's life. Like a growing cancer, they start interfering with normal life including education, friends, relationships with parents and of course, their relationship with God. If they are not restrained, these evil 'weeds' at some point will destroy a person's life. God uses the parent to train the child to control his selfish desires. As the child gets older, he assumes this responsibility.

Pause for Reflection:

Do you 'indulge' yourself occasionally? Do you have urges that you do not control? List them. These are areas that are not carefully guarded against. The child's tendency is to indulge in the areas that their parents do not choose to exert full control over.

A few observations on parent training problems.

- Parents are 'soft' on setting standards and implementing rules in the areas of their own weaknesses. If the parent watches questionable movies, he will often allow his child to view offensive entertainment. It is through this means that sins pass from one generation to the next.

168

- Even if parents are 'strict' in areas of their weaknesses, seeds of bitterness sprout in their children. They reject parental standards as irrelevant (because they are).
- Parents are sometimes ignorant of the standards that please God. They do not study God's Word to see what He wants for His people (2 Timothy 3:16-17).

When parents model godly behavior, their children see this as the only way of life and become accustomed to it. As they grow older, they will see other people living in different ways, but they will be able to choose the best because they have seen the good results in the lives of their parents. These children will not be easily deceived like those who are bitter. They have a good relationship with their parents and desire to maintain it.

Good parents live great lives before their children. Fathers and mothers have flaws, but they will show how to humbly apologize and deny themselves for the sake of others. They choose to serve God and put the needs of others above their own.

Pause for Reflection:
In what areas in your personal life do you have battles? Where do you find defeat? Where are you hardened and unwilling to change? Have you instituted high standards in these areas for your children? What are the results?

B. Drawing Boundaries

Once parents know what they want (standards), they need to know how to train and enforce (discipline) it. The parents must study God's objective Word to set standards. The parents then define these boundaries and communicate them to their children.

| Scripture Verse | ⟹ | Biblical Principle | ⟹ | Parenting Principle | ⟹ | Family Application |

Let's look at an example. Galatians 5:14 is common scripture verse that helps us make many practical applications, "For the whole Law is fulfilled in one word, in the statement, You shall love your neighbor as yourself.'" The whole family should memorize this verse!

The main Biblical principle taken from this verse can be summarized, "**People should care for others the way they like to be cared for.**" We must not stop there, however. The parent needs to turn this principle into a parenting principle. "We should care for others in our home just like we like to be cared for." This, though, can be too broad, and the parent must look for more specific applications to his family.

- We will pick up toys after we play with them so that the next person will have a clean room to play in.

- I will use gentle, kind words when speaking to others because I like to be spoken to with gentle, kind words.

- I will not hit my brother because I do not like to be hit.

Parents often look at what other families do to gain ideas. This is good. Sometimes, we simply have no idea what the child can handle at a certain age or what a parent can enforce. The parents, however, will be accountable to God for the standards they set. It is mandatory that they examine their goals in light of what God desires.

Many times when parents think about standards, they only look at actions such as: to play nicely together, do not hit each other, etc. These are important but parents should also train the child's attitude. We should train our children, even if they do not know the Lord, to rightly respond to life situations. (Actually, children are learning all the time how to do this from us!)

Say, for example, we notice grumpiness around the home. You as the parent might feel something needs to change. Good. You look to God's Word and find that joy and gratefulness are two character traits God wants and expects of us (Galatians 5:22-23).

How can we train our child to be joyful? Certainly the child will have his or her own temperament and personality. We need to go beyond his own personality, however, and nurture the character quality of joy.

Joy is being glad in the Lord who tenderly guides His people through all of life's easy or hard circumstances. (It helps to define the meaning of the different terms.) The parent then needs to set specific boundaries for his children, things to do or not to do. Include what kind of perspectives, attitudes and actions will and will not be allowed.[3] Remember do not focus or have your child focus on what he is not to do, "Don't be so grumpy!" Identify and encourage positive attitudes, words and perspectives. "Everyone remember to wear his smile today!" The older a child gets, the more difficult it is to train attitudes. Start early.

In the case of developing joy, we would not allow complaining, grumpiness, negative attitudes, or any expression of disappointment due to the child's own inconvenience. Instead, we would model and teach how God exercises His goodness, love and sovereign hand over all the affairs of life. Share with the children the ways God cares for your family. Teach them about Bible characters that did their best even in hard times like Daniel, Ruth and others. Point out the desirable results.

Joy comes from fulfilling God's purpose through loving Him and serving others. We will go to church and serve. We will learn how to serve each other in the home and get joy from the opportunity to help our neighbors. We will cultivate a glad spirit even if we are inconvenienced by the pride or bitterness of another.

My son told us that our elderly neighbor asked him to help bring in his groceries. My son had volunteered his help many times, but the neighbor never wanted his help. Mom observed at the dinner table that our neighbor could ask him because he had previously volunteered his services. He learned the joy of having a servant heart (and even got a can of soda as a reward).[4]

Pause for Reflection:

How have you done in setting up boundaries for your children? Have you been affected by modern culture which defines a child's goals as fulfilling his wants? How so? What attitude do you need to work on as a family?

Getting Practical on Setting Boundaries

The following section focuses on four different areas that need clear boundaries: 1) At home, 2) At the table, 3) In public and 4) At church meetings. These provide a good representation of various situations that families find themselves in. Each of the four sections will have a short three column chart.

The charts provide an overview of the results of modern parenting techniques in four different settings. The seed is man's innate selfish tendency that resides in all, though not fully grown. This seed aggressively takes different opportunity to express itself. This is the sprout. The plant represents early growth (i.e. short-term results). The grown plant with its fruit represents the distortion that happens over the long term if parents allow the seed to germinate, take root and grow.

After presenting the home influenced by 'modern' values, we will look at how biblical principles are worked out practically in the home.

Let us now look at these four scenarios, one by one. Each scene will first be introduced by a commonly found scene (a typical approach).

Area #1 At Home

What standards do we need to set for a child so that he lives a good and proper life at home?

Typical approach - parents avoid setting standards

The parent spends his or her time chasing the child around to keep him out of trouble. The parents' motives are good, trying to ensure that the child does not get into danger and damage things. This is only guards the child from danger rather than trains him to act properly.

Each child has a desire to seek his own will. This is his selfish nature. He will go out of his way to gratify these desires. He will want to go places, eat things, climb things, etc. If these desires are not restrained, then the situation described above can easily occur.

Sprouts (nature of evil)	*Plants* (short term results)	*Fruit* (long term results)
Seeking one's own will; self-gratification.	Exhausted parents, disobedient children, lack of self-control, ignorant of standards, friction between parent and child.	Child believes that there are no boundaries. They believe they are most important and that others exist to meet their own needs; relativistic; unreliable.

God's Way

The child should be trained to control himself to do everything the parent wants. Take one room at a time. What is it that you, as the parent, want the child to do or not to do? Communicate these to your child.[5] Make sure that they have heard you by looking directly at them. Have them repeat you if necessary. If the child is young, the parent will only think about what the child should not do. Here are some starters:

- Do not touch the ...
- Do not go into the ...

- Do not move the ...
- Do not jump on ...
- Do not run in ....

The parent must be specific as to when (do not touch the stove when hot), where (do not play around in the living room) and what (do not touch the books on that one bookcase). When the child is younger, we should set standards that do not change. "Do not go near stove." "Do not touch any bookcase in living room." They cannot easily differentiate between why one thing is permissible at one time and not another. Positively, we can identify things that they can touch such as their books and crayons.

Property

Children need to respect property (the things that exist, be it living or nonliving). People are stewards of the things God has made including other people, bugs, trees and toys. As the child grows, he will learn that certain objects belong to certain people. Permission must first be gained before using other peoples' things. Even if there is no specific owner, the child must learn that God has given us what we possess or have access to. We must take care of it. If we cannot properly care for something, then we have no right to possess it.

Even if a toy belongs to him, he has no right to destroy it. I tell our children, "If you do not rightly care for that toy, then we will find someone that will." They have no right to smash something that is good. They are better off if they give it away. This is because we are not the ultimate owners; we are the stewards of what God has given to us.[6] If we cannot properly use it, then let us find someone that will.

We are stewards over things. Furniture is not a toy and must not be jumped on, including beds. On the other hand, we allow them to jump off certain things (they need to learn exceptions). As they learn to take care of property at home, then they can extend that principle to caring for things that belong to others when in public. This principle of caring for things helps supports the idea of keeping things clean.

Clean up

If the child makes a mess with food or toys, they should, if old enough, pick it up and make everything nice and clean. They should even sweep up the mess. When the child is 4-5, the parent or older sibling can work together cleaning up. Later on, they will be able to do it on their own.

Throwing things

Children are taught the principle, "Do not throw things in the house." They are to apply this to all sorts of objects, but sometimes a parent might need to clarify the rule. They are not allowed to throw food. Paper airplanes and balloons are allowed in our house (but they might not be in yours).

Coming

If called, they are to say, "Coming." If they cannot come, they are to ask permission for delaying. Children are expected to speak honestly and obey their parents the first time they say something.

Five Minute rule

When the parents call the children to go somewhere, it is wise to give a bit of time for the children to finish what they are doing and put things away. Even adults need time to get ready for another activity.

For meals, we use a bell system. On the first bell, they are expected to stop their activity such as playing the computer, come in from playing outside, watching television or playing with some toys. They are to shut off electronic devices and put their toys away. On the second bell, they are to wash their hands and proceed directly to the table. This simplifies the procedure for Mom who is preparing a hot meal. This also helps foster in the child the responsibility to pick up after themselves. They are expected to pick up at the first bell.

Hygiene

The parents are to train their children to practice proper hygiene. We must not leave it up to the children to decide what they do or do not want to do. They would rather make art designs with the toothpaste! Instead, the parent must ensure that the child has brushed his teeth properly, toilet needs rightly cared for and hands washed well with soap.

They should be trained at age-appropriate times to take over from their parents. For example, the young child needs the parent's help with hand washing. As the child grows, he should be trained how to clean his own hands. Include on how to care for the towel after use.

Orderliness

God is a God of order. Routines are good. The parent should set the bedtimes and awake times, not the child. The parent sets the mealtime, not the whining of the child. Parents should even set the detailed routine for getting up or going to bed. This would include awake times, getting dressed, dirty clothes, hygiene care, eating, etc.

Training the child to care for his own needs makes an orderly house. After a bath, a child should put away his clothes and properly hang the towel rather than having the mother do everything for him. At first, do it together and then as they get older, you can appoint them to be in charge of doing it. If it is done in the right spirit (e.g. "You are getting big!"), they will want to do it on their own. These times will leave good memories of doing things together. They need to be shown how to fold clothes, step by step. You do one step. They do the next. Before they know it, they will be able to do the whole thing.

Serving others

As a child begins to walk, the parents will look for opportunities to train their children to help others. Part of the training includes helping them notice the needs of others.

Yesterday, I came into my home office to find my study immaculate. Even my chair was nicely tucked under my desk with my sweater neatly hanging over the back of the chair. Later, I found out that my six-year-old daughter engineered that surprise all on her own. We want to foster that kind of serving spirit. We show great delight at their thoughtfulness and do our best at telling others how special it was that he or she went out of the way to do that.

Summary

Early on in training and in life, children are intentionally allowed very few choices. We choose for them. We work with them from the start to make sure they know what and how to do things. Then at the appropriate time, we gradually turn the responsibility over to them to manage on their own. They learn how to prioritize matters by what their parents say and enforce. This is the way to build parental respect without much confrontation. In the end, they have the freedom to do things the ways that we think is important.

Pause for Reflection:

Do you chase your children around trying to keep them from wrong or do you train them to do what is right? Are you consistent?

Area #2 At the Table

How do you train proper table manners into a child? How do you teach a child to make good meal choices?

Typical approach - give them what they want

Many parents ask the child what he wants to eat and then prepares it for him. Parents do this because they fear that the child will reject what they prepare or not like it. The child may throw a temper tantrum when he does not want to eat a certain item. As a result the parent leaves it open for the child to choose.

The parent ends up focusing more on getting the child to eat than on nutrition or the training of self-control. The child gets whatever he wants. Whenever he fusses for something, then he gets it. This is the way to make a picky, ungrateful eater.

Sprouts (nature of evil)	*Plants* (short term results)	*Fruit* (long term results)
Self-determination. Not willing to be ruled by the parent.	Unthankful, demanding, tired Mom, complaining, picky eater, junk food addict. Does not finish eating.	Lack of gratefulness to God and wife, poor health and lack of manners.

God's Way

The child does not know what is best for him. Determine what the child's needs are according to his age. Serve him good, nutritious, well-balanced meals at regular times.

Expect the child to eat what he is served. If he does not eat, he goes without until the next meal. If he learns what good meals are, then he will form good eating habits. Snacks should be given sparingly and should not interfere with a good appetite. Beware of giving milk or nutrition-less juice after weaning because it can interfere with eating well. Gratefulness springs from a good appetite.

He will learn thankfulness by observing his parents. If Dad expresses real thanks to God and his wife, this will go a long way in creating a grateful heart. The child should be trained to give thanks to God for the food as well as Mom for her love shown in preparing meals.

This is not to say that children do not develop likes and dislikes. Everyone is different, but catering to a child's likes and avoiding his dislikes never gives him an opportunity to learn to endure unpleasant things. The child simply has to trust his parents' judgment when his parents ask him to eat something that he does not like.

If a child does not respect his parent, he will certainly make it known on this issue. The table will turn into a battleground. The child can be picky about color (dark toast), snack (want something else), size ("His is bigger.") or practically anything. The parent must make the choices.

Purpose of eating
Parents should ask, "Are they honoring the Lord by what they eat, how they eat and the way they show gratefulness to those who prepared the meal?" Along with being thankful, the child needs to learn not to waste things. He should not take more than he can eat. More often than not, there will be enough for second helpings. This is better than throwing food away. Start with a smaller amount.

Saying 'grace'
Expressing thanks to the Lord is very important not just before meals but for all things.[7] We train our infant children to hold his or her hands during prayer. We do this at first by holding their hands together. This will work for a long time. The young child gets used to it. (The child does not know better.) Later, the child will want to fold hands on his own. Be prepared, though. He will go through a stage where he will refuse to fold his hands. Then the parent steps in and holds both his hands.

In this case, the parent holds the child's hands until he is willing to fold his hands on his own. If he fusses, just calmly keep holding his hands. We do not want children playing during this time but showing respect to God. Children should wait for 'grace' to be said before serving himself (under most circumstances) and eating.

Eating problems
A parent might wonder how to encourage a child to eat food which he does not want to eat. If we start at an early age, Mom feeds the child what she decides he needs. She does not ask him what he wants. When this is done, the child gets used to eating what is served.

Remember that a young child should already respect his Mom's 'no,' and will generally respect her 'no' in the highchair. If the child was not trained this way, then a switch will be needed to establish respect for the parents' authority.

In infancy (4-6 months), hold the child's hands away from the dish. As the child grows, he will go through different stages of training. The child will first learn to keep his hands away from the food while Mom feeds him. As time goes on (about 15 months), Mom will begin to aid him to eat part of the meal with a spoon. Later yet, the young child will be able to eat parts of the meal (easier to handle) by himself. Later, he will graduate to completely feeding himself. This happens around two.

Does not like

The idea that a baby does not 'like' something may come from a parent's misinterpretation of why the child spits out food. A baby is just learning to eat food at that stage. The baby has not yet trained his tongue to work properly. The mother might think that the baby does not like it when, in fact, the baby is learning how to eat it.

When the baby spits out food, the mother's face might express dislike because she thinks the baby does not like it. The baby can learn to reject it from the Mom's negative response, facial expression or words. "Oh you do not like that!" Instead, Mom should show confidence on her face and verbally express how the child will like it. "This is good!" Then help the child eat happily.

Eating together as a family

Eating together as a family should be a joyful event. Parents and children should gather around the meal to spend time. There should not be any distraction from television or radio except for special events.[8] Our family talks a lot together. We do not allow accusations about the failure of others but pleasant conversation of the day's events. We might even read aloud from a chapter of an interesting book after the meal.

Summary

Much mealtime stress can be avoided if the child is trained to eat what is served. The parents transfer God's goodness to the children by purchasing, preparing and providing nutritious meals and a pleasant mealtime atmosphere.

Pause for Reflection:

What are your mealtime manners? What good things would you like to happen at the dinner table?

Area #3 In Public

How do you train a child to act properly in public?

Typical approach

Parents desire to socialize with others at public events. The untrained child often distracts the parent. The child wanders where he should not, runs about making disturbances, or acts naughtily so that the parent cannot pay attention to their company. It is not uncommon for a child to go into a fit of rage to get what he wants. The parent typically bribes the child to behave with many unhealthy snacks. This persuades the child to disobey again so he can get more snacks!

The child will disobey to get what he wants in public and in other places. Without constraining the child's willingness to disobey, his desires will get out of hand. Notice the results below.

Sprouts *(nature of evil)*	*Plants* *(short term results)*	*Fruit* *(long term results)*
The child uses anger and other antics to get his own desires.	Parents cannot accomplish much; do not often go out; become embarrassed. The child manipulates the parents and learns how to get what he wants. Cavities.	He believes he is above the law. He manipulates situations and authorities to get his own way. Arrogant.

God's Way

A parent should expect politeness, orderliness and obedience from his child in public. The child should be other-conscious. Children should respond to their parents' wishes.

Manners

Rules of etiquette come from the scriptures. A person should act as if others are more important than himself. Rules might change within cultures but the principle of regarding another more important than oneself remains the same.

> *Do nothing from selfishness or empty conceit, but with humility of mind let each of you regard one another as more important than*

himself; do not merely look out for your own personal interests, but also for the interests of others (Philippians 2:3-4).

One rule of politeness our children have had to learn is to take their shoes off when they enter a home. Because we largely work and worship with Asians, we go by their cultural expectations. This helps keep the house of our host clean.

Careful words

A child needs to learn to control his words and actions in such a way that he attends to the needs of others. If a parent is talking, then he should observe that he should not be noisy. If he catches himself being too noisy or hears and sees Dad's warning signal, he should instantly quiet down.

Orderliness

Orderliness is very important. It protects others from inconvenience and distraction. Disorderly behavior includes doing things that might cause him to bump into someone, throwing things, accidentally hurting someone, being a loud disturbance, not properly caring for things, or not cleaning up after himself.

I remember once that a church closed the child's playroom after church instead of allowing the children to play there when their parents were otherwise engaged. The toy room was no doubt the best and safest place for children to play. But because the children left the place in such a mess, it was closed after church during fellowship time.

Would it not be better for each child to be trained to pick up after himself? Would it not be better if the whole group of children would cooperatively and speedily pick things up before they had to leave? That church did not know about training. On the other hand, I have seen a messy room cleaned up in moments by trained children.

Learning at home

We cannot expect the child to know all the specific rules of the parent when in a public place, especially if it is a new setting. If you do not allow your child to jump on your furniture, then the child should know that he should not jump on other people's furniture either. The general rule would be, "Do not do to others (or other things) what you are not allowed to do at home." When trained properly at home, the child will act properly in public places.[9]

The parents' expectations

The child ought to pay careful attention to the parents' desires. The parent should clearly communicate his general expectations to the child. (Boundaries like: where to stay and what not to do.) It helps if the parent has arranged a hand signal to let the child know to quiet down. Failure to pay attention to the signal means chastisement at home. When the parent calls, the child should come as soon as possible. No exceptions. At home, have the child answer, "Coming Daddy," or "Okay, Mommy." This is not as appropriate in public places, though. The child should just come.

A parent's attentiveness
When making trips outside the home, the wise parent takes into consideration nap times, a child's age, a child's hunger, health problems and general crankiness from not sleeping well the night before. An attentive parent must not abuse his authority but be attentive to the child's needs. Keep a good balance. If a baby seems to be unnaturally cranky, perhaps the his tooth is coming in or he is not well. The parent should leave a little bit early.

Summary
Child training takes place at home, over a long time. Well-trained children will be well-behaved in public. People will take notice of your well-behaved children.

Pause for Reflection:
Are you embarrassed by your children's behavior in public? Does your children's unruly behavior keep you from attending activities? Do people like to be around your children?

Area #4 At Church Meetings

How do you train a child to act properly in church?

Typical approach
Parents are often embarrassed to go to church or to attempt to sit in church meetings because of the disturbance their young children make. Frustrated parents resolve not to go anymore or the mother stays in the nursery.

Once the child knows that he or she can get away from quietly sitting still for a one hour service, you can be sure that he will do what is needed to 'escape.' The parent will then say that his child cannot sit still. If the child hears this idea enough times, he will be convinced that he cannot sit still.

The child will tend to move around to do something that he likes. He would rather eat a sweet than eat nothing, run about than sit still, play with toys than have nothing to do with his hands. He will even disobey his parents to get these things even when he knows it is wrong.

Sprouts (nature of evil)	*Plants* (short term results)	*Fruit* (long term results)
Arrogance. Delight in self-pleasure over reverence for those in authority.	Disrespect towards God and parents. Parents are manipulated and not aware of it. The child does not learn self-control.	Children despise those they manipulate. They will avoid those whom they have despised.

God's Way

Sitting still

Children can learn to sit still. There is a longer training process for littler ones, but it does work and is needed. Children tend to be impatient in worship services. Parents think it is wrong to expect their children to sit still. These same parents should notice how they can sit still in front of a television set for a long period of time without moving an inch. Children need to learn to control the physical to be responsive to the spiritual.

> *Now it shall be, if you will diligently obey the LORD your God, being careful to do all His commandments which I command you today, the LORD your God will set you high above all the nations of the earth. And all these blessings shall come upon you and overtake you, if you will obey the LORD your God (Deuteronomy 28:1-2).*

Many parents convince themselves that their children are naturally 'active.' More often than not, this is an excuse for the lack of proper training. Parents only need to be sensitive to their child's shorter attention span. If the parents want their children to sit still for part or all of the worship service, or any other meeting, then they should train them to do so.

Curtailing noise in a church service

Our philosophy is to train them so that they know nothing else. This does not mean that they are always quiet. They are noisy without even knowing it. Our cute little 18 month old is a very good girl, but she cannot be quiet in church for so long. She does not really understand the command to be quiet. She might be singing when people are praying or happily talking on Daddy's lap. (Of course, no one can understand her.) Unfortunately, these responses make too much noise. So one of the parents takes her out.

If we take our child to a playroom, then she would soon make a connection: be noisy and go to play room. If we do this, we have just set ourselves up for a repeat performance. The child was not originally manipulating the parent, but we can easily train her to think this way. Once children get the connection, they just make the noise, and the parent makes the move. This is not easily solved once the pattern becomes well established.

We all can do it!

Parents used to think our children's quietness in church was because they were girls. People actually told us this. They made excuses for their children. "You only have girls. You do not have a boy, do you?" They were inferring that girls are easier to care for.

Our first three children are girls. The facts, however, prove that it was through long training that enabled them to sit through one and a half hour worship services. It was no accident. God has now given us three lively boys to prove how training works even with boys! Boys are a bit more restless, but they can sit through meetings just as well as girls if they are trained. They might move about a bit more, but they can be quiet. How, then, can we train our children?

Training

We begin before they know anything different. We do not want them to think that there are any alternatives. Once they taste freedom, they are harder to train, though it is not impossible. Bringing the infant to the nursery is fine. Having them accompany you to the service is fine too. Just remember the mother has a harder time concentrating with her baby there. She is very attentive to the baby's needs.

The key to training occurs when the child can start observing his change of circumstances. At about 6-8 months, the child starts to become familiar with the worship service. By ten months, the child should be with the parent for worship at least part of the time. One parent will need to prepare his or herself to take the child out if he disturbs others. Sit towards the back. There is no need to chastise. The child is unaware of the disturbance he is making. In our case, the Dad took the baby out when needed. He did this to help Mom concentrate. He could usually focus on the message even while holding the baby.

Usually, the child will fuss for a couple of months during the training process, but the parent refuses to take him to the 'fun' room or feed him candy to bribe him. The parent needs to make it very obvious to the child that his noises do not reward him with anything. Dad does not even put the child down just in case the child thinks he could then run around. He just holds his son or daughter.[10] After about six months of this, the child starts discerning the noises he makes and can be trained. When the child can understand such boundaries–such as obey his parent's word, be quiet, etc., then he can be chastised. We do not chastise him in church but at home. The age of understanding is not fixed and depends a lot on what training he has had at home.[11]

Our children sit through those 'long' services. If the parent shows boredom, the child will pick up on their impatient attitudes in an instant. This makes it even more difficult. The parent in many cases is too embarrassed to openly show his lack of desire to be there. The child does not care about this! As parents convey their true excitement about meeting the Lord, the child will not mind being there. They also sense that expectation. My six-year old daughter (still an unbeliever at the time) said that her favorite day was Sunday because of church.

Remember that there is room for change. Parents need to think through special occasions and try to work something out. If things will be different at church one Sunday, then the parents should discuss this ahead of time. We try to be more flexible. We prefer not to send our children to Junior Worship when available. We are not legalists nor prideful that our way is better. We are merely thinking about what is best for our children short and long-term.

Each couple is responsible to work out how they are training their children to respect God and others. We have found that Junior Worship, in most cases, trains the child not to respect God but keeps them busy through activities and sweets. They are not trained in patience but with distraction. This makes it harder for the parents to train their children to sit attentively through church.

Purpose of worship

Man is commanded to worship the awesome and mighty Creator. We are not wrong in training our child to treat this hour more special. They need to be trained how to rightly come before the eternal God with a humble heart and mind. Manipulating the parent to take him to play is exactly the opposite of what should happen.

We do not go to church for entertainment but for meeting God. We do not go for friends or food. We serve God. This means we need to train our children how to regularly assemble before Him and put away their toys and fun. There are higher objectives at stake.

Pause for Reflection:

What are your goals for your children at church? Do these goals please God? Do you love God more than anything in the world? How do you know and show this?

C. General Guidelines for Implementing Boundaries

The areas of frustration are more often than not the areas that we need to work on. For example, the parent desires for the children to clean up the room after playing. That is a good thing. The children, however, do not comply. These frustrations often reflect a deeper standard that is being violated.

In this case, the parent knows the child should pick up but does not. Many parents have a difficult time isolating what is wrong. In this case, our sense of order, respect for property and cleanliness are being violated. We should keep this issue in mind as we remember the following general principles for implementing boundaries.

1. Think about what you want each child to do. The young toddler cannot sweep, but he can pick up papers, put away toys and straighten up the bookcase.

2. Break down the whole project into different tasks. These tasks might mean different areas of the room to be cleaned, kinds of activities to be done, time to be cleaned, etc.

3. Choose one task that the child can learn to do. He can put away the alphabet toy.

4. Do the task with the child. Make sure he can do it. Note where he needs help. In this case, he might not know how to happily put the tray away. Show him how to do it in a fun way!

5. Make adjustments. If the task requires something that the child cannot do, such as reach the high shelf, modify the task. Perhaps you could make a place for it on a lower shelf.

6. Follow up on the child's tasks. Ensure compliance. A good way to do this is to happily work alongside him in another part of the room.

7. Once the task becomes easy for the child, train him to do another task until he is able to do that one also. Pass on the responsibility. With time, he will be able to do the whole room himself or, better yet, with his siblings who helped make the mess.

8. Settle on a time when the job needs to be done. We might say the room needs to be cleaned right after dinner or before he wants to play a computer game or watch a program. (He still cannot tell time.) Perhaps Mom can read a book after the job is finished!

9. Settle on a consequence for disobedience. Communicate this to him. Follow through with chastisement when appropriate. Unfortunately, even though he can happily do the job, at some point he will test parental resolve.

10. Look for ways to encourage your child. Praise his developing virtues: being cheerful, thorough, attentive, faithful, etc. Do not praise his looks or natural gifts (things which he is not responsible for) which can easily lead to pride.

Pause for Reflection:

Work through these steps. Start with one frustration you have. What is it that you would like your child to do that he is not doing? Follow through the steps. What problems do you have carrying them out?

Summary

Parents can really train their children to obedience! This is our God-given responsibility. We need to identify the areas requiring improvement. Break down each of these 'projects' into different parts and train the child to care for each part. Once accomplished, the parent can go on to another part until the child can do the whole project. This enables the parent to move on to other areas of training. The process gets easier because the child is learning to follow your leadership and training.

Encourage *Encourage* *Encourage*

Parenting Principles & Practices

- God expects parents to compel their children do what is right.
- Each child has an inborn tendency to do what is wrong. They must be trained.
- Wherever the parent neglects to cultivate godly actions and attitudes, sinful actions and attitudes develop.
- By focusing on right training, the parent eliminates wrong attitudes and behaviors and sets the child up to good disciplines.
- Routines are good and necessary for raising a healthy child.
- Children need to learn how to obey and honor God and parents.

Parenting Questions

1. What gives the parent the right to rule over his child?
2. How does the parent compel the child to do these things?
3. Why is it so important to train children to high standards?
4. How should a child treat property?
5. Why are routines important?
6. Why should the parent determine what and when the child should eat?
7. What Biblical basis do common manners have?
8. Why is it so important for children to learn to sit still to worship God?
9. Should we praise virtue or achievement? Why or why not?

Notes from Chapter #8

[1] Chapter two is about parental authority; chapters five and six are about discipline. Chapter one is about goals and is also related to this topic of setting boundaries.

[2] We acknowledge that many of these tasks, such as folding clothes, are not moral issues on their own. But once a parent requests this of the child, it becomes a moral issue. The child needs to obey.

[3] The scripture teaches us that if we want to eliminate bad habits, like bad words or poor attitudes, we should replace them with positive ones. This can be learned from the Bible verse, "But I say, walk by the Spirit, and you will not carry out the desire of the flesh" (Galatians 5:16).

[4] Dad started the whole dinner conversation by asking, "Anything special go on today?" That is when he started talking about helping our neighbor.

[5] Remember that if you start training your children when he is young, then the rules are added gradually as the child grows. However, if you try to catch up from the past, then the rules can feel overwhelming. Focus on the major rules and then fine-tune them as you see progress. Instead of expecting a clean room from your child, help him first know how to order his bookcase. Do it with him each day until he has it done. Then, you can expand to other parts of the room.

[6] God is the Maker. Everything belongs to Him. We will give an account to Him on how we use what He has given to us.

[7] "In all things give thanks for this is God's will for you who are in Christ Jesus" (1 Thessalonians 5:18).

[8] Different cultures have different ways of conducting mealtimes. Most of us, however, are or soon will be learning how to live in the new modern culture of electronic gadgets. Building family ties during mealtimes is much more important. Television and games can wait! Or do like our family did growing up. Play at the table while eating! *21 Questions* and *GHOST* are two games.

[9] Unruly peers can lead a child into mischief. The parent needs to foresee this and train the child to handle such friends.

[10] The parent must judge his or her circumstances. There are no laws. Each child is different. Our one particular child at this age is more noisy than the others. Do not put them in the play room because they cry. Either put them in the nursery and wait until they are old enough to understand what it means to be quiet. Or patiently do your best to keep them in worship. Or as some parents do, bring them to the nursery at a certain time, like just before the sermon. The parent decides what is best, not the child. In each of these cases, we have not rewarded their naughty behavior and still leave lots of room for good spiritual training.

[11] Training in spiritual disciplines should take place at home during family devotions. We will discuss this more in a later chapter.

Chapter #9

RAISING GODLY CHILDREN

Purpose: Explain and apply the needed biblical principles to provide proper spiritual care for our children.

"I pray for you Johnny that you will be a godly man who loves God and is willing to sacrifice your money, gifts and time to glorify God and help others."

Introduction

Do we want good children or godly children? This question lies at the heart of our true desire for our children. Surrounded by the influence of a secular society, it is easy to leave God out of our children's training.

If parents were honest with themselves, they would have to admit that their desire for a comfortable life sometimes shapes their parenting more than their desire for godly children. We just want 'good' children. Parents simply want their children to obey them because it makes things easier around the home. Down deep, however, they are not very concerned about the child's life before God. This is the stain of our secular society that pollutes Christian families and claims our children for itself.

While 'good' children might enjoy God's world and His gifts of life and health, they do not necessarily recognize God's care for them. They might go to church, but they feel no serious obligation to obey their Maker. In the end, our children live with a secular mindset rather than God's way.

Unless parents are clear in their focus, most of our children will be lost to the world. We must strive to train them with a passion to love

God and to serve others. Everything else in life, their educational opportunities, home situation, career, contacts and friends, all becomes a means or opportunity to express their commitment to God.

We want godly children who go beyond seeking God's general blessings and pursue knowing God through Christ. We desire our children to have a love and passion for God that overflows in a love for others. Without Jesus Christ, our ability to forgive, have compassion and to love is greatly limited. In Christ, we have the means for Christ to live His life through us.

Our goals for our children must go far beyond what we can do in our own strength. We must train our children to trust God and live a supernatural life walking in His Spirit. There are many voices telling us how to parent, but the majority of them reject God's real purpose for our children. Because many Christian families have bought into secular thinking, their children are living as immorally as the society around them. They might think of themselves as 'good' or even call themselves a Christian, but they are not living for the Lord.[1]

It is now time to change the course of history through our own families. God can do great and mighty things through a small number of families that live by His glorious promises and purposes.

In this chapter, we will first focus on God's principles for raising godly children from Deuteronomy 6 and later conclude by mentioning some practical points on implementing these life-changing principles.

A. Observations from Deuteronomy 6

There are seven principles from Deuteronomy 6 that need to take root if we are going to cultivate godly families.

Principle #1: Establish and live by God's standards (Deuteronomy 6:1)

> *Now this is the commandment, the statutes and the judgments which the LORD your God has commanded me to teach you, that you might **do them** in the land where you are going over to possess it (Deuteronomy 6:1).*

Godly people must adopt God's standards. When calling a new generation to follow Him in faith and go into the land of Canaan, the Lord restated the Ten Commandments. That was Deuteronomy 5. In Deuteronomy 6 the Lord tells Moses to teach the people so that they might <u>know</u> these commands. Without God's Word, they would be unable to accomplish the purposes God had for their lives. <u>Knowing</u> God's Word, however, is not the end goal. God provided His Word that they might "do them."

God is holy, therefore, we must do things His way to please Him. He gave us His Word so that we might know what pleases Him as well as what displeases Him. It is quite insufficient to think we can please Him by only owning a Bible or attending church. He wants His Word to shape our thoughts, lives, words, decisions, attitudes and purposes. In order to obey Him, we must know His Word and then do what He says. Moses taught the Israelites God's commands to help them live out godly lives among the heathen nations.

The same is true for God's people today. Jesus the Great Prophet came to tell us God's Word that it might have an impact on our lives. God's standards must become our standards. A willing heart is insufficient. Passion is often misdirected. Religion is often distasteful to Him. He wants obedience from us.

Many parents have failed right here. Calling yourself a Christian does not make you one. Does your life reflect what God loves? The truth is that as long as we do not obey the Lord, we are an offense to Him. A large proportion of our youth today are not turning to the Lord even though they have been brought up in church. Clearly, one problem lies in the unwillingness of their parents to obey the Lord. Another problem is parental lack of passion for the Lord.

Pause for Reflection:

Do you know the scriptures? Do you study them each day? Do you obey them? Are there places that you reserve the right to do what you want?

Any compromise parents have made is open disobedience and become glaring signs to the children that their parents do not love the Lord. Every disobedience shows them that they love something more than God. This is the idolatry that John warns us of, "Little children, guard yourselves from idols" (1 John 5:21). Godly parenting requires a revival of our own hearts so that we can fervently love and obey His ways again.

Pause for Reflection

Are you learning God's ways so that you can love Him more dearly? Do you eagerly seek Him in your daily Bible readings?

Principle #2: Pass it on to the next generations (Deuteronomy 6:2)

So that you and your son and your grandson might fear the LORD your God, to keep all His statutes and His commandments, which I command you, all the days of your life, and that your days may be prolonged (Deuteronomy 6:2).

God wants us to think in terms of generations. We are not only to think of ourselves but also of our children and our children's children. The 'you,' 'your sons,' and 'your grandson' reflect three generations. What we do with our lives greatly affects the lives of the next generations. The 'fear of the LORD' is the conscious presence of God, which influences our lives. Many professing Christians live their daily lives as if God has nothing to say about what they watch, say or eat.

The chart below depicts how lukewarmness settles into the lives of our children and grandchildren. If we are not careful to live out God's Word in our lives as He prescribes, our families will fall into this situation. This is why each Christian must constantly live in the fear of God or they will begin to leave Him.

When God's Word has minimum impact on what a person does, we can say he is secularized even though he might be religious. The 'fear of God' is no longer a key element in his life. Our purpose is not just to pass down the knowledge of God's commands but that our children might fear the Lord and keep His commands. Knowing is good but insufficient. Knowledge must be translated into life change.

If a generation only has knowledge of His commands and no love for His ways, then the next generation will depart from those commands. This is how Christianity degenerates into a mere religion without life.

How do we avoid this generational drift? Parents must pass on the fear of the LORD to their children and children's children. The Christian parent must do everything to pass on the heart and passion for the Lord as well as knowledge of the Lord's commands. We can only pass on what we ourselves possess first.

We do not need to worry if this is happening. If we live out godly lives before our children, they will most likely pick up that passion. We must, however, be careful to instruct them about who the Lord is and all about His ways. Neglect of this will lead to a coming generation that has respect for our ways but no real power to live it out.

If we live with compromise, then we already live in the second generational stage. Our children will, for the most part, leave the Lord. They do not believe because we do not really believe. Genuine faith always touches our life's priorities. Only a false religious faith permits a division between life and belief. Our children look at the goodness of our lives rather than what we say. They are right. If we do not live by what we say, then they see only our hypocrisy. They naturally reject this. Did you ever take a swallow of sour milk?

Pause for Reflection:

Are you excited about what God is doing in your life? If so, have you shared it with your children? If not, do you really expect your children's zeal to be greater than yours? Have your children started imitating your prayers, singing and devotional time in God's Word? It is wonderful to come down the steps into our living room to see my son reading God's Word.

Principle #3: Convinced of the need for God's blessing (Deuteronomy 6:3)

> *O Israel, you should listen and be careful to do it, <u>that it may be well with you</u> and that you may multiply greatly, just as the LORD, the God of your fathers, has promised you, in a land flowing with milk and honey (Deuteronomy 6:3).*

God's ways always bring the greatest blessing. To the degree our lives are shaped by His teaching, we are able to live by His high standards. When we carefully apply these teachings to our lives, then we see how God's promises fill our lives. Part of this blessing is material.[2] The blessing normally includes the multiplication of children. God wants to increase what is good. Having many children is a blessing of our

LORD which should not be hindered.[3] "And He will love you and bless you and multiply you; He will also bless the fruit of your womb..."(Deuteronomy 7:13).

We will either believe our welfare is dependent upon keeping God's Word or we will not. To the degree we obey, we will be blessed. Our goal should be to run after His commands. Only in this way do we have a passionate love for God that would be worthy of transfer to the next generation.

Pause for Reflection:

Are you enthusiastic about the ways God cares for you and your family? He wants you to trust Him. Do you hold back from having children? Why? Does it have anything to do with the fear of not being able to properly care for them? If so, confess your doubt and repent. He is faithful!

Principle #4: Undivided loyalty to Yahweh (LORD) (Deuteronomy 6:4-5)

> *Hear, O Israel! The LORD is our God, the LORD is one! And you shall love the LORD your God <u>with all your heart</u> and with all your soul and with all your might (Deuteronomy 6:4-5).*

Since the Lord is one, we must not divide our affections between Him and something else. If there were several gods, then our loyalty would be divided. Since He is one, all of our devotion, inspiration and strength must be used to do all that He says. His words take a priority in our lives. God is asking, even demanding, that we rework all of our work, family and personal plans so that He becomes the center of our lives. A doctor, for example, should give up his occupation if he is required to do abortions. He should not murder. The commitment to life requires him to care for and heal people.

Jesus told us that we could only love Him or wealth (mammon) (Matthew 6:24). If a family worships money, then their decisions will be made with those commitments in mind. In the end, we will only prioritize one, the Lord or another.

We need to commit to serving the LORD Yahweh as a family. This decision sets our family apart from others. This is important to communicate to our children. We should not fear the isolation that comes from it. (The topic of developing friendships will be discussed later.)

Identifying with the Lord's ways helps them accept why they live differently than their immoral neighbors. How else will they be at peace with not being able to listen to certain kinds of music, watch television or go certain places? Dad and Mom joyfully fulfilling God's commands helps them live out God's ways. Our children will judge what is right or wrong from out point of view. This is God's purpose for extending the period of training children for up to twenty years.

Pause for Reflection:
Is faithfulness to God your life priority? If things got real bad like Job, would you give God up?

Principle #5: Devoted to His Word (Deuteronomy 6:6)

> *And these words, which I am commanding you today, shall be on your heart (Deuteronomy 6:6).*

We fool ourselves if we think that we can raise our children to become godly men and women without having a passion for God and His Word ourselves. His words must be on our heart. Notice, although the theme of teaching our children is very strong, He asks us to focus on whether we as the parents are keeping His Word.

God communicates His Word through the father to their children.

We can judge our commitment by discerning how much time we spend keeping God's Word fresh on our hearts and minds. When we do spend time in His Word, is it because we desire His Word or because we are obligated to? We do go through ups and downs in our spiritual life, but the real test is how much we love God and His Word through all those times.

Pause for Reflection:
Father, how many times do you meditate on God's Word throughout the week? Compare this to how much time you watch the news, stocks or sports.

Principle #6: Committed to Teaching his sons (Deuteronomy 6:7)

> *And you shall <u>teach them diligently</u> to your sons and shall talk of them when you sit in your house and when you walk by the way and when you lie down and when you rise up (Deuteronomy 6:7).*

There are two commands here. First, we are instructed to "teach them diligently to our sons." This describes formal teaching. Second, we are to "talk of" His ways. This is informal teaching.

Formal teaching

The father is responsible for diligently teaching his sons. Interestingly, we do not see God charging pastors, elders or Sunday School teachers to do this at church. The father must, therefore, refuse any tendency to pass off his responsibility as a father to formally teach his children. Instead, he is to embrace his responsibility as a charge from God. What is a father to do?

Fathers need to diligently teach God's Words to theirs sons. The content of their instruction is God's words or commands. They need to teach them both the positive and negative commands. Since many of the commands are set within the contexts of interesting historical situations, they are also to recite those narratives. The Lord brings that 'God-conscious' perspective to their children through their fathers. This, in turn, brings great blessing to their lives.

Many Christian families go wrong right here. The fathers simply do not teach their children. Some children have heard their fathers teach others but not them.

I myself did not get a hold of this truth until recently. I was pondering how my children were going to be better prepared to face the wild world out there than other children. It was then that I realized that, though, I personally discipled others, I did not disciple my own children one on one. I knew the advantage of personal discipleship but had not applied it to my own family. I was humbled by my neglect of personally meeting with my two older daughters. I decided I would start meeting regularly with my oldest son and teach him God's Word.

After I had understood more of the procedure and need, I expanded to meeting personally with each of my younger children that could read.[4] I did not totally neglect my older children. We have had family devotions each night since the beginning, but this personal acquiring of God's Word into their lives has become a very important building time with the younger ones. As a result, I can naturally talk about personal issues with them that other older children never share with their parents.

One of the greatest problems with this idea of family devotions or personal discipleship of our child is that the father usually does not know God's Word very well. It is to a father's shame if he does not love God and devote Himself to knowing His Word. He must study it. His children will reject his empty religion because that is all it has become. If a father really loves God, then he would really love and study His Word and pass it on to his children.[5]

Another obstacle for fathers is the notion that since they are not gifted teachers, they cannot teach. In other words, they believe that only the few gifted teachers or fathers can and should teach. It is urgent that we reject this notion. Let us instead ask what the Word of God demands of the father. Does He, our Lord, not teach us that we should love His Word and teach our sons? Yes.

Then let us not let this notion of being a gifted teacher get in the way. If we expose ourselves regularly to God and His Word, then He Himself will give us things to teach. We can teach what He teaches us.

Along with this wrong notion is the thought that only those trained in seminaries can rightfully teach doctrine. This is nonsense. Again, it goes clearly against what we have learned from this charge to fathers. Fathers are responsible to teach their sons. Ephesians 4 tells us that pastors and teachers are to equip God's people. This means that God charges pastors and teachers to exhort and instruct God's people. Among them are many fathers. These fathers are then to instruct their children.

Fathers are responsible to teach their own children. Every father has to develop and carry out a formal plan of instruction. Without it, the children will be missing out. We have partially chosen to home school for this reason. This gives us even more opportunities to instruct our children using God's Word rather than daily exposing them to secular curriculum with all of its biases.

Pause for Reflection:

What formal teaching of God's Word do you bring to your family as the father? How much time do you spend doing it? Where? To whom?

Informal Teaching

And shall talk of them when you sit in your house and when you walk by the way and when you lie down and when you rise up (Deuteronomy 6:7).

This passage catches fathers off guard. Some fathers do have family devotions with their children, but many are too busy to spend any significant time engaging in worthwhile conversation with their sons. This whole approach works only if the father really loves God with his whole heart, mind and with all his strength. Passion for God is normal. Anything else is backsliding.

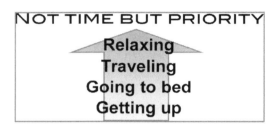

Yesterday, for example, my head was extremely congested with allergies. I was uncomfortable, but my heart was joyful. When I lay down, I thought about my Lord and His love to me. Later, I shared with my children how the Lord kept me from complaining or doubting His care for me despite how poorly I felt. We must in a similar way share our life experiences with our children. When should a father do this? The passage gives us four settings.

Sitting down in your house

Some Dads are so busy working, watching television, surfing the web and going to sports events that they do not spend any significant time with their children. Others have the time, but the Lord is not on their hearts. They will talk excitedly about some soccer match, some recent purchase or about some project that they are working on. Their main project should be to know God and His Word. This lack of passion becomes obvious to their sons and daughters. Their hearts go somewhere else but not to Lord. They are only doing what Dad does.

Walking

Walking would include driving, riding a bus or taking a train. Often, the father is intently listening to music or watching some television show. He has no patience with children that interrupt him. We need to make room for personal conversations with our children when we are working around the house, looking at our personal finances or cleaning out the garage. The children love to talk and ask about things. Do you ask them about their day? Do you like to talk to them? They really like to talk to you.

Lying down

Lying down would be the time the children or parents get ready for bed and settle down. In the old days, houses were smaller. Sometimes, guys would sleep in one room, the girls in another. This provided many opportunities to share. I remember some of my good conversations with my Dad happened when camping together. Just before going to sleep, we talked a bit. If children have their own bedrooms, then the parent should pause and talk with each child before they go to sleep. Give the chance for the children to ask questions. Recount the day a bit. Give them a hug and kiss.

Getting up

Getting up is the time early in the morning when one is arising from bed, getting dressed and perhaps eating. The morning sets the pace and attitude of the day. The father should share some reflections from his morning devotions or say some statements that help the children properly look at each day. The father should be an early riser so that he can help encourage the family when they get up.

Everyday, we face many situations through which the Lord wishes to teach us and then pass those lessons on to our children. We have refused to get cable. We can barely get five stations on our television (neither do we have an antenna). Sometimes it is in the family room but at other times it is moved to the attic.[6] The urge to watch television, a movie or surf the web must not distract from our times together.

Mealtimes are another great opportunity to share about what you are learning. Informal teaching is not to be the only kind of teaching. It is a good companion to formal teaching.

Pause for Reflection:

When was the last time you talked with each of your children in a personal way? When was the last time you talked about life or God's Word with them in a personal way?

Principle #7: Display God's Word (Deuteronomy 6:8-9)

And you shall bind them as a sign on your hand and they shall be as frontals on your forehead. And you shall <u>write them</u> on the doorposts of your house and on your gates (Deuteronomy 6:8-9).

We surround ourselves with what we love. If we love God's Word, then it will be all around us. We can put scripture on our computer screens, walls, plaques, etc. We should throw away some of those old items that show our old treasures and replace them with our growing love of God's Word. Throw away those Buddha statues and anything else associated with different religions. Take down those pictures of movie and sports idols. If your paintings are depressing, replace them with Bible themes such as from Psalm 23. Take a step further. Memorize these verses with your children and learn to treasure them.

The best place to store God's Word is in our hearts. What is on our walls should reflect what is in our hearts. We put scripture around our home not because it is mandatory but because that is what we like.

Pause for Reflection:
What do you decorate your walls with? Would anyone know that you have a great love for God from walking around your home?

Summary
Dads need to rethink their calling from God. They are not just husbands; they are fathers. They need to lead and teach. Leadership is an inherent part of marriage and fatherhood. It is from verses such as Deuteronomy 6 that we understand the true importance of the family to a great society.

When the family disintegrates, the society disintegrates. When the family is strong and fathers take the lead, the society does well. Will we, fathers, begin to take our role seriously or let our children be drugged by modern teachings and be caught by the pull of the secular world culture? Our response to God's charge shows our answer.

Behold, I am going to send you Elijah the prophet before the coming of the great and terrible day of the LORD. And he will restore the hearts of the fathers to their children, and the hearts of the children to their fathers, lest I come and smite the land with a curse (Malachi 4:5-6).

The above verses show that either fathers are going to get serious about the Lord and renew their relationships with Him and their children or that judgment will come. Only one thing in these verses indicates what will stop God's judgment on our land. Will you and I, as fathers, arise and begin instructing our children in God's ways?

B. Reflections on Family Devotions

Family devotions is a name for the structured time a family has together before the Lord. Although most people now seem to think more in terms of 'cell' groups, family devotions or the 'family altar' served as the original small group meeting. Families now are so small and dispersed that the church needs to create (rightly so) specialized group meetings. We have no problem with the cell groups, but they should again remind the father of the importance of formally teaching his children. The family must regularly group around the father to learn of his love and knowledge of God.

Like personal devotions, family devotions often have singing, memorizing and discussion of God's Word, prayer and personal sharing. The more the teaching and prayer time is related to people's personal lives, the more helpful the time is. We will now share some details on how to conduct family devotions with a particular focus on the handling of toddlers. Some have made a catastrophically wrong decision to wait until their children grow up and understand God's Word before implementing family devotions. Please do not do this. Children really can start learning quite young. The longer the parents hold off, the more bad habits and attitudes will develop in their children and will need retraining.

When do you start?

Devotions should begin before the children are born! That is right. At that time, it will only be the husband and wife, assuming no other relatives are present. Once the first child comes, the whole family passes through a transition time for about 3 months. It is important for devotions between the husband and wife to continue even if it is a brief ten minutes.

My wife and I personally pray and share each night as a couple. We do not watch television but talk and pray. This does take a commitment of time but think of the benefits. We do not fight. We are a harmonious couple. We enjoy our marriage. We save much time that would otherwise be spent in aggravation, worries, and fears. Even more, together through prayer we significantly and positively alter people and situations around them. Our prayer time is a ministry time.

We can sit the child in our lap starting at about four months. If they are sleeping, we will not disturb them. Even though we have family devotions, my wife and I still meet separately as a couple. We like to do this. Besides as a couple, we cannot share on the level that is needed during family devotions. Neither can we pray for many with the intensity that we need. With our children, we need to carry on at a different level of conversation and focus depending on their age and spiritual maturity.

Instead of reducing our conversation to the level of the youngest child, we choose a higher level which challenges the older ones. We never want our children to get bored with God's Word.

Singing

We sing both simple children's songs as well as old hymns. Little children love to join in even if they do not know the words. They clap or move their bodies. Before children can read, they can learn to sing hymns together. We simply need to train them. The younger they are, the more you need to use repetition. Repetition is how they learn. Have them repeat some words after you. Their memories are fantastic. Most young children like to sing.

If we find a child not singing a familiar song (usually a bit older), it is not because they do not know the song. They are displaying 'quiet' rebellion. They are choosing not to sing. If we want them to sing, then we should have them sing with us. They might need to be chastised otherwise their rebellious spirit spoils the worship atmosphere.

In this case, we would first remind (warn) them of our expectation that everyone is to sing. And then, if necessary, chastise them in the other room. They join in nicely after that. We have also asked the child who refused to properly sing to write the words of the song down. In another case we might write one good sentence at the top of a blank page, and ask them to write the same line fifteen to fifty times. The sentence might be, "It is good to give thanks to the Lord with all my heart." The sentence positively instructs them what they should do.

God's Word

We want children to learn God's Word. We read, quote, and sing God's Word. Our real purpose is to get us to think about what God's Word says. Some use books such as Bible storybooks to help them explain the scriptures. We suggest using those books as extra reading material.

It is better to focus on a theme for a month such as fear of man, being kind, etc. Memorize some appropriate verses. Discuss them. Read other applicable verses. With search programs on the web, one can do a search on the word 'patience' (which we are doing this month) in a moment and have a whole list of passages to work on.

We especially like the virtue theme calendar that gives us a Christian theme for each month for the whole family to work on. We have preferred to discuss doctrinal topics as they come up, but it is good to supplement and enrich what we know about God's Word.[7]

Memorizing Verses

A child is capable of memorizing a great amount of scripture verses. It would be a shame if we did not believe this and neglected to act upon this capability. The parents must memorize along with the child, but this is fine! Why not get God's Word into our children's hearts early on so it shapes their lives? They do not necessarily need to know its meaning right away. They can learn that later on.

The parent decides what to memorize. We usually review our memory verses at devotions time. Our children can quote Psalm 1, 23 and 100. This is easy for them (and harder for Dad whose memory is going)! Should we stop there? No. We keep going on and on. Here are some practical points. During home school, our children have memorized much more such as Matthew 5, 6 and 7.

Have a folder for each child. Keep the verses that the family has memorized together printed out there. We also keep the hymns we have learned together in a three-prong folder. Bilingual families can learn some songs and verses in one language and some in another. Make it fun. I remember after learning Galatians 5:22-23, we would often go around each saying one word at a time. It is much fun! We even learned a song about the fruit of the Spirit.

Pause for Reflection:
What verses have your family memorized so far? Which ones do you think they should know? List two worship songs that you would like your family to learn to sing together.

How do you get your child to sit still during devotions?

The most difficult time for many of us is to have our children sit still for prayer time. If we start training them early on (4-6 months), however, then this problem is largely eliminated. For example, when the child is an infant, the mother holds the baby's hands and gives thanks before feeding the baby. Once in the highchair, the same thing happens.

During devotions, I (Dad) have always liked to take the youngest one and hold him or her in my lap and hold his or her hands. When the baby has learned to fold hands during prayer, they need to go through a time of keeping them folded. If they resist, we just go back to holding them again.

We cannot force a child to be quiet, but we can help them sit still. For example, toddlers will sit with Daddy or Mommy. When they start wiggling around, I hold them tight in my crossed legs. Unlike church time, we can ignore their baby sounds.

How do you pray?

This really depends on how old the child is. It is proper to teach children to confess their sins, ask God for help and encourage them to pray for others. Sometimes it is good to review the day and see if we as a family need more patience, kindness or obedience.

We take prayer requests. The children are great at remembering special needs. They often like to bring different needs up and then get a chance praying. We can get the same request over and over, but this helps develop our perseverance in prayer. We pray until there is an answer.

We also pray for missionaries. Make sure you have some missionary focus as a family. We never dare just pray for ourselves. The Lord wants to do greater things through us as a family. He wants to bless those around us through our lives. We cannot pray for all the missionaries we know of but do pray for a good number of them each night.

Since we have many children, we take turns praying. With fewer children, it is fine for each to pray. In our case, I open in prayer, and two other volunteers pray after me. They are chosen before we pray. We do not force our children to pray. Children usually want to start praying very early on. Our two-year old hardly talks but has caught on by watching the older children eagerly raising their hands to volunteer to pray. I say a few words and then give the little one time to repeat. Sometimes it is as simple as one word at a time. They are eager to join in though. When they are very small, just take their hands and in prayer say, "Thank you God for every good thing! Amen."

Does God hear the prayers of our unbelieving children? He does not. However, we still encourage our children to pray in preparation for the time that they will believe. Because we are praying along with them, God is pleased to hear our joint prayers.

Summary

Devotions can be shortened for nights when children are sick or tired. If the family comes home late, try to sing songs in the car and pray for them with a hand on them while they are in bed. The family altar is not a legalistic matter but a marvelous opportunity through which the family day by day seeks what the Lord wants of our lives and ask for grace to live out our lives pleasing to Him.

C. Thoughts on Spiritual Nurturing

Let us now take a look at some other specific aspects of nurturing our family with spiritual teachings.

Praying for your child

Each child is special. Each child has his or her own voice, facial shape, body size, palm prints and finger prints. We should have a special prayer for each child. Prayer is not magical. It is the parent's earnest plea for the child to be all he or she should be.[8] This prayer is a growing prayer. As we see the child grow, we are aware of different gifts and challenges that a particular child will have in life. We need to sharpen our focus and prayers for that child.

Usually we see both strengths and weaknesses in each child. We should encourage them and pray for them that they would overcome sin, bodily weakness, difficult situations and fulfill God's good plans. We specially equip them with verses we have memorized with them.

Most people have one predominant sin pattern. As parents, we need to realize that this is the child's biggest enemy to becoming a godly person. Our prayers serve as their shield as long as we live. Our tender love reminds them that we care more for them than the things that they do. Satan would love to convince our children that we do not personally care for them but only for standards or religion. Love and joy in the family largely protects them from such attacks.

As we increase in such observations and prayers, we become full of expectations that our children will be godly persons, full of the Spirit of Christ. We have found it helpful to focus on the name that we have given them, much like the scriptures do. What does it mean? Why were you inspired to give it to him or her? (See more of this in the last chapter.) Pray for a godly fulfillment of that name.

The Mother's Role

Some wonder why Deuteronomy 6, Ephesians 6 and other passages address the father and his spiritual responsibility in bringing up the child before the Lord but do not mention the mother. This is because the father is held responsible. We can see this in verse 4 by the special way fathers are addressed. Fathers are heads of the home. We also see, however, that the father is not the only one actively shaping the child's life.

> *Children, obey your parents in the Lord, for this is right. Honor your **father** and **mother** (which is the first commandment with a promise), that it may be well with you, and that you may live long on the earth. And, fathers, do not provoke your children to anger; but bring them up in the discipline and instruction of the Lord (Ephesians 6:1-4).*

Verse 1 shows us how children are to obey both father and mother. This is reaffirmed in verse 2, in case we should have any doubts. Children are to respect both parents' commands and wishes. Generally, we see the mother's intensive care for the child's nurturing when small,[9] but the father must see to it that instruction in the Lord and the whole discipline process is rightly implemented. The wife works with the husband to help implement family goals. The wife has special insight and ability to help the children. The good father knows this and works closely with his wife. Notice how the wife is expected to operate in the home.

> *That they (older women) may encourage the young women to love their husbands, to love their children, to be sensible, pure, workers at home, kind, being subject to their own husbands, that the word of God may not be dishonored (Titus 2:4-5).*

The children should gain a great experience of warmth and love from their mothers. This does not mean that mothers do not chastise. Chastisement is a sign of love. Any child that gives a mother great difficulty should be told that his father will properly deal with him upon his return. A wife, however, dare not pass all such situations needing instruction or chastisement on to her husband. Surely the father does not have the mother's advantage of timing and the understanding of the context which superb training requires.

As a helpmate, she works with her husband in carrying out discipline. A mother is a major means through which God communicates His tender love. Father and mother work together in harmony as one. We can understand a mother's influence even more when we understand what the scriptures say regarding a Christian mother with an unbelieving husband.

Unbelieving Husband

In some marriages, one spouse is a Christian, but the other is an unbeliever. Believing mothers should not lose hope. A godly grandmother and mother raised Timothy. He became a great pastor in the early church. The apostle summarizes this influence, "For I am mindful of the sincere faith within you, which first dwelt in your grandmother Lois, and your mother Eunice, and I am sure that it is in you as well" (2 Timothy 1:5).

Later, we read that Timothy got his understanding of the scriptures from them, "And that from childhood you have known the sacred writings which are able to give you the wisdom that leads to salvation through faith which is in Christ Jesus" (2 Timothy 3:15).

This only confirms what Paul the apostle stated in 1 Corinthians 7:14, "For the unbelieving husband is sanctified through his wife, and the unbelieving wife is sanctified through her believing husband; for otherwise your children are unclean, but now they are holy." As long as the unbelieving husband (or wife) is willing to stay with the believing spouse, the believing spouse can have great impact on an otherwise lost child.

Maintaining A Family Purpose

We need to think beyond our goals for our children. As we look through the scriptures, we find that God does great things through families. Children are seen as a multiplication or expansion of what the parents stand for. As Christian parents, we must reject a purely individualistic perspective and understand that God wants to perpetuate our ministry, vision and love through our children.

For example, if we see that a couple is hospitable, more likely than not the children will learn to be so. We can see the compassion, care and love through the parents, but we can also see it through the way the children imitate their parents. We do not mean that parents should force careers and positions upon their children, but that there should be a general expectation of how the Lord will be working in our children. This should encourage us to set up a good positive model so that our children will pass those great things on to others.

Take a look at Abraham, Isaac and Jacob's lives. Note their disharmonious marriages. It negatively affected their children. We can also note on the positive side how their faith in the Lord held firm. They held onto the land and the promises of the Lord.

We need to be cautious, though. Children will not only catch the good but also the bad. While we have time, we can confess our sins and find the Lord's strength to change. This encourages even older children that have already been affected by bad modeling. If the parents have changed, the children need to know about this change and listen to what God is doing in their lives.

The clearer we are on these matters, the easier it is to go forward developing this purpose and sharing it with our children. "Do you know how our great God uses our family? He has used us to help poor people who live near us. Let me tell you about one family…." Sharing instills a great vision that goes beyond an individualistic perspective. Instead, the children gain a perspective centered on the Lord's purposes rather than money or position.

Pause for Reflection:

What is the Lord doing through your life as a family? What gifts do you have? How does the Lord bring His grace to others through you as parents?

Positive Instruction

Although we have said this before, we should mention it once again. We are not just passing on negative admonitions. They are necessary. Our children, for example, are not to lie, and we need to rebuke them for such things. Our instruction, however, must go far beyond this. We also must teach them what good things are expected of them. A child who only focuses on the things he is not to do might very well develop an unhealthy legalistic spirit.[10] The more we can focus on the virtues of godly living, all encompassed in that one command to "love our neighbor as ourselves," the more we can instill a vision for godliness in our children.

Positive instruction becomes the child's road to walk on. They will wonder what positive things they should be doing. We should give them answers to that important question. Let me give an example. I heard our three year-old crying because he wanted something that another brother had. I told him that he was <u>not</u> to cry to get the things that he wanted (negative). I went on to tell him what I <u>did</u> expect (positive).

First, I got his attention. I wanted to make sure he was listening. I told him that I expected him to share things with others. This is how we ended our conversation. This is what I want him to remember.

Pause for Reflection:
List the positive instructions that you have given to your child in the last week. Please remember that this can only be effectively done when the child can start to understand and reason, but we can start training ourselves!

Salvation of our children

Every child needs to come to know the Lord. Many churches practice infant or immersion baptism. In either case the ceremony does not save the child despite what the parent thinks. We are looking for a deeper work within the heart of the child known as regeneration or being born again (John 3).

Remember that a child should respect both God and their parents. We can train even a non-Christian child to do this to some degree. To love God and others, however, requires the power of the Gospel. Children are born with a sinful nature. They are sinners because they are born to sinful parents (yes, we must confess our part– see Ephesians 2:1-3). We are sinful because of our sinful parents. And it goes on and on this way all the way back to Adam. Paul summarizes it well in Romans speaking of Adam.

> *So then as through one transgression (Adam's sin) there resulted condemnation to all men, even so through one act of righteousness (Jesus' righteousness) there resulted justification of life to all men (Romans 5:18).*

When Adam sinned the whole human race was contaminated. All people everywhere need to be saved. Young children need to be saved too. People do not come to a point where they become morally responsible and then confess their need to be saved. They are born sinners as it says above.[11] The process of salvation is the same with all people, but special care is needed for children because they respect their parents and desire to please them. This desire to please the parents is not the same as being saved.

In evangelical Christianity salvation is equated with a decision. The problem with this is that there are different parts of a decision. A decision includes the mind, will and emotions. When a child feels he needs to please his Dad or his pastor, he might say that he wants to be a Christian or nod his head to their plea to be saved. This is probably just an emotional decision. They might not be saved at all. Instead, we should look for other signs of salvation.

We should speak clearly of their fallen state and need to be saved from the wrath of God (Ephesians 2:3). We need to point out the child's sins. We do not do this accusingly but as a matter of fact. We should remind him just for that certain sin of lying alone he would go to hell. We are not exaggerating matters but just telling them the truth. Children seem to understand this more easily than adults.

During our family devotions, one of my sons said that he stole a penny. We can point out that such a sin reflects a sinful heart that needs to be saved–even if most people would not bother saying anything about a penny. It is not the amount but the heart. Early on, they will understand their sin and equate their guilt with the displeasure of God. We must not pressure them to say they are Christians. This does not change their heart.

We are looking for an awareness of their sinfulness. We should see a repentant spirit about them. They should be asking questions about the Lord, heaven and hell, etc. on their own. Then we know that the Spirit of God is starting a work in them. We can encourage children to believe by saying things like, "I hope that you soon become a Christian. You would not want to live without the Lord."

Right now, it seems that all but our two youngest children are Christians, but I am not sure.[12] Six of them have not yet been baptized. I ask myself, "What keeps the older ones back." They know that my love for them is not dependent upon their believing. They hear how I pray for them to come to know Him. They know becoming a Christian is the best thing in life. I could easily persuade them to say a sinner's prayer but that does not save them. They need the Holy Spirit to convict them of their sin so that they would seek salvation and the cross.

Unfortunately, the word 'decision' has become a replacement for 'repent and believe in Christ.' We need to return to scriptural language. Notice the power of God at work in salvation in the following verses.

> *I tell you, no, but **unless you repent**, you will all likewise perish (Luke 13:5).*

> *For our gospel did not come to you in word only, **but also in power and in the Holy Spirit and with full conviction** (1 Thessalonians 1:5).*

> *For they themselves report about us what kind of a reception we had with you, and how you **turned to God from idols** to serve a*

living and true God, and to wait for His Son from heaven, whom He raised from the dead, that is Jesus, who delivers us from the wrath to come (1 Thessalonians 1:9-10).

Repentance starts as a spiritual conviction from God that a person's sins are the most dreadful curse upon him and that he fully deserves the condemnation of God. Repentance's work is done when a person turns away from the sin in his life and seeks refuge in God's salvation. Reading a book like Pilgrim's Progress can highlight this process.

When our children are rightly trained, we see much good in them. Do not be mistaken and think that this is the same as salvation. It is not. In fact, it can lead to great deception if the parent believes it is the same. The parent will convince the child and the pastor that they are saved when they are not. The child will have the form of a Christian but not the heart.

Repentance and belief go together. The child must believe that Christ is their Savior. God will give them this faith (Ephesians 2:8-9). It is not the mere knowledge that Christ died on the cross for their sins that saves them, but a deep confidence that this Savior indeed has saved them from their dreadful sins. Even the best child, when under conviction, knows that he is a wicked sinner deserving judgment. A truly born again child will love God and want to obey Him.

Pause for Reflection:

Are your children saved? Have you seen them go through the stages of repentance and belief? Have they desired baptism on their own? Have they shown signs of salvation (e.g. hunger for truth)?

Raising Godly Children

Parents should have goals of raising godly children. We should hope that in early childhood they come to know God through the Lord Jesus Christ. We should also expect that they have a sense of love for God, His Word and His ways. We should encourage a regular habit of personal devotions such as reading the Bible, praying and worshiping God.

Parents should encourage their children to maintain these habits. However, we refrain from forcing these habits upon our children unless they come to know the Lord, and even then, only gently nudge them in that direction. As Christian parents we do these things but prayerfully wait for God to stir our children's hearts. We want to see them respond to God, not to us. We steadily pray behind the scenes. They will see what to do by noticing us in our private devotion times. You will help them to have good routines so that they can learn to have regular devotions to seek God on their own.

We do encourage our children to have a faithful time with the Lord. For example, during family devotions, I sometimes ask everyone who spent time with the Lord that day to raise their hand. If I see our ten year old exhibiting a bad attitude, I will privately meet with him and show him how his bad attitudes are directly connected to the lack of reading God's Word. The mentoring relationship becomes an invaluable tool for the parent to train a child to grow into maturity.

The parent should carefully listen to their children's prayers during family devotions to see if thanks, worship, asking for forgiveness and mission (praying for the needs and salvation of others) are included. This is part of the instruction that a father can give. Attendance at family devotions is required in our home. Personal quiet time is a way the child can seek the Lord individually.

Our secular society has so shaped our ideas that many Christians read the Bible as a book rather than the Word of God. They do not even know the difference. They have not learned how to listen to God through reading His Word. As parents eagerly seek God in His Word, they will find Him and can share those experiences with their children. In this way, they pass on a spiritual inheritance.

In summary, we should remember that a godly child is more than a virtuous child or well-trained child. A godly child has those qualities, but he also has a great affection for God, His Word and His ways. We should pray, train and seek God's work in our child's life so that he or she would love God from the heart and not only outwardly conform to His ways.

Pause for Reflection:
Are your children godly? What makes you think that is so? Do you pray regularly for this?

Summary

There is no doubt that proper spiritual instruction stands as one of the most important aspects to parenting. How tragic that it also is as the most neglected aspect!

The scriptures clearly outline how God expects parents to care for their children. Whether man or society has these expectations, it does not matter. We are accountable to God for passing on both instruction from His Word and the wholesome example of our lives. Parents need to seriously take up the challenge to both formal and informal instruction. Families have a lot of conflicts to distract them from carrying out God's instruction, but if we set ourselves to obey God, He somehow gives us grace to stand strong in an evil society.

May God give each parent grace to be faithful. May He raise up fathers and mothers who will be bold in their stand to train their children in the love and ways of the Lord. May He raise up a new generation of children who have parents that truly love God with all their heart, soul and might!

Parenting Principles & Practices

- God expects the fathers to take charge of spiritual instruction in the home.
- The whole family is commanded to love God with all their heart soul, mind and strength.
- The father's love, obedience and zeal for the Lord will greatly affect the family.
- The wife assists the husband in carrying out his responsibilities.
- There are two ways a father must instruct his children about the Lord: formally and informally.
- Family devotions are important and necessary to train the children and inspire them in their worship of the Lord.
- Parents should point out to their children their need and the way of salvation but wait for God to stir their hearts unto repentance.
- Parents should pray for each child's future and pray that they would grow to fulfill God's purpose.

Parenting Questions

1. Who is in charge of instructing the child in the Lord? Why?

2. In what two main ways is this person to carry out this spiritual duty?

3. Why is it that many children leave the Lord?

4. Is living a good life the same as being saved? Why or why not?

5. Why are family devotions so important?

6. What are three things that should occur during family devotions?

7. Should parents press their children to have personal devotions? Why or why not?

8. How should a parent learn to pray for his or her child?

9. What should a parent look for in the child when trying to discern whether a child is close to salvation?

Notes from Chapter #9

[1] The increase of wealth does not help us in this process! Jesus Himself says, "How hard it is for those who are wealthy to enter the kingdom of God! For it is easier for a camel to go through the eye of a needle, than for a rich man to enter the kingdom of God" (Luke 18:24-25). Remember this man was 'good' in his own eyes but fell far from God's standards. By God's grace we must live out a life whose joys and strength does not come from money. Our real problem as parents is that we think it is the money that gives us a good life not God. We are idolatrous. In the end, we pass this idolatrous mindset onto our children.

[2] We should understand that this does not mean that God will not test us. Deuteronomy 8:2-3 tells us that the LORD deliberately tested His people to show them what was in their hearts. He caused them to go hungry to see how they would respond to Him. The discipline (8:5) is for their good. It is hard for the time but great for the long run.

[3] Birth control methods hinder God's good purposes in 99.9% of cases. The exceptions should be left only for serious medical reasons, if at all. Historically, Christians rejected any use of birth control.

[4] The first lessons are on the web for those wanting to learn more. They show you step by step how Paul met with his son in those very first lessons from the Book of Proverbs.. Drawings included! www.foundationsforfreedom.net/Topics/DiscipleshipConcepts/Sons/IntroSons.html.

[5] Some fathers need renewal. Look at 'Renewing our Personal Devotions' on how to renew one's love for God at www.foundationsforfreedom.net/Topics/Devotions/Devotions000.html.

[6] At times the television comes back down for a while. Some people focus on not having any television at all. This is a requirement if parents and children cannot restrict the time and content. Swearing, immoral scenes and improper father-mother role models are typical. Parents constantly must monitor what is seen and for how long. If things get out of hand, I simply put the television back in the attic. Our children largely watch old trusted programs recorded on a video or DVD.

[7] You can find catechism booklets in the question and answer format that drills doctrines into children. Both the parents and children are to memorize both the question and answer.

[8] Ephesians 2:10 emphasizes how each Christian is a special workmanship of God's grace. Each person is specially equipped to do the works that God has appointed for them to do. In a similar way, we are readying our children to know God and to do these good works.

[9] "… As a nursing **mother** tenderly cares for her own children" (1 Thessalonians 2:7).

[10] It would be good to study whether or not a legalistic spirit gains its strength from parents who only tell their children what not to do (second generation Christians) and are not inspired to live for Christ.

[11] This is the reason abortion is strictly a tool of the devil. They are doomed to perdition because of the sin they have in Adam (see Romans 5:12-21). They have not volitionally sinned but still live under the wrath of God.

[12] During the teen years, each child goes through a time of objectively analyzing their life and faith. Do not be shocked by this or their questions. We do need to pray, though, and keep them from scoffers. Coach them (keep open conversation with them) through this time and you will see them affirm their faith on their own. I do not pressure them into baptism because I want this to be a decision made on their own.

Chapter #10

DEVELOPING INTERGENERATIONAL LOVE

Purpose: Enable new parents to show God's love and truth to their parents and in-laws during extended visits.

Every family is happy to hear of another child coming. But for some, the near birth of a child raises much concern. The parents or in-laws will be coming to help, but the relationship between them is not very good. How is the young couple going to handle this time?

The number of difficulties that arise from a visit from parents or in-laws is rarely overestimated. We can honestly say that what should be a good and pleasant occasion often becomes a nightmare. The new parents are usually shocked by such a visit and feel powerless to change things.

Let us reflect on God's Word as we try to discern what the issues are and how to overcome them. It seems quite probable that God wants to use these situations to restore family harmony.

A. Establishing Family Harmony

Three important points help establish good relationships with one's in-laws/parents. They are like steps. They need to be followed in order.

#1) Be Humble: Cleanse away your sins

Good communication with family members is dependent upon how much we are able to apologize for our sins against our parents and clear up any past misunderstandings. Once we have cleared up our sins against our parents, we can stop reacting to what they say. Instead, we can genuinely begin to honor them and to have compassion upon them.

Watch out! Past offenses and pride are the source of many misunderstandings and arguments.

#2) Be Honoring: Consistently respect your parents

God commands us to honor our parents. We must remember that our parents are God-appointed. We assure their value by giving them special respect.

Watch out! The relationship you have with your parents is most likely the one you will have with your children. So now is the time to change! Your children are learning how to relate to you by the way you relate to your parents.

#3) Be Honest: Patiently share and hold to God's standard when with your parents.

Family harmony is dependent on how much God's love and truth shapes our relationship with our parents. Truth must be shared in the context of love to be accepted.

Watch out! Whenever we tolerate a lesser standard than God's Word, we open the door for disharmony. By disobeying God, we keep God's love from being fully revealed in our lives.

Summary

These three steps: humble, honor and honest have been briefly mentioned here but will be explained in detail in the following pages. Remember God's design is always the best. God knows how crucial it is to maintain good relationships with our parents but at the same time not to compromise the truth.

Pause for Reflection:

Have you sought harmony in your relationship with your parents? What steps have you taken? Which ones could use improvement?

B. Understanding Parent/In-law Irritations

The fact of conflict between new parents and their own parents and in-laws is widely testified to in the different literatures of the world's cultures. Of particular note is the traditional Chinese culture. The struggles between the new wife and her mother-in-law are recorded in famous novels and are still being written in the family stories of modern times. In some ways, the Confucian ethic made the problem worse by unbiblical principles perpetuated over long periods of time. Like a bent wheel, it will only get increasingly out of shape as time goes on.

We would be silly to think this problem only affects the Chinese culture. Cultures around the world face this same difficulty. The longer an unbiblical principle becomes entrenched in a culture, the more havoc it wrecks on the family.

A little wobble is okay, right?!

What seems ironic is that nobody thinks these family problems will occur in **their** family. But again and again, year after year, what everyone hopes to be a grand family reunion becomes a bitter memory for the families involved. One would think this tension would be hidden with the birth of a grandson. It is not. Let us think of why there is so much tension between the new parents and their own parents.

1) Married without Parents' Approval

If a couple wants to guarantee problems for their marriage, they should start by not getting their parents' blessing for the marriage. Young people are naïve when it comes to understanding the need for parental approval of major life decisions such as marriage. Why is this so important?

Marriage not only unites two people but also two families. It is not just one person and one person. More is at stake. Only the more mature person can see this. God knows it and categorically reminds children of the need to honor their parents. Parents are offended when their children decide marriage matters without sincerely seeking their advice and agreement.

The young would be protected if they worked with their parents in the process of seeking a spouse rather than against them. This problem is made worse by the clash of modern ways with traditional ways of seeking marriage partners. Parents no longer have confidence or understanding to properly relate to their children. Children do not expect their parents to have any real contribution to the process. This is a shame.

The intergenerational struggle can often be seen at the wedding. If the young have pursued a marriage partner without their parents' advice, they have behaved rudely toward their parents. Instead of building up trust, they have given offense.[1] The parents will disdain their child's decisions in the future. The grown child, meanwhile, will continue to ignore his parents' counsel. Each sees the other as foolish. A wall of mistrust has been placed between the newly married couple and their parents.

The young couple wrongly assumes that nothing much is wrong; time will heal all. They are very wrong in thinking that having a baby will make everything better. On the surface, this seems to be true. The couple is delighted in their new child. The grandparents are happy for a new grandchild. This scene, however, will become the next showdown, a place of serious confrontation.

We will not go into discussing the confrontation at this point, but we do want to stress the fact that the harm from not seeking their parents' opinion has not gone away. The only way to begin to unravel the bitterness is to confess your foolishness, admit your lack of honor and respect and ask for forgiveness. Some people have learned to forgive; many others have not. For those who have learned to forgive, they will forgive and the relationships will move on. Otherwise, bitterness will stay in their heart as a long lasting enemy. God will forgive our sins and work through our difficult situations, but we cannot force a person to forgive.[2]

Before moving on, just think of the deepening of trust that comes as the adult child works along with his parents in seeking a spouse together. The parents would give valuable insight to the inexperienced couple. They would help protect from foolish decisions that he or she otherwise might not understand. Since the in-laws are part of the process, they would be honored. They would see that their child really treasures their insight. This would build up a strong trusting relationship.[3]

> *Children, obey your parents in the Lord, for this is right. Honor your father and mother (which is the first commandment with a promise), that it May be well with you, and that you ay live long on the earth (Ephesians 6:1-3).*

Before marriage, children must obey their parents.[4] We should not make exceptions since God does not. Parents are parents whether they are Christians or not, wise or foolish. Children must learn to trust God to work through their parents. It is one of the important ways God reveals His will. If we look back in history from God's perspective, I believe that we will be surprised by how much God has shaped our lives through our parents. By contrast, the young person seeking his or her parents' advice shows great maturity. He is willing to delay marriage or end the relationship if necessary.[5]

In the above verse, Paul directs children to obey their parents "in the Lord." This recognizes that sometimes the parents will ask their children to do immoral things.[6] These are things that the child is clearly not to do. Whenever the parent compels a child to clearly do an immoral thing, then the child should refuse. In other words, a child should seek to fully comply with their parents in everything even when it is not their preference.

If the parent asks the child to disobey the Lord by forsaking their faith or to stop reading God's Word, then they must choose God. If a child has consistently obeyed his parents, then they most likely will not be offended by a child's insistence to obey higher orders. There are exceptions, however, and every child must be ready to face the cost. The child should still speak kindly and graciously to his parents.

Pause for Reflection:
What do your parents think of your marriage? Did you ask them for advice and permission? Did they agree?

2) Sinful struggles from the past

If you offended your parents with your engagement and wedding preparations, it is highly probable that there is a whole set of improper and sinful habits that are barriers in your relationship with your parents. One problem leads to another. Many little problems add up. Have these sins from the past been cleared up? If they are not properly confessed, then these sins will come back to haunt you.

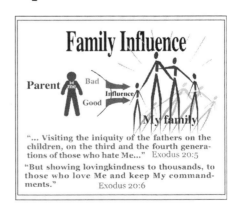

The story of Jacob in Genesis highlights these problems.[7]

The Christian has the grace to be forgiven by God but also the command to forgive. If sins are not cleared up from childhood, then the child will act independently of his parents. This leads the grown up child into sin. Sin always affects the relationships between people. If the child offends the parent, then he will naturally 'hide' himself from his parent. John describes this process, "For everyone who does evil hates the light, and does not come to the light, lest his deeds should be exposed" (John 3:20).

The sins of youth negatively impact the relationship he or she has with his parents. This is fact. Trust is built up by obedience. Mistrust is built up by a young person's resistance to honor his parents. Youthful rebellion is seen in all the independent acts that have been done including the bad attitudes.

Everyone needs to make sure that they have identified and apologized for any sins from the past and the resulting attitudes that have poisoned the relationship. The best way to do this is to write a list of all the outstanding sins and offenses, including wrong attitudes. Tell your parents that you have not properly valued their relationship with you but would like to do that starting now. Although your parents no doubt have also wronged you too, do not mention this. Focus on clearing up your own sin.

It is best to confess each wrong individually and then, in the end, ask for forgiveness for them all in one big swoop. "Will you forgive me for these things?" You might find it necessary to separate one or two areas out for further elaboration.

An angry parent might not forgive you. Others will say it is not important. It is! Tell them how much it would mean to you if they would forgive you. After this, whenever you sin against your parents, immediately apologize. This is the way to maintain an excellent relationship. "Confess your sins to one another, and pray for one another, so that you may be healed" (James 5:16).

Although these steps might seem to make it easier for your parents to oppress you, they are essential to restoring a relationship and establishing the trust that is needed. Agreed, it is very humbling, but it is also what the Lord has instructed us to do. There is no greater way to honor your parents than to show them how much you desire a close relationship with them all through your life.

Pause for Reflection:
Have you ever asked your parents to forgive you for your past sins? Has this included your bad attitudes? Commit yourself to seeking God so that you will do this in His time.

3) **Intergenerational sins**

We need to be aware that our sins against our parents are often related to other family problems that have been passed down. In other words, we cannot rightly understand or deal with these sins by looking at our lives alone. They have become our own sins but more likely than not have been passed down from our parents and grandparents.

Notice in Exodus 20:5 how God promises to pass on sin to the third and fourth generations. "I, the LORD your God, am a jealous God, visiting the iniquity of the fathers on the children, on the third and the fourth generations of those who hate Me."

Whatever this means it should include the sense that somehow the consequences of the parents' sins will be passed on to the next generation.[8] The most likely way this is done is by simply allowing each generation to adopt their parents' sinful lifestyle. Each generation falls into a deeper curse. (This is the exact opposite to what we want for our children.) We see this in families battling with bitterness, alcohol abuse,

"For you who judge practice the same things." (Romans 2:1)

SIN

SIN

We tend to be more critical of those who do the wrong things that we secretly do.

arrogance and immorality. The reason this is being brought up at this point is that these very sins are often the ones that cause the worst problems in a person's life and cause disharmony between us and our family members especially parents. These sins lay unresolved because they are not easily detected in those under their influence.

If a parent and child have similar sin patterns, then we should expect that they would have little tolerance for each other. For example, if the parent is given to outbursts of anger, it is likely that the child will similarly express himself.[9] It is hard for the parent and child to communicate well when they share similar sins. Romans 2:1 gives us a clue to the reason for this.

> *Therefore you are without excuse, every man of you who passes judgment, for in that you judge another, you condemn yourself; for you who judge practice the same things (Romans 2:1).*

Paul indicates here that those with a sin problem often are able to see their problem in others but not in themselves. In many cases, the person is hypersensitive to this sin and judge others but excuses himself. He is blind to his own guilt and sin. When we apply this to the parent and child relationship, we discover that there is a tendency for the parent and the child to have the same sin pattern. They easily notice the pattern in the other but are blind to their own area of weakness. This situation magnifies misunderstandings because each considers the other irresponsible while they cannot see their own fault. Both sides accuse the other and excuse themselves. Can you see how this can contribute to the lack of communication between the generations?

When parents come to visit their children and grandchildren, old animosities are revived. The solution is not to change the parents. Honestly evaluate yourself with the help of your mate (they are always ready to help here)! We just need to remember that this process is not easily done. Expect to find many areas of sin that have affected responses and attitudes over time. As you work on eliminating and hating these sins, then you can begin to understand and have mercy on your parents.

I (Paul) have seen God do this in my own life. I had a great deal of animosity in my own heart towards both of my parents. God has completely changed my heart through the process of reconciliation as mentioned above. Now, I genuinely love and care for both of my parents. While it is sometimes very difficult for my siblings to deal with my parents, it is easier for me. They think it is because of my nature. I assure them that it is not. It is because of the power of forgiveness. Because I have forgiven and asked for forgiveness, God has given me an unbelievable amount of patience and respect. It has really changed the way I relate to my parents. Only after this line of communication is open, can we possibly address other misunderstandings.

Your parents' behavior might still be annoying. Some of their decisions still might disturb you, but you are suddenly pro-parent! The change in our hearts will remove the hatred and pride that would make this otherwise intolerable. The relationship between parents/in-laws and children is critical. Whether we resolve these problems or let them stand, they will affect the way our own children react and respond to us.

Pause for Reflection:
List three predominant sins of your parents. Ask your spouse if you have any traces of these sins in your own life. Remember to check attitudes as well as behavior. Properly deal with them.

4) Unclear or unacceptable lines of authority
When grandparents visit their grandchildren, they must also visit their children. Many of them would rather not do this because of the

problems mentioned above. God has used the cute little grandchildren to bring the family together when they otherwise would not. These reunions are opportunities to discover and overcome past sins. Many never see it as an opportunity but only as a point of endurance.

If the past problems have been properly dealt with, or at least have begun to be dealt with,[10] then the young couple can begin to understand and explain lines of authority. We are referring to what was originally mentioned in Genesis 2:24. God, Jesus and the Apostle Paul all state this concise but strong statement.[11] "For this cause a man shall leave his father and his mother, and shall cleave to his wife; and they shall become one flesh."

The 'leaving' and 'cleaving' principles are clearly laid out here. Unfortunately, there is no further explanation of what 'leaving' means. Whatever it is, it is essential to a good marriage just as the cleaving is. God sets up newly married units by separating them from their parents. Like flower bulbs in the garden, they must be dug up, pulled apart and then planted as separate plants. If left together, they will end up being unhealthy and small.

Many parents do not understand this foundational principle for a good marriage and how it affects the harmony of the family. The young couple is often afraid to bring up such issues. If God's truth is not acknowledged and obeyed, however, further troubles will develop. I am thankful that my parents try (it is hard for them too) to implement this principle. Our purpose here is not to address all the ins and outs of this scripture passage. That would take a book. Instead, we are trying to limit our conversation to situations that have to do with how parents can negatively affect the marriage of their children and the training of their grandchildren.

When the man gets married, he is forming a new unit. He is no longer bound to 'obey' his parents but only to honor them. Some cultures worsen this problem by equating obedience with honor. Obedience means to comply while honor means to give consideration to. Obedience requires doing what the one in authority asks. Honor means to respect and admire. In some cases, honor will lead to imitation because it is good, but it does not require submission of the will to the wishes of another. The Confucian ethic requires even the married son to both obey and honor. This has exacerbated the tension felt in the newly formed families affected by Confucian teaching.[12]

The parents of the newlyweds should respect the couple's freedom to live under God's rule now rather than under their authority.[13] They should not make decisions for the new couple. The newly married couple should delight in talking with their parents and gaining wisdom from them. Wise parents will release the couple (i.e. make the child leave) to manage their own affairs. Birds illustrate this when at a certain time the little birds are cast from their nests to live on their own.

Both parents and their married children should know these principles. Some parents might threaten their children with loss of inheritance if they do not comply. The young husband must, however, not be intimidated by this threat, but act properly and with respect to his parents. He must be willing to abide by God's truth even if it means letting the inheritance go. Sometimes the desire of inheritance strongly figures into the married couple's willingness to 'go by' their parents' decision. They must reject this threat as the basis of their decisions.[14]

Trust is a much better way to go. Trust leads to harmony. Some parents fear that their children will abandon them once they marry. While this might be true in some cases, the wise newly married couple must assure their parents that this will not happen. Our parents' fears tend to increase when they, sometimes unconsciously, begin to pressure the young couple to conform to their ideas. If the couple senses this manipulation, they tend to pull back and withdraw from their parents. It is at this point that the couple's parents (i.e. grandparents) feel even more fear. Their fears are heightened as they sense their child and spouse avoiding them. As fear increases, doubt and mistrust grows. As mistrust grows, so does misunderstandings and animosity.

God's design is the best way because it allows for relationships to grow through trust and love. Even though the couple feels that their parents are trying to manipulate them (maybe they are), they, filled with love and respect, still graciously care for them.

God enables us to obtain that much desired harmony. The married couple wants the support and company of their parents (when they are pleasant). The parents want to see their children and grandchildren. God wants to have it this way too! That is the reason for the command for couples to leave their parents' rule.

Pause for Reflection:

Have you ever thought about what 'leaving' means practically in your family? Have you left your parents' authority? Do they still control you? How so? What kind of tension develops in these situations?

5) **General difficulties (money, attachment, etc.)**

There are other difficulties that interfere in the relationship between the parents and the newly married couple. They often have to do with money but not always.

➢ The son might be obligated to his parents by loans for education or other business deals.

➢ Some couples become dependent upon their parents to care for the grandchildren. The grandparents will watch the child if the couple does what they want.

➢ Still other parents have strong expectations that create much stress on the couple. I recently heard how one father told his son that even though he had got married he still expects him to fully obey him and not let his wife interfere. This was not a hidden tension but an open one!

➢ Some newly formed couples are expected, or because of difficult circumstances required, to live with their parents after marriage. This makes it nearly impossible to leave the parents emotionally.

➢ In some cases, certain cultures and local laws act as the substitute father and put much pressure on newly formed families to conform to its own expectations. Some societies with strong modern philosophical influences put a lot of pressure on the wives to work. They tend to push for a limit to the number of children a couple should have.

These situations and others, like economic factors, make it hard for a couple to 'leave' even though they know they should. Special circumstances of divorce, adultery or separation further complicate carrying out God's design. Sickness or death can greatly affect a family and their circumstances. The loss of employment has caused havoc in some families often resulting in a spouse living away from the family to earn a living.

Some parents like to control their grown children. In some of these cases, they themselves were oppressed by their parents and feel it is now their turn! Usually, these parents convince themselves that they are helping the young couple when in reality they cause much damage. In a positive way, we should recognize that many parents are trying to help young couples handle special difficulties. It is kind of them to do this. They need to be careful not to tie their gift to their control.

Pause for Reflection:

What pressures do you (or did you) feel from your parents that indicated 'leaving' was hard? What other circumstances in your life add to the confusion of trying to have a good relationship with your parents and in-laws?

Summary

The key to understanding God's design is to compare the standards and expectations our parents have with God's own standards. In all cases, God is to be trusted and obeyed. Parents are to be honored. At times, obedience calls for brave decisions, but they always must be based on God's love and design. Only then, will we find solutions. Otherwise, the sins of our generation will pass on to the next generation.

C. *Looking toward a Solution*

God knew the potential problems of marriage from the start and provided an effective solution. The problem can be better understood by thinking about Adam who lived a long 930 years. He was a very influential man, to say the least. If he acted in direct authority over all his children and grandchildren, there would have been many frustrated

families out there. He would rule over them for almost a millennium! It is much like the parent who does not let a child grow up. The children are 'tied to their mother's apron strings.' They become emotionally unstable. Instead, God has arranged it so that when a couple gets married, the husband becomes the new head of his immediate family.

How did God solve this problem? He simply included in the institution of marriage a clause that required the new husband to become the new head of that new family under God's authority. The groom leaves the jurisdiction of his father and mother and becomes the head of the new family. The man leaves both father and mother and cleaves to his wife.

God's design is established in wisdom and conveyed to us in love. God not only has the knowledge of the best order for marriage but also desires to pass that on to us so that we can take advantage of it. Ignoring God's teaching is like having a fruit tree with gorgeous fruit but not realizing that it is good to eat.

This command of God is not largely recognized or desired. Parents feel more secure doing it the way they were brought up. The parents should take the lead in explaining how the leave/cleave principles work out. Unfortunately, few children have such wise parents.

Instead, the children, now grown up, need to both understand this truth and share with their parents how it needs to be worked out among them. This is awkward. If the new couple does not clarify this truth with their parents, then the family will face disharmony. This situation can be even more sensitive with those who have recently come to know the Lord.

God's design is established in wisdom and conveyed to us in love.

So how do grown children share this truth with their parents? First, start praying for them and yourselves as you discuss what can be a tense topic. You need to respect your parents and speak politely to them about God's better ways. Remember they might not be open to hearing about God's ways. Honor their decision. Below are some questions that you can ask your parents to help them gently understand God's truths. At the same time, the questions will help you better understand your parents' experience and why they do things in certain ways. Use and improve these questions as God leads, but God's truth does need to be implemented for the sake of your family, your relationships with your parents and His honor. Please remember that they do not need to be asked all at one time. When you sense some tenseness, slow down. Follow up at another time.

Questions to ask your parents

❖ **Did your parents expect you to do everything they told you after you were married?**

If this question is asked in a genuine and sincere way (rather than accusingly), it helps accomplish three things. First, it helps clarify the point of tension between parents and their older children. Second, it reminds the parents of pressures that they have had in the past. Third, it enables the young couple to politely point out the pressure their parents might be placing on them. Many parents dominate the lives of their married children because that is the way it always has been done. Tradition. It is likely that the parents are either imitating their parents or reacting against them.

❖ **(If they did) Did you have problems doing what they asked?**

Here we are trying to help our parents see the inferiority of their method of insisting that their married children obey them. By recounting their past problems, we can begin to point out why this system does not work.

> ❖ **Why do you think your parents insisted on this even though it was so hard on you?**

By this question, we are helping our parents to both identify the origin of what they do and begin to examine the inferiority of their method. The parent will probably not know why they used this method but will supplement their answer with their own thoughts or opinions. From this, we can better understand why it is important to them.

To have a good discussion, we need to know what our parents value. If we first suggest another way, they will feel threatened and become defensive and maybe accusatory. Perhaps they will mention the need to protect the children or to follow tradition. Others might suggest keeping harmony or peace in the family. Depending upon their answer, we can continue in one of two ways.

If they answer to protect the children or follow tradition, we should go on and ask,

> ❖ **How do you think it protects the children?**

> ❖ **How does the tradition help create peaceful families?**

Their answers will probably lead to the question in the following section. We need order, protection, strong families and good interpersonal relationships. Good relationships are not easy to find. If they are found, it is because they are going by God's command.

Once they see the goal of keeping harmony or peace in the family, you should ask,

> ❖ **Do you see it working? If I look around at the families around me under these circumstances, I get discouraged.**

Only the keeping of God's Word brings harmony. Recount a few examples that you know of in the same cultural situation to show how this method does not work. Ask if you can share how God's design addresses these problems and provides a solution. Depending upon their background, you need to phrase this question in different ways. If they are atheists or belong to an Asian religion, they might not clearly understand the idea of Creator. They still might be interested in knowing.

> ❖ **Do you know the way the Creator of mankind has told us to have family harmony? Could I share it with you?**

This is a key question which can lead to the description of God's better way. It is to be hoped that they will be open to listening. They might not be. If they are not, the couple will have to keep praying until their parents are more open.

It is important that your answer is respectful and addresses your parents' concerns. Many of them think that the biblical way will steal your allegiance away from them. You need to explain the difference between obey and honor (see above). You hopefully should be able to show them ways that you have honored them since you got married and became Christians. If you recently became Christians, tell them how you now respect and honor them compared to before. Remember that you must clear out past offenses by apologizing before talking about these matters. Here are a few points derived from biblical instruction.

- God desires harmony.
- God designed marriage (not to mention male and female).
- God asks the groom to leave his parents' authority and lead his new family under God's authority. (leave)
- The couple is still to honor their parents.
- God wants the husband to be loyal to his wife to support, protect, and provide for his wife. (cleave)

The above questions are used to stimulate helpful and gentle conversation. We realize that this model cannot suit all situations. However, if the children do not bring the truth to light, they will face more misunderstandings. In this case, at least the parents know why you do what you do. Rarely would a conversation actually use these exact words. What is more important is the gentle flow of thought and sincerity of heart.

Pause for Reflection:

Do you need to explain this 'cleaving' and 'leaving' truth to your parents? Have you done so? Was it easy or hard? Why?

D. Understanding Difficult Parents

What do we do if our parents still do not understand or are unwilling to talk about such issues? This is a tough question. Instead of challenging our parents, we should prayerfully go back and ask them if we have offended them in any way or caused them to think that we did not honor them. If so, we need to apologize and change where appropriate. All the offenses must be removed to the best of our ability. Do not point out their faults. As you confess your faults, they are reminded of their own.

If you have rightly humbled yourself and cleared out possible points of misunderstanding, go back and see if they will hear you. Remind them of how you have honored them. This will help assure them you really do respect them.

Can they be wrong in their expectations?

There will be times when we think our parents' expectations of us are wrong. They might be demanding parents who are ignorant of the spirit of love and service. For example, they might want us to make much money instead of serving in the church. If we spot such attitudes, we need to humble ourselves because without God's work of grace in our lives, we would hold to the same values. When I see my parents' mistakes, I am often very humbled because I see what I would be like if it was not for His abundant care for me.

If they are non-Christians, they cannot easily understand our new set of values. Yet, we see Jesus dealing with such people every day. Somehow, His love and explanations would work together in the lives of many people and bring desirable changes. We must hope for our parents that they, too, in time will see Jesus in us and change.

We must realize that we should not cave into our parents' unreasonable or unbiblical demands and expectations. These manipulations have ruined families in the past and must be rejected. After prayer and counsel with an elder, the husband (i.e. son or son-in-law) must gently explain that they cannot fulfill what his or her parents are demanding. Remember to clearly state the reason you cannot fulfill their demand.

For example, you might not have money to do certain things like take them on an expensive trip. Do not go into debt to do it even if it is embarrassing to state that you do not have the money.

They might want to hold, rock, or carry the new baby from day to night. For one or two days, this would not trouble the baby, but if their visit is extended for a month, then the couple must explain why you do things differently in your home. (Some have given this book to their parents to read!)

If they insist on giving the children candy day after day, you might ask them to explain why they like to do that. Help them understand how a friend's child lost all his teeth because of the sugar in the candy. Remember, your parents want to help and show love but often feel very limited in the ways that they can do it especially if they are visiting you in your home. Give them alternatives. Explain your routine and the reason for it. They generally want to be helpful.

On the positive side, when they do something right, reassure them of its positive effects. For example, they might not think it very special when they walk their grandchild down to the swings, but heartily thank them and tell them how much it meant to that son or daughter. You might even encourage your child to draw them a thank you card.

If you feel frustrated over something that is happening between you, your child and your parent (or in-law) try to follow these procedures.

✢ Refocus with a prayer.

"God my Father, I want so much to honor You by honoring my parents. Please help me to understand them and help them so that they can see Your love through my life."

✢ Identify what is troubling you.

It is not always easy to identify what is troubling you. Do not worry. Trust God to show you as you seek Him in prayer. If you still cannot figure it out, it might be good to write a chart of the times you sense that frustration and note what it is that you have seen or heard just before those times.

✢ Understand why your parent does such things.

Ask yourself a series of questions to better understand your parents. Has he or she always done this? What have they experienced in the past that make them think or react in that way? We should remember that sometimes people react rather than act. That is, their experiences and feelings over rule certain normal protocol.

For example, they might not have had any candy when they were little, but consider it a very special treat. When they give it so regularly to your child now, you are very concerned. You can ask your parent what it was like when they were little. Note if they are just imitating their past experiences (eating much candy) or reacting (doing the opposite of their experience—giving lots of candy). This is often true of the parent who was raised in poverty. They 'force' the goal of making money on their children, thinking it enables them to live without the problems that they experienced. Share with them how money does not solve but creates a whole new set of problems. Share some stories of some real life situations. They are probably very unaware of the problems that you face.

✤ Genuinely thank them.

Thank them a lot for their desire to give their grandchild the very best care. Sometimes it takes us a while to appreciate their help because of some existing friction. No matter what, we should still be thankful for their good intentions. They are trying to help even if it is based on inaccurate information. (Please note how we are trying to lessen the misunderstandings between the generations generally through sincere and quiet conversation.)

✤ Give them an alternative so that they will change their ways.

Give one piece of candy each week rather than each day. Give a cracker instead of candy. An alternative helps them retain their original intent to some degree.

✤ Be patient.

If their 'way' is not harmful, patiently tolerate it and help your children tolerate it. They might spoil the child some or hold the baby when he should be laid down. If it is for a short time, however, then it should be tolerated.

✤ Instruct them.

If their 'way' is physically not good, use books and authorities to help them understand the damage that treatment will bring to the child if continued. Many grandparents do not understand how their well-intended care could bring harm to their grandchild.

✤ Gently warn them.

If their 'way' goes against biblical principles, explain as a Christian that the Creator's ways are best. See the example above.

✤ Gently explain to them.

If they try to force you to go their unbiblical way, such as taking the child to some temple to worship some idol, explain the difference between honor and obedience. When you became a Christian, you were obligated to obey God. When you became married, you needed to leave their authority and cleave to your spouse. Gently explain that God's ways are best. Furthermore, explain as much as possible how God's way in this particular case is better.

✤ Refuse them.

If the parent demands that you obey him rather than God, you must explain that you can do many good things but not bad things like: lying, stealing, molesting, idol worship or gambling.

✤ Intervene

If your parents are insisting on some unbiblical way or irritating your wife in some bad way, the husband must intervene (we certainly hope it doesn't get to this point). He is to speak firmly but gently. He is always to be respectful. Explain the principles behind the problem. They might not understand God's better way, but do your best to explain its abuses in the past and how God's way is meant to bring the needed care and love to the family.

✤ Confrontation

If your parents are staying with you, it might come to a confrontation. It might be best to first have an elder share the difficulty with your parents.[15] Perhaps your parents have some problems with you, and you do not fully understand the situation. If they cause havoc in your home, however, the young husband will need to clearly share with them the lines of authority.

Explain they are welcome to share their insights (you should welcome their advice), but they are not to push you to obey. You might not be able to stop them from getting drunk (if this is their problem), but they should not think that you should join them in such drinking or that they can cause disruption to the home. If their behavior is unacceptable, then you will have to limit your welcome to them. There are alternatives.

You could shorten their time of visitation, or you could visit them, with or without your children depending on how difficult the circumstances are. Lastly, you could meet them at a certain place for vacation. Have separate accommodations.

Summary

We all desperately want family harmony—unless it means change. Change is not easy. It takes us from our comfort zone. Speaking to your parents might not be easy. You might have fears of "What if they …." Just remember to trust it all into God's hands. Fears do not lead us into God's will but generally away from it.

Start off and enjoy the opportunity to better understand your parents. Use all sorts of questions to find out what life was like for them when little. Become interested in them. They generally will not mind it. They will consider it an honor that you want to learn from them. Look at old pictures together as you talk.

God's ways are always best. Sometimes, we will need to stand up for God's ways. If we avoid the issues, we will tend to have persistent problems with our in-laws and pass these sins on to another generation. Most problems, however, arise from married couples who really do not care for their parents and hold on to bitterness from past situations.

Be determined to be a new generation for the Lord and set up high standards that will bring great blessing to your children and your children's children.

Parenting Principles & Practices

- Family harmony comes from knowing and observing God's ways.
- We are to take the initiative in apologizing for our offenses against our parents.
- After a couple gets married, they are still to honor their parents but no longer obey them.
- The couple should esteem their parents' wisdom and try to learn from them.
- 'Leaving' refers to the way the young married couple become their own independent unit under God.
- 'Cleaving' means that a husband should protect his wife from bad outside influences including dominating in-laws.
- A young couple should not be manipulated or influenced by their parents' money.
- A young couple should do everything they can to help their parents understand and tolerate God's ways for the family.
- Sometimes confrontation is required. Do it sensibly and quietly explain your actions.

Parenting Questions

1. Why is it so hard to get along with our parents?
2. If you could grow up again, what are some things you might do or say differently?
3. How do you treat your parents? Would you like your children to treat you the same way? How so?
4. What is the difference between honoring and obeying?
5. Explain the ideas of 'leaving' and 'cleaving.'
6. What steps do you need to take to have your parents not interfere with your own family (wife and children)?
7. Are there any influences that your wife needs protection from?
8. What ways do your parents interfere with the raising of your children? Are they unbiblical, unhealthy, or cultural issues?
9. How can you approach your parents when they seem to dominate your family?

Notes from Chapter #10

[1] It is right to honor our parents by including them in the big decisions of life like marriage. This is a simple application of the command to honor and obey our parents. The parents might not say much, but they should feel the couple's warmth.

[2] We can and must forgive others even if they do not forgive us (wrongs are rarely only one-sided). Check out this series on confession and forgiveness: www.foundationsforfreedom.net/Topics/Overcomer/OC3/OC311.html.

[3] It is for this reason we state that dating is an unbiblical concept. Dating leads to important decisions being made without the parents' consent or input. This happens when couples make the preservation of their dating or courting relationship more important than God's command to obey their parents.

4 There are some other situations that might be exceptions. For example, a son might not marry until 28. He has been living on his own and caring for his own needs for a number of years, perhaps far from his parents. However, even this situation points to the need of honoring his parents by seriously considering their judgment in the matter of seeking a spouse. It would be reckless to marry without caring about their opinion. It would be foolish to try to establish a good family without seeing whether the in-laws approve. "Listen to your father who begot you, and do not despise your mother when she is old" (Proverbs 23:22).

[5] A trust in God to work through parents brings about a big step in developing parent-child relationships. This is virtually impossible if you do not trust the Lord.

[6] What does a child do when a parent insists that their Christian child marry a non-Christian? Here, we have a tension between the command not to marry a non-Christian with the command to obey parents. Although, the young adult is under the parents' jurisdiction, he must recognize that this is not 'in the Lord.' The child must insist on not marrying if possible (They might have the power just to marry you). Remember, however, the cost of obedience can be great. The grown child might not be able to marry at all. This grown child needs to tell his or her parents the truth: he would like to marry, but if it means marrying a non-Christian, then he cannot because of God's command. This is one application of Luke 14:26. "If anyone comes to Me, and does not hate his own father and mother and wife and children and brothers and sisters, yes, and even his own life, he cannot be My disciple."

[7] Sins always catch up with God's people. We can see this clearly in Jacob's life. Check out this mini-series on his life. www.foundationsforfreedom.net/References/OT/Pentateuch/Genesis/15JacobSin/Genesis25-37_0Discipline.html .

[8] The scriptures are not saying that the children will be liable for their parents' sins. They will be judged for their own sins. The point is that the next generations will learn the same sin patterns and thus reap the same consequences. "Behold, all souls are Mine; the soul of the father as well as the soul of the son is Mine. The soul who sins will die" (Ezekiel 18:4).

[9] The child will not have <u>all</u> the sin patterns of the parents but usually one or two more prominent ones.

[10] I am still noticing hidden sin patterns that have eluded me for many years. I am just beginning to hear how I used an aggravated voice to reprimand or speak to our children. I have been married now for 25 years!

[11] God stated it in Genesis 2:24; Jesus in Matthew 19:5 and Paul in Ephesians 5:31. Jesus and Paul's quotes are slightly different due to translations. Instead of 'they shall become one,' they use 'the two shall become one.'

[12] Filial piety is a doctrine deeply ingrained in the Chinese culture. The many good aspects of this teaching become corrupted when the son does not 'leave' (move out from under) his parents' authority upon marriage. Filial piety also does not rightly embrace our true Father's will because it puts human relationships higher than our relationship with God.

[13] This does not enable the couple to do anything that they want. They are responsible to obey God just as before. If they abuse their children, surely God will judge them, perhaps through the earthly courts. This verse is only stating that the parents are no longer responsible to make decisions for their children when they marry. This is a hard but necessary change for some parents.

[14] This is an example of how intergenerational sins are passed on and broken. It is not easy to break out of the pull of sin. Other factors of religion and money are often involved.

[15] Wisdom from our elders can often help shed light on our weaknesses. This does not imply that you should confront your own parents. The husband must remember his role. He might be wise if he uses mediators in the process. He needs to be very careful to first share with the mediator what his values are unless the mediator does not represent him well. The husband should seek God's wisdom in solving the problem.

Chapter #11

REGAINING THE TRUST OF OUR TEENS

Purpose: Help parents of older children who have not been well disciplined or tenderly loved to take steps to regain the hearts of their children.

A. Regaining Hope for the Family

Many parents are greatly surprised to discover that the Bible teaches us how to raise children. When parents are first faced with God's biblical principles for parenting, certain questions are on their minds. The expressions on the faces of parents with older children are different from those with small children. Lesson by lesson they see the things that they <u>should</u> have done. Scenes of marital spats in front of the children come to their minds. Perhaps they feel a great dread deep in their hearts for not having exercised authority over their children.

There is a silent fear or desperation written on their hopeless faces. Perhaps it can be summarized by their own words, "We now know what we should have done, but it is too late. They are already grown up."

In this chapter we want to provide hope and ideas on how you can set your family back on God's track. We cannot guarantee how your children will respond. That is always the case. On the other hand, we can honestly say that if you follow these steps, you will have the best hope that your children will begin to respect you and follow

The Window of Reconciliation

God's way. The alternative is scary.

Too many children are being placed on the altar of materialism and sacrificed to the world by their parents. The parents have gained such devotion to the values of the world, that they neglect the real needs of their children.[1] This is no longer a novel of the future. It is reality now! As a result of their parents' sins, children are uncontrollable and even outright nasty. They are, as Jude says, overrun by their lusts. "In the last time there shall be mockers, following after their own ungodly lusts" (Jude 1:18).

We have a hope, though. "Just as the Holy Spirit says, 'Today if you hear His voice'" (Hebrews 3:7). Although family sins are piled high to the sky, you can still by God's amazing grace look to Him for solutions. There is hope. Every once in a while a child running on his wild path will turn his head back, in hope, that his parents will have changed. They are hoping that maybe, just maybe, their parents will begin to really love them.

This is where we start. We start with what God has built into each child—the need and desire for the love and support of his parents. Even though a child has been repeatedly rejected, that child will hold on to a slender hope for change. Children have a desperate need for this love and attention. Animals grow up very quickly. Within months or even days, in some cases, the little ones are off on their own. However, God has given parents an extended opportunity to care for their children, some of which are not so young anymore. Because of this natural affection, we can greatly influence our children for good even if we now are grandparents!

Many parents are astonished at how miserably they have failed God and their children by their unbiblical parenting methods. Through a book like this or some crisis, all their mismanagement becomes obvious. This chapter encourages and enables such parents to regain the trust of their older children. It is not too late. We are glad that through God's grace we can offer hope even for our stubborn and rebellious children. Do not give up hope!

Our Needy Children

Did you ever try to change another person? It does not work! It is easier to change ourselves than to change others (and even that is not easy)!. How then, can we change our children? Not a few parents have tried working with their recalcitrant children only to find rude words shouted back at them. They might even do the very things that their parents do not like just to spite them. Behind all the recommendations below, you will need to bathe your whole family, including your own lives, in sincere prayer.[2] Put on your spiritual armor. We need to take steps to make sure that nothing in our lives interferes with the process of restoring our children.

Whenever parents do not raise children according to God's biblical principles, troubles will arise. If we are consistent in our neglect, these troubles develop deep problems in the attitudes, habits and perspectives of our children. One result of improperly raising our children is bad communication. There seems to be a towering wall between our children and ourselves. They might hear us if we shout over it, but usually they misunderstand what we are really saying, blocking good and effective communication between us. Here are a few symptoms of bad parenting.

- Children have lost respect for their parents. The parent says one thing but does another.
- Children are bitter at their parents' anger and rage.
- Children have sought the company of other undesirable friends because they do not have their parents' love.
- Children accept the bribes (i.e. material gifts) of their guilty parents but would rather have a good relationship with their parents.
- Children reject themselves because they do not feel loved.[3]
- Children purposely do wrong just to get their parents' attention. (Negative attention is better than no attention.)

Parents, appointed by God, are the chief vehicle through which He passes on His love and truth to the new generation. When the parents fail, the children flounder. This is why there are so many modern physical diseases and emotional problems. The parents are too busy in the world with their 'own' lives and have laid aside their parental responsibilities. Unresolved problems will only worsen as the children grow up.

Handling our failures

We are not saying that every parent is as bad as he or she could be. We are asserting that parental 'mistakes' leave scars in the lives of the children. The apostle describes the non-Christian as "Having no hope and without God in the world" (Ephesians 2:12). They are stuck. They simply have nowhere to go. It is hard to fathom how dark the world is for those who have not met the Lord.

The Christian lives in totally different circumstances. Romans 5:5 states that "hope does not disappoint." The Gospel of the Lord Jesus brings amazing hope into every area of our lives. Unfortunately, many of us are not aware of our disobedience until our children are older. By that time they have scars. They have no love for the Lord. They are caught up in this world's parties and lies.[4] In our hearts we know where they are going. We must wake up from our slumber and first correct our own path. Hope only can be found on that road.

The World	God's People
"Having no hope and without God in the world" (Ephesians 2:12)	"Hope does not disappoint" (Romans 5:5)
failures	failures
Hopeless	Hopeful!

Pause for Reflection:

Are you a good parent? Can you see or admit to your own faults? Have you changed your approach yet? Have you confessed your sin?

The Place for Biblical Truths

This book on parenting focuses on biblical principles because they bring light and love into our families. We do not want good-looking patches to hide our wounds. Those untreated wounds will lead to serious infections down the road. We want the wounds healed so that we can tell others how God has made us and our children better! Does this not sound like the Gospel message when people meet Jesus? They come away from that encounter excitedly telling others about Jesus. This is what He wants to do today in our families.

God wants each parent to take these biblical truths (i.e. His light), to be aware of our failures (conviction), to seek forgiveness (confession), to point out the right way (instruction) and to create testimonies on how He has helped us (praise). We cannot save. We need help. Before turning and seeing the path out of our miserable mess, let us first pray.

> *Dear Father in Heaven, You are perfect in your ways. We, however, have failed miserably. We grieve over some of the decisions we have made as parents. We have chosen promotions over time with our*

246

families. We have chosen work over the home. We have chosen entertainment over taking a walk with our children. Lord, our home is a perfect candidate for a miracle. We cry out to you now, "Save us Lord!" Help us be good parents for the short time we have left. Help our children to break from their hopeless path in the world and follow your glorious ways. In Christ's Jesus Name we pray, Amen.

Renewed Hope

It is impossible to point out all the ways we have for one reason or another neglected to carry out God's Word. Even God does not bring up all our sins at once. He selectively works on one or more areas at a time. Training is a process.

As we go continue this series, God will begin to prod you about certain failures. This is not me. God is speaking to you. He convicts us through the Holy Spirit. He points out our failures so that we understand what to turn away from and what to turn toward. When we have elbow pain, it is because our elbow hurts not our knee. When we feel guilty watching a movie rather than spending some time with our child, God is making us aware of something He may want us to change. Listening to His promptings to make changes will bring significant help to you, your children and others you influence.

The need for prayer

Our tendency is to avoid thinking about our failures. This is because we are humbled and shameful of our mistakes.[5] Our desire for acceptance, more often than we would like to admit, influences our decisions. As long as we feel reluctant to admit and confess our sins, our pride continues to destroy and cause havoc to our lives and families. God's way back to His blessed path is always through the door of confession. The Great News is that there is a path back. Do not fight confession; just follow through with what you need to do.

Some parents want to disguise their sin by claiming that bad parenting is not sin. I disagree. Bad parenting means we are not carrying out one or more biblical principles or instructions. Whenever we violate God's Word, we are sinning. We hurt ourselves and others even if it is out of ignorance. If we love others, we will not sin.

Parenting failures are sin. We must turn from them. "He who conceals his transgressions will not prosper, but he who confesses and forsakes them will find compassion" (Proverbs 28:13).

If I speak angrily to my child, is this not wrong? If I am too busy with my schedule to pay attention to a child's need, is that not selfishness? If I chastise too harshly due to my former reluctance to solve some problems, I sin. If I do not enforce standards for my children that I believe are right, I am not loving my children. If I bribe my child to get my way, I have strengthened their lustful flesh. If I am critical, am I not withholding love and care from my children? If we are too prideful to confess our sins, we destroy any trust left in our relationship with our child.

If, however, we respond to conviction, we are responding to God and allowing light to shine in the darkness. This is the beginning of good change. The parent always starts with himself, not the wrongs of the child. The parent's confession allows the child to see that there might be hope. He sees something, a humble heart, that shocks him. A ray of light comes through the clouds of despair and touches his heart.

Parents taking this step are taking a giant leap forward. The child probably will be caught off guard. They will no doubt be very cautious. They do not know where this might lead. It is enough, though, to allow them to begin to have hope (even if they do not show it). This sets the scene to tell your child that you have made a number of mistakes in the past and would like to talk to him or her more about them later. It is here that hope is birthed.

> *"Blessed are the poor in spirit,*
> *for theirs is the kingdom*
> *of heaven" (Matthew 5:3).*

Understanding Suspicion

Trust is essential for a good relationship. Why is it so important? Trust enables a person to accept what another person does or says because they believe that he or she has said it with good motive. When he hears, "You are a good friend!" he feels good. There are no hidden motives to darken that trust. When bitterness, anger, or lack of love is repeated, however, he can no longer simply trust what the parents say is with good motive. From their experience, they are convinced that their parents are ultimately selfish or hypocrites. They believe (and they may be right) that there is a hidden motive to hurt, hate or reject them.

The child is conditioned to accept lies about the parent and distort issues out of proportion. It is as if there is a lens over their mind, which interprets everything in a certain way just as a blue lens would make everything blue. Because of their lack of trust in the parent, they more readily believe lies from the evil one. The worst part is that even if you say something truthful or with genuine concern, the child still mistrusts your words and may interpret them wrongly. This is the key problem with poor communication. Failures and suspicion lie behind it.

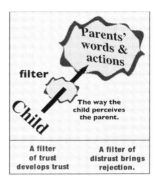

Relational walls create isolation and mistrust. This in turn creates vulnerability to the evil one. Their minds become receptive to the evil one. Hatred is amplified and rejection is blown out of proportion. Hebrews 12:15 says that the "root of bitterness springs up causes trouble and by it many be defiled."

The Way Back Home

So how do we reach our child? The most important thing we can do is to straighten up our own lives so that our children may perceive God's special love radiating through us. We want to destroy any reason for them to mistrust us. We make the new love in the home irresistible.

Please remember perfection is not the goal. This cannot be reached. We should, however, strive for excellence. The Lord desires for us to be great parents. When we approach parenting this way and combine it with a heart of apology and forgiveness, it becomes a powerful influence in the lives of our children. Through proper confession, we legitimize our parental love. Our children still might disagree with us, but they still must respect us for our stand. The restoration process can take a while. Remember it took a long time for us to get where we are–not days but years. Fortunately, it is easier to take down walls than to build them.

Parents should not just change their attitudes. Repentance will also require important lifestyle changes. Perhaps it means a successful business woman will quit her job and return home to be a successful Mom. That will get the children thinking, especially if they share why they are changing their ways of life. If the children are older, do not forget to share the difficult financial picture with them. Perhaps, however, the family can take a real family vacation and have fun together. This is very significant for families who rarely spend time together.

If we are honest, we will see how we have repeatedly disappointed our children and even driven them away into isolation. They have had nights of tears because our pride would not let us apologize for blowing up in anger at them. We will need patience to win them back. The good thing is that God's love is patient. Our constant shower of love will be shown in consistent discipline, prayer and time together. God will supply the persistence. We just need to hang on. I look at it like this. God has called me to love so love I will. From now on, I will just plan on going the extra step. My focus is not on my child but on how I respond to my Lord.

Pause for Reflection

How about you? Will you make this commitment? "I will by God's grace consistently love _____." Just put your children's name in the blank. Then cry out to God to see His love shine through you so that your children will see His light and feel His love.

This is the Matthew 'shine' principle applied to our children. By the way, our spouses would not mind this either!

> *Let your light so shine before men in such a way that they may see your good works, and glorify your Father who is in heaven (Matthew 5:16).*

Now let us see how we can accelerate this process. Little time is left.

Considering the Importance of the Family

Since we cannot force a change in our child, we need to focus on changing our own hearts. Fortunately, God in His rich grace enables us to take these steps. The more sincere we are, the quicker the process. We should ask how much we really want to change. Be desperate. If you aren't, get desperate. There could be nothing quite so important as these matters. The questions God will ask us in heaven will not be about the promotion we got but whether we sacrificed that promotion to spend time with our family.

About 14 years ago, I was taking a shower early one Sunday morning. Everyone else was sleeping. I felt a sharp pain in my chest and felt dizzy. I quickly finished my shower and went to my study. I realized that this could be the end of my life. I knelt down to pray. My life rushed through my mind. Although I loved the pastoral ministry (I was pastoring at the time), I had trained the sheep. God would care for the church. My concerns, though, focused on my dear wife and children. I wept for them. I cared for them. God used this time to crystallize my care for them and to prioritize them. I asked for forgiveness for not properly praying for them. God healed me from that chest pain, but from that time on I had a renewed love and affection for my wife and children. God was making me desperate.

I knew my children's love for God and belief in Christ was all-important. Without Christ, they would perish. I took special steps of commitment that day that would lead me into praying daily for each child by name. I also desired to enter more into their lives while I had time.

Jobs are important, but they are to support you in your service toward God and your family. What do you gain if you are rich, but your child is spoiled and misuses the money? God has not made us responsible for much in this vast world, but we had better do a good job with what He has appointed us to do. God wants to work along with us, but we need to make some real adjustments in our lives so that we will focus on what He wants. I speak so dramatically because I fear you will not make those needed changes. Will you?

Pause for Reflection
Here is a possible commitment statement.

> *"I will make whatever changes that I need in my life to be faithful to God in my responsibilities to care for the children He has appointed me to raise."*

I do not encourage making quick commitments. This pledge, however, plays an important role in accomplishing His purposes for you and your family. The determination and faith behind such a commitment becomes the backbone to the persistence needed for the struggles ahead.

B. Restoring the Home

Much needs to be done to establish a godly family. After reviewing the Lord's standards for our home, we will look at three practical steps to not only restore the relationship with your children but also to rightly administer your home.

1) Our Standard: Being More Like Jesus

As we confess on our own failures, we will ask God to show us what needs to be changed. He will faithfully help us as His children. We have a tendency to fail in one of two ways. We either are permissive or tend to be authoritarian.

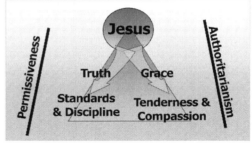

Remember we need to be like Jesus and live out both <u>truth</u> and <u>grace</u> to our children. Permissiveness and authoritarianism are perversions these truths.

Permissiveness (perversion of truth)

We have shown before that when we compromise truth, we tend to be permissive (chapter 3). Our intent is to be close to our child so we give in to their desires. Often what they want, demand or desire, is not bad in itself, but timing or appropriateness is off. Jesus Himself said that a father would not give something bad to his child. Whenever we carry out less than what we sense is right to do towards our children, we are doing evil. Below is a chart that depicts many ways sin patterns our children's life because we distort genuine love.

Distortions of False Love	
Parent says ...	**Results in ...**
"I want my child to know I love him so I give him what he wants."	**The child is discontent and ungrateful. He shows signs of rebellion.**

"I love my child too much. I could never discipline him."	The child doesn't learn right from wrong. He feels unloved or rejected and has difficulty with obedience.
"I love my child so much that I always pick up after him."	The child doesn't learn to take responsibility. He looks to be served.
"I love him so much that I never want to hurt his feelings."	The child has his feelings easily bruised. He hasn't learned to accept criticism or advice.
"I love my child too much to say no to him."	The child interprets that as rejection and feels uncared for.

When a child grows up with one or more of these distortions, he has more difficulty maturing and transitioning into adulthood.

Authoritarianism (perversion of grace)

When a parent focuses on the rules—the law, he often does it without grace. This is the other extreme. A father might want a quiet house or feel as if he is in control. He demands obedience. His love does not come through in situations at home because it is missing! He cares more for himself than about the child's overall needs.

Families without compassion and love are known for being excessively strict. The child's compliance is on the outward rather than from the heart. The Heavenly Father indeed has standards and carries out discipline, but He always does it in love. The authoritarian parent[6] ruins the relationship with his child by caring more for the rules than for the person. Here are some symptoms of an authoritarian parent.

- He is unable to apologize when he does wrong.
- He chastises children for things he himself does (double standard).
- He does not have a warm welcoming home.
- He shouts in anger when disobeyed.
- He is overbearing when he disciplines.
- He does not encourage times of discussion.

The parent makes no way for the child to be reconciled to him, and the child does not even feel like he wants to be restored. The parent tends to be unwelcoming, arrogant and hostile. This is the way barriers between parents and children are built.

The authoritarian parent needs to seriously evaluate his life. He should start by examining whether he is carrying out the principles of grace in his affairs. He focuses so much on the standard, he is unable to rightly look at this area of grace.

He needs to take a close look at how Jesus conducted His life. How did He confront people in sin? We agree that Jesus was not the father of the people He met, and yet, He was very sensitive to them while confronting their sinful acts (i.e. the woman caught in adultery John 8). Jesus did speak abruptly to His disciples but always with good cause.

A Blend of Problems!

The problems in the family are probably a blend of these two perversions of truth (permissiveness and authoritarian). Each parent might operate from one of these deficiencies. In both cases we have compromised living like Jesus. We need to humble ourselves before God with our spouse. Then have a conference with your children. We must get honest about our failures, ask forgiveness and then clearly set out the way the home is going to go and why.

If we do not get honest about our failures, then we have no chance in winning back our child. Why? Our failures, deliberate or not, have caused bitterness, anger, and worldliness to swell up in our children. They no longer trust us like they did when they were small. As we humble ourselves, however, they discover a desire to restore their relationship with us. Our sincere apologies produce a seed of hope.

When high barriers have been raised, we should not expect the child to break down that wall. Dad and Mom need to lead the way. The goal is to help the child restore his respect for his parents. Remember that if the parents have not properly raised their children and are now only discovering this, there is a wall between them and their children. The wrongs have piled up. The wrongs have been grouped together into a mass of rejection. For example, a father might have yelled at his child (two times a week) for twelve years. That is a total of twelve hundred times! The problem is not just the yelling but also how many times resentment has been built up in the child. After all, when there is no forgiveness and restoration, then that dividing barrier between parents and children will be quite tall and strong. The question is then, "How do I take down such a wall?"

Breaking down the wall

There are three steps to taking down this wall.

Step #1 Alone with God

Get right with God.

Find a time to get by yourself with God and ask Him to help you get an honest look at your life. Admit your failures to Him. Ask for cleansing by the power of Christ. State that you look for His help and direction to restore your family. Make a written list of your deficiencies before you, it is much easier to properly follow them up and discuss them with your spouse and children.

After doing this, you need to commit yourself to take the necessary steps to follow up what the Lord has put on your heart.

Step #2 Along with your Spouse

Meet with your spouse.

It is best to start anew as a one husband-wife team. You do not surprise your family by a sudden conference call. Instead, you first meet with your spouse. Your husband or wife might have his or her own suspicions as to your sincerity. This is the time you need to share with your spouse what God has been doing in your life.

For example, maybe in this instance, God has been convicting the father of his failures. He would like to regain the trust of his two teenage children. He is greatly distraught over the whole situation and seeks God's help. He should first meet with his wife and explain what God is doing in his life. She might need time to catch up with what God is trying to do in her family. Be content to only deal with your own sins. Focus on where you have failed as a father, where you want to go: a godly home marked by God's love and grace in Christ Jesus.

After you are able to share your changed heart with your spouse and talk about your family's true needs, then call a conference with your children. If your spouse has no interest in this, then as a father you still need to continue, only be kind. It might be that your wife does not trust you. Pray and show a new willingness to be a good husband first. After detecting your sincerity as a husband, she will be much more able to understand your heart to be a good father. If your husband is not interested in how God is prompting you as a mother, then you must trust God to reshape the whole family in His time. On a personal level, however, you can still follow through the steps below and gather hope from 1 Corinthians 7:14.

> *For the unbelieving husband is sanctified through his wife...for otherwise your children are unclean, but now they are holy (1 Corinthians 7:14).*

This verse shows us that even one sincere Christian parent has great influence on her spouse and children. We hope for both husband and wife to work together, but we start with what we have in hope of greater things.

Step #3 Conference with our older children

There are two main parts to this third step: There is confession and correction. Confession focuses on restoring your broken relationship with your children. Correction refers to stating positive instruction so that the home can function rightly.

At conference time, you will need to carefully go through this list. Each step is important.[7]

a) Confession

The 'confession' part has the expressed purpose of restoring the relationship with our older children. Do not force the meeting to work out all the details. Make another time for that discussion if needed.

If there are younger children, only gather those that understand the problem. Those that are six or seven will have been hurt and should be part of that conference. You have the option to meet privately with them after you have held a conference with the older children. It is important that you are fully restored to all your children. I remember after an angry outburst that I had to search out the younger ones and apologize to each one (this was not easy). They could understand. They learned that apology is a way of life in our home.

We should make an appointment. Do not get upset if no one seems to make it easy to get together. Keep searching until you find a good time. Pray that God would work out the best time. Our family usually meets in the living room, but the kitchen can serve well too. Make sure that no one needs to leave early and that there are no disruptions. Shut the phones off. Do not answer them.

Sit in a circle and tell your children that you have several things you need to share with them. Mention that they will have their turn to talk but first the parents must talk. You respect their cooperation. If they have questions, they can simply raise their hand.

✤ Dad should open in prayer.

In your prayer confess your sins as a family and specifically your sins as a father. You as a whole have fallen short before the Lord. Do not be specific with people's names at that point. You will have time for that. Ask for general forgiveness and cleansing through Christ.

✤ Initial confession.

Tell them how you have not kept the standards the scriptures have set. This confession sets the tone for the meeting. Acknowledge that each time you have compromised, you have hurt them (and your spouse). Tell them how slow you were to learn this.

✤ Tell the story how God got your attention.

Your testimony of how God has gotten your attention is a special work of God. Share it with them. Acknowledge His work but also that you have plenty of room to be humble and many opportunities to live it out. Tell them how God has led you to desire a real godly family. Set the vision before them.

✤ Confession time.

You need to quickly move on to confession time or their rebellion and struggles will surface. You can take out the list you made. Before you start you might give them a quick show of how long the list is (this will shock them–include bad attitudes and poor speech). Go down the list one by one and tell them how you, their father, has failed them and God.[8] Tell them that this does not mean that you will be perfect but that you are going to strive to be a Dad that pleases God. You want to honor the Lord and help your family to reach God's good design for each of their lives. Confession is simply admitting certain things were wrong.[9]

Make sure you identify the specific areas that you have compromised God's standards (i.e. rage, unforgiving, materialism, etc.) Again state that your behavior has negatively impacted them. For example say, "Don't you remember that time I spoke to you rudely, and you refused to speak to me for a week? I must have hurt you very badly." Focus on your fault not the other's.

Tell them, as the head of the household, that you have not been properly leading them but now are going to by God's grace (definitely by His strength and wisdom because you do not know how). Share how you will need their prayers because you have lots to learn that you should have learned a long time ago.

Once you get going it is a lot easier. Be thorough. Give illustrations. Ask some questions to help you understand how badly you hurt them.

After you have gone through your list, you must ask them to name other things that have offended them. Give them time to answer and do not be defensive! It is to be hoped that you have gone through this procedure already with your spouse. Your spouse should not add to your list at that time but she can help clarify or join in the confession if needed. Work together as much as possible.

✤ Apology introduced.

After getting all the hard facts out, ask them to forgive you. Tell them that you cannot pay them back for the emotional harm that you have caused them. Acknowledge how sad you feel that they had to go through painful times.

Be sensitive to the fact that they might want some time to think about it. Do not let them think you are just trying to put it off indefinitely. Insist on it and yet do not push too hard. Remind them that it is important for your family to get better. Forgiveness always precedes restoration. The illustration of the barrier between the parents and children can be shared if you think it helps clarify how your parent and child relationship has been affected.

✤ Apologize

Be direct. List all the wrongs that you have committed. Mention that you want a personal response from each of them. Say something like, "I have not been a good Dad. I am so sorry. Will you forgive me of all my wrongs against you?"

Then one by one seek a personal response from each child, starting with the oldest. "Jimmy, will you forgive me for all the things I did against you?" I recommend hugging him or her right at that moment in front of the others after the child has said, "I forgive you." Then turn to the second child and continue on until each child has had a chance to forgive you.

Afterwards, your wife might want to do the same. Do not push her. Let the Spirit work. Right now He has been prompting you. Focus on doing your part and be open to how else He might work in others.

Pause for Reflection:

Have you ever apologized to your child before? When was the last time? Have you done wrongs for which you have not yet apologized?

Further Thoughts

You should tell your children that some feelings of resentment, bitterness, anger and rage could still be in them. You as a parent are confessing your part. When the child forgives, then you both can have fully restored relationships. Indicate that you plan to make some real changes in how things are handled in the home. Do not get into this now. If each of them does not forgive, then hold off on new plans. Reconciliation must precede restoration.

If a child refuses to forgive you, do not be surprised. You have greatly disappointed them in the past. They might be testing your sincerity. On the other hand you might not have confessed the area that has particularly hurt him. Privately ask him or her what might be the problem. Prod around a little bit. Ask for wisdom from God.

One time I remember that my son did not want to give the regular kiss and hug at bedtime. I tried to talk with him for several minutes trying to see what was wrong. I could not think of anything. He denied anything was wrong. The scripture, however, says not to go to bed with anger. I persisted. Finally, I started going through the times I met with him through the day. The second thing I mentioned hit the buzzer. I knew that was it. I had wrongly chastised him (at least he thought so). It took me a while to understand and appreciate his perspective and even more time to be able to swallow my pride and apologize. When I did, however, he forgave, and we were back to normal. Barriers indicate resentment and bitterness.

Another suggestion. When there is deep rebellion, sometimes they are unwilling for you to make a direct hit on that area. Start by asking forgiveness for other less traumatic situations. This is especially true when one child is unwilling to forgive you for some matters.

Please remember the rules of confession.

- Do not be defensive. Try to listen. If you do start speaking when they are speaking, quickly apologize and then say, "Continue on. I need to hear what you have to say."
- Confess only sins that you have done. Admit there are misunderstandings but there are real wrong things that you have done. We usually could have handled things better than we did.
- If certain issues pop up, ask for more time to think on these issues, especially if it is not very clear what happened or what you did wrong.
- Speak only for yourself. In this case, the parents should not state any of their children's sins. Speak only of your own. Unless agreed beforehand, you should not confess your spouse's sins. The one that has made the offense needs to ask forgiveness in almost every case.
- Mention how you have hurt them and are sorry there is no real way to make up for it. Do not bribe them, but if there is need for financial restoration, they should be paid in full. You might need time to work this out. If so, tell them your plans.
- Ask for forgiveness. Expect an answer like, "I forgive you." Do not accept the polite, "Oh it does not matter." Answer that statement by saying God says it really does matter (they know it does). Explain how it has specifically hurt their feelings and your relationship with them. Then repeat your request for them to forgive you.
- What about their sins? Deal with them privately. Let them come out as they may. Do not let it interfere with this special work of breaking down the mistrust and animosity they have toward you.
- Future changes. If you have time and stamina, tell them that you would like to go over how the family needs to run according to God's ways. If you are tired or still need to straighten out a relationship or two, then postpone this to a future time.

b) Correction

After the confession time, you need to set down the new goals the Lord has given you for your family. Humbling our hearts and calling a family conference are important matters, but we must not stop there. We must also establish a good family structure. Nehemiah did not only take control of the city. After observing the broken down walls, he strategically built them up in record time. He shared his plan with others, and they all worked together to accomplish the common task.

Because your children are older, they should be involved in this process to some degree. You are to lead. You are not undermining your authority when you do this but are using this opportunity to instruct them. Since you have not done this before, then you need to tell them what is right and wrong and why.

You might have a series of short Bible studies to highlight the way your home should be. You might read Genesis 6 and see how much God does not like violence and so will no longer tolerate evil television shows. Then have a discussion of what makes a show violent or sensual. Bind yourself to the newly adopted standard without any room for slackness! This flows nicely with one of the father's responsibilities to instruct the child how they should live. If you did it consistently when they were younger, they would have been better equipped for life. Now, however, you must work with them and discover and establish these rules.

At some point you should let your pastor know what is happening. You need his support and guidance in these matters even in suggesting Bible study materials or showing you how to lead your family in studying God's Word.

Summary

There are two things that must be discussed with everyone: standards and enforcement.

Discuss with them what changes your family is going to face. Share a few real changes such as family prayers each night. Tell them what standards the Lord wants for you all. No lying. Complete obedience to parents. You can be honest and say you are just learning, but are excited how the Lord is leading you. Read the fruit of the Spirit from Galatians 5. Let them hear the goodness of God's goals. This is where you all want to go.

Also share how you are now going to carry out discipline God's way. Depending on how old the children are, you need to tell them how you are going to enforce these standards. For younger children, you can use the rod.[10] As they get older, you need to turn to consequences and freedom that has been discussed earlier on.[11] You need to tell them how consequences works. You might want to tell them later how the whole correction process works. If they are older, they can read the appropriate chapters in this book. Being older, they need to mentally understand.

Let us now look at some more specific things that can be done to rightly establish family order according to God's way.

C. Resolving Conflict

Let us take a broader look at what constructive work needs to be done to properly set up a godly home. We will then look at a few specific examples to more clearly understand how each area can be implemented.

1) Correction: Areas of Instruction

Below we have suggested areas that, in time, will need to be thought through and dealt with. This is not a complete list but helps us focus on real changes that need to be studied, understood and applied to our families. The most immediate need is to fully restore broken relationships. More will be said about this below.

- Goals for our family (Galatians 5:22-23, Greatest Commands, Great Commission).
- Authority structure for family (Ephesians 5:18-6:5, Father, Mother, children, servants).
- Purpose and means of discipline (Hebrews 12, Proverbs).
- Need and process of reconciliation and forgiveness (resolving conflict).
- Habits: Viewing and listening to media and playing computer games.
- Expectations for different settings (table manners, getting up, going to bed, school work, etc.)
- Developing schedules that please the Lord (including devotions).
- Develop accountability for special areas of need (e.g. self-control, manners, etc.)
- Organize family fun (avoid spending much money; focus on walks, cultivating relationships).
- Set up and attentively attend family devotion times.
- Discuss values that come from God's Word for friends (study from Proverbs).
- Honor the Lord's day; worship; pray; tithe, serve.
- Cooperate: Discuss mutual expectations (use of car, wanting to go places, privileges).
- Explain and implement 'Trust and Freedom' consequences.

- Write up a family mission? What distinctive ways does God want to bless and work through your family knowing their special gifts, burdens and abilities.

- Family vision: define what you want your family to be like. The godly family is not too austere but fun, friendly and delighted in the way God rules their home through their parents. Home is a place everyone likes to be. Love rules through politeness, apology and acts of caring. Your home should be a place where people can increasingly learn to love God.

What is a parent to do first? Let us look at this for a moment.

2) Guiding our First Steps

It might overwhelming to know where to start. We cannot give a complete answer. This somewhat depends on your past practices. It also has to do with past failures. We tried to list the things that must be worked through, but there is a need to prioritize. It is a process. Think of the  whole restructuring as a life process. You might follow these steps to prioritize what you need to work on first.

• *Conviction*

Try to remember exactly what areas the Lord has convicted you on. Write down those scriptures and situations that He has used. We need to remember that God does not point out all our weaknesses at once. He does not want to overwhelm us with too many things. Write down the two or three most important things that have been on your heart. Start here. If you already went through a time of confession, then you have already begun on the right road!

• *Prayerfully seek the Lord*

Pray through those areas and ask God to lead you. Maybe you know three areas that have been bothering you (think conviction): bad friends, too many bad computer games, and your child has been rude and ignores what you say. The father should meet God and ask Him how he should lead the family into His paths for peace. He should pray that God would make the necessary corrections in their lives. Look back in this book for suggestions.

• *Focus first on the plan God has for you*

Children watch for reform in the parents. They have heard many words but really want to see genuine change. The father and mother should first share some of the changes they plan to make in their own personal lives. Be specific.

Ask the children to keep you accountable. For example, you will no longer watch movies with sensual images. Explain how God convicted you and how you want to please God and rightly lead the children. The children will see that everyone is changing and that the standards come from God's Word.

Make sure you tell them what is happening. Do not just secretly do it. They need to learn from your positive instruction and example at this critical time in their lives.

• *Identify the issues that have to do with relationship first*

We cannot progress far if the relationship issues are not cleared up. Do they still have a bad attitude? Do you still see the 'filter of mistrust' operating?

If so, slow down and focus on the relationship issues that must be dealt with first. We will give an example below to show how you can continue working through an area of need. Remember, however, there is the happy and bright side of building relationships. Do things together. Learn to like to be with each other. Do special things for the other without thinking of getting anything in return.

3) **Dealing with rude behavior**

In the three examples above, rudeness was the one that did the most damage to the relationship between parents and children. If it is not caught right at the beginning, relationships will go sour and hope will dissipate faster than ever. Let us look at this issue very specifically.

1. Express the urgency of keeping a good parent-child relationship.

2. Discuss the importance of this. See if they can identify its importance. Remember these children are older. If they are slow to respond, think up a few past circumstances where you rude. Ask if they liked it. What happened as a result?

3. Stress that you want to live the way God wants you to. Ask them if they can think of any verses that speak of the importance of this issue. In this case, Exodus 20:12, Ephesians 6:1-3 (provoking from father's point) and generally loving one another. When they say 'honor' their parents, make sure they use their own words to explain what 'honor' means. Then have them work out how a person can practically express kindness instead of rudeness. What

happens when someone is rude? You can fill in where they leave out. In this case, you might mention:

- Always speak respectfully.
- Never interrupt the parent unless there is an emergency.
- Never respond in disagreement with outburst, whining, sassy, crying or talking back.
- When answering your parents say, "Okay Daddy" or "Okay Mommy" or however you think is best.
- If you catch yourself with the wrong words or attitude, stop talking and humbly apologize saying, "I'm sorry. I should not have responded that way. Will you forgive me?"

4. To make it easier for the child, tell them that you will also eliminate rudeness from your speech. A parents' willingness to live by the same standards helps a child realize how important a new rule is.

You can tell them (though this is by no means necessary) that though you have the right to command them to do different things, you recognize that they are getting older, and you will treat them as an adult. You will politely ask them to do things. You can ask them that if they note that you are not being polite, then they can make some kind of sign like a crossed "t" or something to let you know. (They need to know how to honorably pass correction on.) They should not tell you of your rudeness in front of others.

Summary

We hope you get the idea. There is so much to say and much needs to be gleaned from other chapters in this book. This includes polite rules, devotions, public behavior, making or having friends, regulations on television or movies, phone use, etc. We would like to make one more suggestion to help evaluate priorities.

4) Examine Schedules Together

We would suggest to write out a schedule of your activities and share this with your older children. This might seem excessively strict for some families, but this is not as rigorous as it sounds. Our lives conform to a schedule more than we would like. When we show our children our schedules, we have a special opportunity to spot areas of potential conflict.

It is easier for your children to understand your wishes and needs when you explain your calendar to them. As children get older, you will

need to do this less as they are more independent. At certain times in life, however, the parent and child need to clearly think through how their obligations and expectations affect each other. This is part of learning politeness.

This is a great time for the child to see how much the parent does for him. It also is a good time to explain that as a family everyone works together for the common good. Everyone has a role at home. Freedom demands responsibility. Perhaps you can explain to your older children that when they were little, not much was expected from them. Now that they are older, things are different. They are learning responsibility. The parents' job is to prepare them for adulthood. They do this by having their children take on increasing responsibility. They share house jobs and voluntarily helping out the whole family. (In actuality, this should start when children are small.)

If this is a sudden change for them, they might react negatively. We highly suggest that before you do this, you specifically apologize for how you have failed to give them jobs in the past. Specifically state how you used to treat them as a little child rather than as a growing young adult. Also state how you have neglected to train them and want to change this now. Ask them to forgive you and get a proper reply.

Children feel wanted, desired and valuable when they share a part of the household jobs. If they have no part, there is no ownership. The parent should not feel like they are being mean or lazy by assigning the children house jobs. The opposite is true. They are preparing for real life.

They are mature and responsible enough to carry out these duties. Just remember to do it with them the first few times. It will be awkward at first, but it will help them see that you are also willing to do it. This also gives you the opportunity to set a standard for cleaning the bathroom or organizing their room. Write down a checklist if necessary. As you watch their work, you will see the child's positive character qualities as well as deficiencies. Applaud them for their faithfulness wherever you see it. Affirm the character qualities you see. "You have been so faithful sweeping the walk each week." They like it, and the positive encouragement motivates them to do better. You also must kindly work with them on the things they did not do well. Clarify, correct and give other opportunities to try again.

Working out a child and parent schedule together helps clarify expectations, areas of conflict and issues that need to be dealt with. Again, we suggest do not fix everything at first. You might see some activity that needs to be changed such as coming home late. At this moment, however, only say that you will need to evaluate that activity in the future but for now it will continue. They will see that you are carefully and prayerfully contemplating what is going on in the home and not just being rash.

5) Mr. Mean & Mrs. Critical

If God is bringing great conviction to your lives, then you will see significant changes. We should remember that many times the Lord is working on just one or two areas at once. We make those changes, good results come and so we are ready for more. This process keeps going on as long as we are on earth!

I remember two big conferences we have had with our children. One was about the way that I (Paul) chastised with great anger and awful facial expressions. The other was my wife's critical tendency which caused our children great distress. After many years by God's grace, we identified these problems. We really should have identified them long before, but we were slow to learn and plainly too prideful.

Becoming a great parent takes a lifetime.

One breakthrough in resolving my angry expression came by thinking if Jesus would have looked that way. Of course, He did not. I needed to learn that this threat of power was going against the goals of discipline. Instead of bringing growth and strength, I was wounding hearts. I finally called the family together, acknowledged my sin and asked for forgiveness from each one, from the oldest down to the youngest. If you have regular family devotions, assembling the family will not seem awkward.

These are significant steps to building a godly family. If we do not walk the path first, our children will never get there. It is through our faith, humility, honesty and love that our children follow. Think of it as deep snow. When the father goes first plowing through the deep snow, he makes both a path and specific places to step. The child can follow much easier. If not properly dealt with, these very sins of ours will plague the next generations causing even more havoc.

At this point it would be good to state how great our Savior is. He is awesome and powerful, fully able to deliver us from any sin. Give praise to God our Savior! Parenting helps us grow and trust in the Lord. It takes a life time for the Lord's love and wisdom to shine through our lives to our children.

Case Study

Before closing this chapter, we want to provide you with a case study on how to properly handle your relationship with your children. In this case, the child refuses to talk. He says there is nothing wrong. He usually is warm and affectionate but in this case he is stubbornly quiet and resistant to talk. The scripture says that you should not go to bed in anger. We have to force ourselves to resolve the issue. More than likely the child will not take the steps to solve it. It is up to Mom and Dad to break through. Threatening does not work. Nor does questioning. He says nothing is wrong. Should we believe him? Something, however, is wrong in the relationship. What should be done?

Go through the daily events, starting with the ones that you and the child were involved in together. In a recent case, I mentioned one thing after another: What I thought he did wrong, how he was disciplined, whether apologies were made. Everything seemed okay. When I started talking about the second time I chastised him, however, he started speaking about how I had not properly disciplined him and hurt his toe.

I stood there next to his bed reflectively praying. Had I disciplined with the right attitude? Had I disciplined for a clear offense? Had I chastised him properly? I failed on the second account. It was real hard to say I was wrong. But I was. After a long moment of silence, I confessed my sin and apologized. After a while, he turned over and hugged me. That was that. Off he went to sleep. Everything restored.

Summary

Teens who live under the supervision of their parents can be taught to respect them. It calls for the parents to be firm in their beliefs that these changes are necessary and vital to the lives of their older children. The children might only conform on the outward. They might already have accepted ideas from the outside world that make the parents' suggested changes unappreciated. At these times the parents must endure with prayer.

They must love their children more than their pride. All the resentment must be chased out so that their children can trust them again. Perhaps the children will rebel at some point, but much love can be given with the new rule. Parents can affect their children for the good. It might not be as much as the parents would like or when they would want, but it will help them in the long run. Anything short of a life change and display of humility by the parents, however, will only prove to the young people how hypocritical parents can be. Real love will haunt the children no matter where they go.

Parenting Principles & Practice

- If we hide our sins, we will not prosper.
- Humbling breaks down the walls of resistance.
- Confession is the beginning of reconciliation.
- Be honest in all communication.
- Reconciliation comes before restructuring.
- Start with the areas that God has put most on your hearts.

Parenting Questions

1. Why do parents of older children sometimes face so much despair?
2. Why should parents think that they can bring restoration to the family despite all their past mistakes?
3. Why have many children given up on receiving what they need from their parents?
4. How should we properly think of conviction? Why is this important?
5. Explain how mistrust keeps restoration from occurring.
6. List three things that keep an authoritarian parent from being reconciled to his child.
7. Write down the three steps a parent must do to restore his family.
8. Why is it important to work along with your spouse?
9. During confession time, why should we avoid bringing up the problems of others?
10. What should characterize a 'good' apology?
11. List a couple of areas that need work in order to set the family on the right track.
12. How do we know where to start fixing so many problems?

Notes from Chapter #11

---

[1] Although many people make abortion a simple choice of life, in view of the Life Giver, abortion is cold and calculated murder. We should not have killed, but our children are now dead. However, by God's grace the parent can find forgiveness through Jesus. He or she only needs to repent and cast their trust upon Jesus. This does not make light of the evil deed. Christ has died for our sins. That child is now lost, but we should focus on bringing life to others.

[2] We cannot go into how to develop your prayer life here but look at this crisis as a means by which God is wooing you to Himself. Remember that there is a greater purpose going on than just praying for the souls of your children. God is trying to deepen your relationship with Him. Once your children are restored, you will want to continue these humble and vigorous prayers to God through Christ for your children and others.

[3] Many emotional problems can be traced back to parental neglect to carry out the principles taught in the Bible. These would include things like stealing, anorexia, gluttony or low self-esteem. The child's sinful response comes out of their own evil heart, but an environment of evil devoid of God's truths lived out reinforces the pattern.

[4] Forty percent of US college students are involved in binge drinking (five or more drinks at a time. They are drinking just to get drunk.

[5] Complicating the issue is our secret or not so secret desire for things that we do not want to give up.

[6] Remember we use this word 'authoritarian' as distinct from authority. Authoritarian describes a person using his authority in inappropriate ways. If parents are filled with grace and love, they can properly carry out their authority because they care for the ones they are exercising authority over (making decisions for).

[7] Make sure you let your pastor/cell group, etc. know of God's work in your life so that they can pray for you and keep you accountable. Some people do not understand accountability. Tell them what would help you. For example, "Joe, I would really appreciate it if you asked me each week whether I was leading my family in devotions together every day that I was home."

[8] Because you are confessing many sins of the past, identify what kind of sin it is, how it is wrong, the way it hurt others and how often it has been done. For example, "You know I have given myself to watching bad movies all these years. I have set a bad standard. I have offended God and led you to believe that what I watch is not important. It is. I have offended God with viewing violent and sensual movies, hurt my marriage and neglected spending time with you."

[9] A half-baked apology without real change is absolutely disappointing. The alcoholic Dad goes out and drinks, comes home, curses and hits. After he sobers up and realizes what he has done, says, "I'm sorry. I should not have done that. No one deserves that kind of treatment. Please forgive me." The problem is that the next weekend he goes out and gets drunk all over again and finds himself in the same situation again. This kind of confession is abhorrent because there is no true repentance. This parent fails to gain the respect that he wants because of the way his selfishness wounds and hurts his family members.

The parent that truly repents of such behavior must first show repentance and then ask forgiveness. In other words, the parent should stay home and spend time with the family that weekend night instead of going out with his buddies. On the way home, he should ask his son (and of course his wife) whether they notice anything different. They will note he is with them rather than getting drunk. He can at that point confess his last one or two offenses and ask for forgiveness. And then continue on with the other instructions. He must be sure about his decisions. They are life changes for him, and they bring a ray of hope back into the situation. Otherwise, the child will not believe anything significant has changed.

[10] There is no clear age that the parent should stop using the rod. At some point, it becomes inadequate and inappropriate. This happens during their adolescence when they are bigger and the fear of the rod is gone. And yet, at very rebellious times, the rod might be the right tool to awaken them from their foolish and rebellious outburst. Be very careful not to lash out at them.

[11] A father came to tell us that one of his daughters could not go with our family to a special event as planned. He explained that she had to learn the consequences of her wrong. This was not easy, but he stood firm. Even though she is good friends with our daughter and tickets were involved, he was willing to follow through. The consequence of her rebellion was the loss of privilege. May the world have more fathers like that!

Chapter #12

INTEGRATING GOD'S TRUTH INTO OUR FAMILIES

Purpose: Encourage families to pursue godly living by recounting personal stories of how God has shaped us.

We can stuff our minds with knowledge and read all sorts of good books, but this does not take us across the threshold to success. The dividing line is clear. Without change, we are the worst of fools. Having acquired the needed knowledge, we can now make good and needed changes in our family. God's biblical principles work! In this chapter we want to encourage you to take the needed steps by sharing some personal life stories. It is to be hoped that these honest accounts will help you get a better perspective on your own life by seeing how God has taken and reshaped our lives.

A. Getting a Real Life Perspective

We are very unlikely candidates to write a parenting book. I (Paul) still remember when the psychologist interviewing us for missionary service said that we would likely end up divorced! This was more than twenty-five years ago now. We only had our first child then. But facts are facts. As a child of parents divorced multiple times, it was likely that I would get a divorce too. Apart from God's grace, we would have been added to the long line of figures in some negative statistical analysis.

Now it is more than twenty-five years later. Or should we say eight children later? We have an incredibly happy and stable marriage. Are there threats? Yes, there are. Are there uncertain times? Yes. Are there times when I hear, "No more children." Yes, there are. We are not trying to pretend that we do not have challenges or difficulties. We have gone through hordes of problems–probably several times over.

One summer in the recent past, we saw two of our daughters at different times come close to death. Probably once or twice a week we face parenting situations that we really do not know how to handle. I remember praying this morning about several family matters that we just do not have solutions for. But frankly, we have learned that this is normal. It is okay for us not to know all the answers and for things not to work out immediately. Like the apostle, we have learned to trust God with the unsolvable. We do not worry or fear. We take the opportunity to see God's special grace come to work in our family.

> *We are afflicted in every way, but not crushed; perplexed, but not despairing; but not forsaken; struck down, but not destroyed; always carrying about in the body the dying of Jesus, that the life of Jesus also may be manifested in our body. For we who live are constantly being delivered over to death for Jesus' sake, that the life of Jesus also may be manifested in our mortal flesh (2 Corinthians 4:8-11).*

Many years have now passed (our oldest is 28 and our youngest is 5), but we have seen the wondrous power of God's truth step by step take hold of our family. To be quite honest, it does not always seem that way when we are in the midst of those trials (which sometimes feels like every day).

We have prayed so long over one of our sons that he would stop sucking his thumb at night. We tried everything: tape, gloves, the rod, warnings of health consequence, threats and, of course, praying. All to no avail. Last week, he threw sand at a car and was badmouthing. On Saturday night, however, he suddenly said he did not need anything for his thumbs anymore. He was not going to suck his thumbs. Moreover, he said that he read the Bible that day. It showed a new beginning for him. We do not say that he is a Christian, but it is likely that God's Spirit is starting to work on him. He was even singing with more participation during family devotions.

Our goal is not just to have him stop sucking his thumb. That is nothing compared to possible forming a lifelong habit to indulge the flesh. He was doing something to satisfy his pleasures against the wish of his authorities. Without self-control, he would not have the confidence that he could stop a bad habit. This is not what any child needs especially in this sensual age with pornography being released all around us! We want him to have self-control so that he could, through his self-control and the power of Christ, resist and overcome any bad habit and use his whole body to serve the Lord. As parents, we long for these 'new' days, these breakthroughs.

God often brings us into these kinds of difficulties so that we can learn to trust Him. Parenting is one of the Lord's greatest tools for training His people. Without pain, there is no gain. It is true that Satan uses God's testings to tempt us. We need to be careful, but as His children we are never put in a totally helpless situation (1 Corinthians 10:13). We are privileged to obtain extra grace, love, knowledge and help so that we might come through these battles victorious. Like our father of faith, Abraham, our trials prove to be the battlefields where our greatest victories are won.

> *Blessed is a man who perseveres under trial; for once he has been approved, he will receive the crown of life, which the Lord has promised to those who love Him (James 1:12).*

Just think for a moment, what kind of children do you want? Do you want spiritually weak or anemic children? We want strong children. Our world needs strong men and women of faith. The Apostle Paul boasted not about his strengths but about his weaknesses. It was there he met God and gained a powerful testimony that prodded him to surmount difficulty after difficulty.

Paul & Linda Anniversary
May 20th, 1978

We celebrated our 29th anniversary in 2007. Linda and I became one in matrimony on May 20th, 1978 at 2:00 p.m. at a church in Massachusetts. Parenting started as a surprise for us just two months after our first anniversary. We had our college plans worked out. Linda would work while I studied. Fortunately, God interrupted our safe plan and gave us something much better, a little girl and some hard financial circumstances through which we learned many lessons of life. Our little girl graduated from college several years ago. We would love to share more about marriage but must narrow our focus to parenting experiences that helped us grow.

The problems in our families during our growing up years put various sin patterns in our personal lives. We had many blind spots which we only noticed years later. We have shared many principles in this book that will help you leap over a pile of problems if you only apply them to your lives. We had to learn the slow way. Our Christian leaders did not equip us for family living. We learned far too slowly. Do you realize that we really did not understand the basics of training of an infant until our fourth child was already a few months old? We both read many Christian books but such a topic was rarely touched upon.

Looking back, however, we have found that we can always trust our Lord no matter what situation we find ourselves in. He is there always ready to help us grow more than we ourselves really want or think we can. Perhaps He is much like the parent that hopes his child will finally learn that one lesson once and for all. The Lord does not want us to repeatedly fall into the same old problem.

We might be hesitant to trust His principles. We were like that too. Ignorance was part of it. We had the Bible. We memorized the verses, but we had no idea how it applied to our own family life. Blind was a good way to describe us. At other times, though, we just did not want to obey. Perhaps we were afraid of what would happen or just plain old selfish. The church as a whole has lost its grip on these basic principles for developing a godly family. Recent generations have proven this. Where are the Christians who love their families? Where are the couples that want large families? And perhaps most revealing, where are the churches that teach their people these godly principles?

Things could be so much better. How we hope that others soon wake up and discover the power of God's love revealed in His truths so that there would be many wonderful families all around us.

B. Organizing Our Thoughts

In this chapter, we want to integrate and expand on what we have learned by sharing how we grew in a number of specific areas. We have taken far too long to learn these things. Parenting courses were not available when we were young. The Christian culture was just beginning to break up. Now that many people have grown up in tiny and broken families, good parenting skills are even more rare.

Many courses and books are being written to help parents with their many problems. Much of this material is based on wrong assumptions which, if adopted, will keep a person ignorant of God's design and hurt their children. Only principles built on God's perfect design will empower parents to raise up good and polite children that respect God and care for others.

Paul will share about his crippled leadership abilities, personal relationships, bitterness and pride. (I told you we are unlikely candidates for teaching a parenting course.) Linda will share about some incidences that revealed personal weaknesses in handling our children.

Our goals for this chapter include:

- To see how great God's principles are.
- To understand the process God brings you through to live out His ways.
- To keep you from discouragement and giving up.
- To motivate you to take serious steps to integrate these biblical principles into your lives.

We will follow the road of our past chapters to help stay organized and review the main points of what we have learned. Every good parent continually seeks God's ways for his own life and for his children. The first chapters have focused on embracing God's vision. This is where parents are better prepared to be able to easily acquire God's truths for their own lives and families. After that, we focus on equipping the children, which highlights how to get your children to where they should be. The last section, establishes the whole family. We are concerned here of making the whole family work together as something that would please God. They are set out below.

EMBRACE GOD'S VISION
God's Goals for the Family
One Great Team: Dad & Mom
Parental Authority

EQUIP THE CHILDREN
Cultivating Self-Control in Our Children
Child Training & Routines
Correcting Your Child
Discipline and the Loving Use of the Rod
Setting Boundaries

ESTABLISH THE FAMILY
Raising Godly Children
Developing International Love
Regaining the Trust of Our Teens
Integrating God's Truth into Our Families

EMBRACE GOD'S VISION

Goals for Biblical Parenting

Possessing God's goals for our children is an essential part to good parenting. We ourselves never thought of having goals for our children for the first many years of our parenting experience. For many parents, the only parenting goal they have is to have no more than one or two children. This is never a way to start off a marriage or a family! We never consciously thought about purposely training the character of the child but only like many others focused on taking good physical and spiritual care of the child.

Now, we think a lot about character training. Character training is spiritual training, the training of the child's heart.[1] Somehow it was separated in our minds. We think and pray a lot about where we want our children to be physically, spiritually and knowledge-wise.[2] Notice how Jesus is said to have grown. "And the Child continued to grow and become strong, increasing in wisdom; and the grace of God was upon Him" (Luke 2:40).

Neither Linda nor I had any spiritual training in the family beyond being taken to church. Our fathers did not train us in what counted the most. We did not have any clue how these things were instilled into children. We thought the child would naturally do what is best if put in a good situation. It just does not happen that way. We were naive. Our children were sinful.[3]

We came to this understanding far too gradually. We had three problems. We tended to parent with our parents' critical and doubtful eye. We focused on our children's problems rather than encouraging them in the right way. We also had a problem with setting positive standards (what we did want in their lives). We were also ignorant about setting positive standards.

- We only had vague expectations of what a family should be.
- We were ignorant of the necessity of training to produce a godly family.
- We faced much frustration after learning what we <u>should</u> pursue but did not know how.

As young parents, we were often frustrated over what our child was doing. We couldn't even identify the problem and make proper corrections. This was because we focused on bringing them back to neutral (out of trouble) rather than positively instructing our children to do right. "Do not cry." "Do not fuss." "Do not have temper tantrum." "Do not throw your food." These were samples of our wishes. I do not remember teaching patience, kindness, generosity, perseverance, etc. in the first years of our family. The bright side was that we physically took care of our child and had family devotions from early on. This made it easier for the Lord to get us to where we needed to be as parents.

It has been an uphill battle to get back to where we should have started off. We should have realized that God has a life goal for each child. We are stewards and are fully responsible to properly equip the child for the tasks God has for them.[4] These end goals help us to better understand where our children morally, spiritually, physically and in other ways need to be.[5] By observing our goals, we see the need for training. This need fosters motivation to bring the needed training.[6]

Project: One of the things that we have started doing (not yet finished) is to connect our children's names with God's purpose for them. Throughout the Bible, the meaning of a person's name is significant. For example, our third daughter's name, Allison Grace, means "Truth" and "Grace."[7] We desire her to be like Christ who was full of Grace and Truth. This is our prayer target. We know we are not there yet. She has significant areas to work on that threaten to undo this. God will help her, though. When each name is linked to a Bible verse, a promise appears. In this case, we

ALLISON
"TRUTH"

Allison means truth. Truth is God's perspective of the world and man. Truth is given so that man might understand and come to God. Truth needs to be both lived out and proclaimed in all its fullness. Allison is to live close to God so that others can see God's truth through her life just like looking through a window.

"FULL OF GRACE AND TRUTH" (JOHN 1:17)

hope our Allison is like Christ: full of grace and truth (John 1:17) who bears light to those around her.

Pause for Reflection:
Do the project above for each child. Have a piece of paper for each child. Write the name and meaning of the name. Ask God to show you how to train your children so that they might faithfully serve the King. Seek Him for a Bible verse and perhaps a picture or symbol that captures that meaning. This project can take a while as we wait on Him for understanding.

One Great Team: Dad & Mom
We had struggles in our marriage like many young couples. We had some advantages though too. We had a short premarital counseling course along with some good modeling of other Christian marriages. We were growing Christians. Our differences, however, challenged and at times interrupted our oneness. We had to break through these differences if we were to grow, but as typical, we were not that clear as to what problems we needed to overcome to get there. We knew where we wanted to go to some degree but simply did not have directions.

What contributed the most to our marriage was regularly studying God's Word, praying and talking a lot together. We had no models for this. We did it because Paul loved studying God's Word and praying together. We did not think much of its implication to our marriage or improving our parenting skills. God taught us through these studies. He would have spoken more to us if we could have handled it.

The impact of marriage on our parenting began to dawn on us when we heard Gary Ezzo[8] speak of having 'sofa time.' My wife, of course, liked the idea of being together more. I kept asking myself,

"What does this have to do with good parenting?" I finally understood that the unity of the parents is integral to the security of the child. If parents love each other, then the child feels safe. Once they feel safe, they can go on growing in other areas. Although this sounds a bit like modern psychology, let us remember the fact is that God prescribes a husband to love his wife. Good things happen when we do what God tells us.

I (Paul) never saw this unity in my parents. My parents were divorced when I was very young. I did not see them together. Even less did I see love between them. My parents eventually remarried others but their relationships were superficial and left bitter wounds. Fairly regular arguing and fighting drove me from home. I left as soon as possible. I realized later that the reason I chose to go out of state to college was to escape the home scene.

Real understanding and joy of God's design for marriage came to Paul when he did a personal in-depth study of God's love in Song of Solomon during college.[9] This would later be solidified by studies in Ephesians 5. Christ loved the imperfect church. It then occurred to him that he knew little of love, including God's own love. Paul's doubt, skepticism, ignorance and unbelief shattered his hopes of growing in trust. He was so humbled. He thought, "How could I ever love if I did not understand love?" God has gradually helped him by specially designed experiences to train him to believe, imitate, understand and model God's love in Christ. Where would Paul be without Him? He hates to think what his wife and family would be like if God did not rescue him.

We are now convinced that God's goal is to give every couple His great love so that they can have a wonderful marriage and family and thus glorify God. Our Lord gave both the husband and the wife one special guideline. They need to focus on this while at the same time grow in observing other principles of Christian living.

Pause for Reflection:

Your love for God and each other greatly shapes the training of your children. How intimate are you with your spouse? How close are you with God? What would help you grow closer together?

Parental Authority

I (Paul) had great problems with accepting the responsibility to lead the family. I knew what I wanted but did not know how to make it happen. So I defaulted to poor decisions. My Mom directed things at home. My Dad was passive and quiet and most my life lived far away. My stepfather did not show me how to do anything, not even how to put air in a bike tire or shave. Mothers tend to become domineering when fathers do not do their job in the family. When the Mom nags, the Dad retires from the scene even more.

I learned to avoid activities requiring leadership (though I did lead devotions). I was crippled. I did not even think I should or could lead. I tended to back away from my responsibilities which then put the whole family off balance.

Theologically, I knew I was the head of the family, but somehow

that never translated into real life. I never knew that I was responsible to make decisions, how to make decisions, or that my decisions were needed. When I started to understand my duty, this made it difficult in some ways for Linda. She had gotten used to not having me make decisions! Before she could do things that I did not even like. One area that suffered was the correction of our children which will be discussed later on.

Leadership training for me has taken place in thousands of ways. No particular way seemed more important than another. It would have been enormously helpful if someone simply explained the difference between leadership and serving. I heard of servant leadership and assumed that it would be fine just to do what was needed at the moment (i.e. to serve). I did not understand that this idea of servant leadership is chiefly given to those in authority who only care about commanding others rather than providing a good example. I focused on serving and neglected leading and used this wrong concept to avoid making the tough and important decisions that needed to be made.

Just think how this one fault would affect setting standards for our family. I might choose to live that standard out, but I would refrain from shaping others under my influence. I allowed many bad things to happen that could have been avoided. Fortunately, steps were gradually taken that enabled me to step out of this pit. Otherwise, my family would have difficulty living out God's ways. On the outward, our family looked fine, but we were being disobedient by not fully carrying out God's ways. A father must both lead and care for his wife and children.

Pause for Reflection:

Are you, husband, a good leader? Can you make and enforce good decisions in love without anger? Explain. What happens when you, as a husband make certain decisions and your wife disagrees? How do you handle it?

EQUIP THE CHILDREN

'Equip the Children' focuses on the particular skills needed to develop godly children. Like a carpenter needs tools, so do parents. They not only need the vision of what the child should be but also the means by which to get them there. Physical discipline is not the total solution. Rather it is only a part of the total process of training our children.

Developing Self-Control in Our Children

I (Linda) am astonished when I think what I was like as a young parent. Before our first child was born I had no recollection of reading anything about parenting. I probably read childbirth and baby care books. I guess I assumed I would be a good parent.

One of the first things that being a new parent exposed was how selfish I was. I no longer had my own free time. A new little life was dependent totally on me. My sleep was interrupted and my body (breast) was in pain. I did not really know much about baby care. Maybe I knew more than some others because I did much babysitting. No one told me what to expect or how to do the best for the baby. Anything I might have read came from our godless culture.

Our number one child was very easy to care for; compliant and obedient. Number two arrived when we were missionaries in Taiwan. She was very different. Looking back, I can see my ignorance all over.

She cried: I fed her.

She fussed; I picked her up.

I did not know about routines and schedules for training her. I had one baby book overseas written from a secular point of view. It told me to let my child eat what she wanted. She would balance her own food needs given the choice. So I tried giving her choices. Paul told me to feed her what she needed and not to give her any choices. I did not listen.

Giving her the power to reject what I gave her carried over into different areas of life. I did not know I had the responsibility to make sure that she obeyed. Everything was negotiable. I cared more for my child's happiness and feelings than for her obedience and holiness. I did not know I was supposed to. No one told me.

As she grew, I might tell her to do something. She would whine or answer back, and I changed my request or allow her 'reasons' to change my mind. I did not insist on obedience. If I insisted, she cried or looked sad. I would feel bad about making her feel bad. And then not insist on her doing what I said. This is the relationship that I established. It has been very hard to change. I have only been partly successful with her. She still makes excuses for not doing what I ask. I accept that. I can see this pattern to a lesser extent in some of the younger ones. I am wiser now so it is not so bad, but I still have to change more and retrain them. It is always easier to train right the first time than to retrain.

Pause for Reflection:
Do you negotiate with your child? What is wrong with doing that?

Child Training and Routines

These lessons on child training and routine were largely learned by repetition. We do not mean that we understood them with our first couple of children (unfortunately), but only later in life, when God granted us more children. We were so slow that God had to give us many training opportunities! Well, now that we have eight children, we can see how important training and routines are in a parent and child's life. Training helps the children rightly respond to people and situations early on so that the parents and children (and other children if there are siblings) can be a happy family.

We often hear the statement, "I do not know how you do it!" Most of these parents, unfortunately, do not stay around for an answer! They just resign their lives to struggling with their children. We now have an answer. The parent can have their child do what they want. When we rightly time things, the little child wants to be able to do things too. So we show them how and then make sure we enforce it when they decide to challenge the authority at hand.

We started training very young on our last few children, as soon as the Mom and baby completed recovery from the birth experience. This made life predictable. Even what is more important, we could clearly identify what the problem was. Routine and clear instructions (for older children) enable both Mom and child to do things the same way over and over so that when things do not work out, the problem can be easily seen. Perhaps the problem is Dad or Mom slipping on the reinforcement of a rule or the child's expression of his inner rebellion against a rule. It does not take long to spot the problem so we can avoid those days of inner frustration, and maybe outward explosion, before trying to solve the problem.

Just the other day, for example, we noted that a number of children seemed out of whack. They were all (it never is 'all' but it feels like it) arguing and fussing with each other. Linda was rather distraught, wondering what was going on. We started thinking about the situation together. As we talked, we came to see that we were beginning to threaten them rather than discipline them as the scriptures instruct. We did not go back and give them all the chastisement that they should have received (that would be the wrong timing). Instead, we just gathered all the children together and stated our observations. Everyone knew that rebellion was not going to be accepted. They changed their behavior on their own.

Pause for Reflection:
Simply ask yourself, what is your child doing that you do not want. Then, (do not stop there!) ask yourself what you would rather have them do. This sets you on your path to training. You train them not to do something wrong by having them do what you want. With a little reinforcement and consistency, our children quickly change their ways. Why is it that we just have not thought of this before![10] It is amazing.

Correcting Your Child
Our ideas of authority, standards and God greatly shape how we correct our children. Parents rarely set clear standards that disagree with what they practice. They would feel guilty! They reason, if they did, their children would reject it. So, if we have not conquered some sin in our lives, then our children learn how to live evil lives from us.

How Bad Habits are Formed

There are two parts to bad habits.

(1) Doing wrong

There is the lack of doing the right thing–the bad habit itself. One gets used to doing the wrong thing from which he gains a little reward and puts up with the consequences. Johnny gained some satisfaction from hitting his little brother.

(2) Hopelessness

There is also the hopelessness of doing it the right way. The person never develops confidence to do it the right way. This is why it is so hard for one with a bad habit to change. They simply do not have the confidence (faith) to do something else even when they know it is better. What might seem easy to some people, is 'impossible' to others.

Our biggest marriage struggle had to do with the way we chastised our children. This seems to be one of the big tension points for many marriages. Because of the Mom's ability to feel for the child, it is usually harder for her to carry out consistent discipline. They need to overcome an emotional attachment to their children in order to do it. They can but they need a strong vision of its importance. It is even harder for those parents who were not properly corrected when growing up. If they were spoiled (not corrected) or if their parents were mean or strict (corrected with anger instead of love), then they will have an especially difficult time correcting their children. Linda also had this root problem to overcome.

She faced many problems with correcting our children because she couldn't see how it was the best thing to do. She did not see the whole process. Once God gave a vision for the family, it still was difficult at points, but the struggle took on a whole new nature.

In the past, she struggled against disciplining our child. She felt she might damage the child or her relationship with him or her. Now, however, she was struggling to get God's way–consistent firm correction when needed. What a difference! She was open to learning where before she was closed to anything that did not confirm her viewpoint.[11]

Correction helps preserve and maintain the excellent relationship that is needed for cultivating rich relationships with our children. Though we have made our mistakes, we find that God can make wonderful patches. He is a Master of healing. Once I (Paul) sensed some animosity building up between my wife (the mother) and my daughters. I needed to get out of my comfortable mode and call for a conference between them. This was not easy for me.

This forced conversation opened the door for some painful thoughts to be voiced which in turn led to healing. If this did not take place, I sensed our older children would have started avoiding the home. Though we avoid conflict, we must not hide it. We best avoid conflict by resolving and eliminating it. Otherwise it persists. Parents do not do everything right and sometimes need to be challenged to live the way we teach.

Pause for Reflection:
Are you humble enough to listen to someone tell you something that needs to be changed? Are you willing to change what needs to be changed?

Discipline and the Loving Use of the Rod

What we believe about the child will influence our decision whether or not to use the rod. Those convinced that the child will flourish by providing all sorts of freedoms will burn the rod. Because they think that the child is essentially good, they give the greatest opportunity for expression so that the child will turn out well. Although some might be shocked at the conclusions seen in the sidebar, they are only being consistent with their assumption that children are naturally good.

This 'Love' Destroys a Child

- *Love means no standards.*
- *Love means full tolerance.*
- *Love means no spankings.*
- *Love means no responsibilities.*
- *Love means I can watch anything I want.*
- *Love means I can eat anything I want.*
- *Love means I set the time to go to bed.*
- *Love means I get the toys I want.*
- *Love means I can do anything I want.*

The scripture says that the child is a sinner by birth, which demands correction. The child must be shaped according to God's standards. When love is confused with treating the child in a comfortable way, the child becomes self-focused. Instead of having a nicely trimmed and planted garden, nothing is cut, and it becomes very unattractive. We have learned that genuine love is exactly the opposite to what the modernist has written.[12] Hebrews 12 states clearly that if we love our children then we will chastise them.

God's vision for what He wants to do needs to stay in our minds. A constant vision will overcome those confusing feelings and thoughts.

This can only happen when we allow God's word to dominate our thoughts.

We personally have made a number of changes in the past twenty plus years of child training. We have gone from using the hand to a rod (mostly). We have grown more consistent in our discipline. Perhaps the most important aspect is the use of the switch (a tiny training branch) to train the child when he or she is a young toddler. We missed this valuable training on the first six children. Not one Christian book mentioned it. We train the child to associate the parent's 'no' with the sting of a little stick. After that, the child simply obeys. If we say 'no' each time we do it, then the child begins to respect our word and the switch is replaced with our word 'no.' I never knew our three apple trees would bear rods for correction!

We were far too slow comprehending this. We just did not start early enough. We never heard it was possible. It might be too late for our generation but hopefully yours will catch on more quickly for the sake of the parents, children and the world.

Pause for Reflection:
Do you think true love means you must chastise your child? Have you always believed this? Explain.

Setting Boundaries

Before setting standards, we need to set long-term goals for what we want God to do in our children. With no clear goals, the standards are often shortsighted and lack the urgency of implementation. Along with thinking about standards, we need to ask ourselves whether we are doing what we are asking from our children.

When things do not go right in the house and the children seem to get a bit wild, we typically start looking for a reason for the chaos. We used to question ourselves: Is it too many sweets? Not enough sleep? Programs they have watched? Or friends they had been playing with? These things undoubtedly affect our children, often for the worse.

Lately, however, we have begun taking a better look at ourselves. Linda tends to get a bit edgy during certain times of the month. I might be in a rush. We might not have met closely with the Lord during the day. We might have argued in front of the children. We have found that the unsettledness that arises from our sins and neglects often negatively influence our children. Certainly, we need to grow in our own lives too.

Examining Media Modeling

We have also had to reexamine our standards. We have had to ask ourselves whether our standards were inconsistent with what the Lord desires and wants. Some of our standards were worldly, that is, accepted and practiced in the world. What would you say to the person who confided to you that he was eating poison? You would probably be alarmed and warn him. But what if he merely responded by saying that he only takes a little each day?

Do you see the problem that develops with bad television programs, videos, DVDs, computer games, web surfing, magazines, books and catalogues as they come into your house? This is the slow poison that is daily being given in various amounts to our children. We must remember everything that they are exposed to becomes a model for their lives. The different means provide models of what they think are acceptable behaviors and responses.

We began to see that even if we watched a 'good' television program that the commercials still could be horrible. We could not allow the poison to enter our children, even if only a little at a time. By strictly controlling or eliminating this effect on our lives, our marriage has improved. We have gained more time together. Our children are being better trained. Things like adultery as a way of life or the use of violence to handle

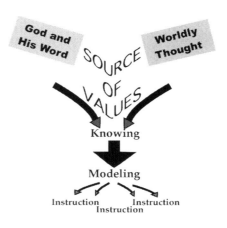

problems are no longer being modeled in our home. The further the television is from our minds, the more at ease we have been as a family.

I forget now when the television made its way to the cold, often unheated and cable-less attic. We do not even have regular chairs there. The decision to move it there was great and has renewed our times together. The children even forget about it. Before it was hard not just to turn it on because it was in the living room, even if it was one of those animal programs that pushed evolution (which assumes the Bible is not true and that God did not make or care for the world). Now we play with each other, read books, play games, etc. The children learn to do things with each other.

I (Paul) personally have been convicted that God is offended at the sex and violence on many programs. Can we ever find a program that actually shows a godly couple lovingly caring for each other? Can we find one example of a smart, good husband or father? Not really. Men are portrayed as idiots who have no goals but to find sexy women, get rich and famous. What a model! The children learn how others disrespect such foolish fathers and transfer it to us. Why do I have to accept the world's standard? We do not. I do not. Away with the television. Maybe someday we will get rid of it altogether, but having eliminated it from my life enables me to spend better time with my children.

We do use a limited set of videos or DVDs instead of television. Once in a great while, we might get a 'G' video and watch it. The children know what to expect. Dad is going to ask a group of tough questions about its meaning and assumptions. Did you ever examine what these movies and programs are 'pushing?' The "*Lion King*" is poised as a 'good' movie. Have we, however, ever examined what it spends time portraying or singing about? I cannot trust "Disney" movies anymore. The *Lion King* pushes everything I hate including witchcraft, laziness, reincarnation, etc. Now a bit wiser, I expect them to be evil unless they prove otherwise. The movie ratings are not God's ratings![13]

God has much work to do on our standards. We are not holy. We would rather catch a show, than pray and contemplate God's love and goodness. We are not saying to eliminate such activities, but our reluctance to give these things up makes it much slower for us to love God with all of our hearts, souls and minds. With the popularity of the internet, a whole slew of new problems have arisen.

We allow our children to watch regulated programming from 5:00 p.m. to dinner time. We also limit our children to 30 minutes on the computer six days a week. Originally, we had separated this into two 15 minute sections, one for games and another for education. For some, however, it was hard to separate and so we combined it. They choose a time and write it on the white board. If they go over the time limit, they loose the privilege the next day.

They have extra time for research projects and developing computer skills such like drawing or learning html (web page language). They need to get permission for these things. This is a freedom that we are quite free to take away. As they get older yet, we allow more time for IM and email. This is the way they communicate with their friends. We need to constantly monitor how much time older children 'chat' through the computer. It seems similar to limiting how long we were on the phone when we were young, except they are not keeping the phone out of use.

One last word of advice. Do not be legalistic. This destroys the delight of obedience. We sometimes allow the television to come downstairs for a visit. We need to train our children: "How do we use it?" "Does it control us or do we control it?" "Is what I watch pleasing to the Lord?" We do not legislate against all television or computer games but strictly govern what is being seen.

Pause for Reflection:

What kind of programs do you and your children watch? Would they please the Lord? Are people acting politely? What is the message of the program or movie? Here is an exercise to train yourselves. As a couple, watch a program together and share what values are being taught. Examine how they relate to each other, carry out responsibilities, morally act, resolve conflict and handle immoral desires.

Dealing with Anger

What about the standard of anger? I (Paul) used to be bitter and angry. I had to work through many problems from bitterness in my childhood. I now have forgiven all. My facial expressions, however, have not yet fully changed.

When I discipline, my voice, I am told, sounds horrible and my face curls up like some horrible monster. It is hard for me to believe. I have not completely been changed by the gentleness of my good Master. I seek Him. It is hard to hear how I blew it again. I do not even know if I should believe it. I need to keep seeking the Lord for a closer walk with Him. My wife has been a great help in identifying my problems and is better at knowing how to let me know of my failures.

If we as parents allow our anger to control us, then it gives permission to our children to do the same. For one, they do not think it is possible to resolve their anger as they see the example of their out-of-control parents. Second, they see anger as a normal means of communicating and defending themselves.

Pause for Reflection:

Are you so desirous of God's standards that you would be open for someone to correct you? How do you respond when someone mentions how you could do something better?

ESTABLISH THE FAMILY

Having the vision, confidence and tools to train our children is fine, but we need to be careful. There are some other pitfalls out there that can easily cause us to be distracted from God's purpose in nurturing godly children. The results are disastrous. We must not turn from the path.

Raising Godly Children

Some parents want good children but not godly children. If the big problems they have with their children are solved, then they are happy. We need to dig deep into our hearts and realize the great difference between a heaven-bound child and a world-attached child. Never minimize the spiritual goals. They are crucial to your children's lives as well as to your grandchildren. We must stamp Jesus' words into our hearts and minds. "For what does it profit a man to gain the whole world, and forfeit his soul?" (Mark 8:36).

Parents can get discouraged when they discover that their children are too old and set in their ways. We offer hope. We need to move forward into taking God's truths and establishing them in our family. We want Him to be pleased with the way we interact with each other. The truths must, however, get from the head to the heart, which is much harder than we would like to admit.

We have found that our goals for our children can only be as good and holy as the ones we have for ourselves. We need to walk the path first. We need to be actively pursuing the Lord all of our lives if we hope to have our children to do the same.

Every parent has the same great challenge to produce godly children in an evil age. Many parents do not care. Most likely, these are the ones that do not care about some of their own evil habits. Other parents that do care cry in despair. What they are doing does not seem to work. The world seems to be gobbling them up. I suppose this frustration sounds like a good reason not to have children–the fear of not being able to raise them to love God and live a pure life.

We can appreciate this thinking but urge you to fight it. We must fight it, and fortunately, God has given us examples of those in the scriptures who believed that God can help parents raise godly children in a wicked world. Just think of Joseph, Daniel and Job. Our grief is that our standards are typically not high enough. Once that personal revival takes place in our own lives, we need to have enough faith for our children.

Spiritual Standards

From the beginning, we had a firm commitment to learn and study God's Word, individually and together. More recently, God has refreshed our study of His Word. This increased excitement has come from two sources.

First, we began to understand that the character of a person was related to Christian growth. This knowledge helped spur us on to eagerly live by God's standards. We knew that if we desired these standards for our child, then we must have them ourselves first. We became more open to God's process of making us more like Christ. These are the standards that we would adopt and implement in our family. Love became something we could specifically teach ourselves and our children.

> *For this, "You shall not commit adultery, you shall not murder, you shall not steal, you shall not covet," and if there is any other commandment, it is summed up in this saying, "You shall love your neighbor as yourself." Love does no wrong to a neighbor; love therefore is the fulfillment of the law (Romans 13:9-10).*

We made a change to another home-school curriculum because it brought God into each sphere of life.[14] The curriculum highlighted a character quality each month. We studied and observed what God's Word said about each monthly character quality and how it worked out in daily life. It taught us how a particular quality like patience made a significant difference in a person from history's life. Education now strengthens our values rather than opposes them.

The other extra excitement has come from learning about the ways God reveals Himself to us as His children. We have heard this over and over, but it finally dawned on Paul one day when God pointed out how Jesus lived day to day. Jesus depended upon the Word of God and received whatever He needed day by day. This brought about an expectation that God was trying to speak to us, but we just were not paying attention–even if we were studying God's Word. Now we are learning how to meditate on God's Word and seek the special insights He has for us that very day.

If we are going to be good Christian parents, we need to grow, grow and grow. Linda lists some significant growing points for her that greatly improved her ability to parent over the years.

➢ Understanding my responsibilities and accepting them as my calling which is giving my life to God so that He can use me in my family.

➢ A growing intimate marriage has helped me know that I am unconditionally loved. This gives me room to try and fail without the threat of rejection.

➢ Learning to love what God loves and ordering my life accordingly.

➢ Growing intimacy with God. Knowing how dependent I am upon Him for everything.

➢ God changing me from a negative, fearful worried mother to a mother or woman that trusts Him and expresses more joy. Still working on this. Still have a way to go.

Turning my Heart to my Children

One of the first issues that God had to deal with in me (Linda) to turn my heart toward my children was that I really did not believe what He said in His Word. I did not believe that children, even many children, are a blessing and reward. I <u>said</u> I believed that, but my actions and attitudes exposed my unbelief. I acted like they were a bother or in the way. I had the "It's easier to do things myself" mentality. This was when we only had two children. I knew nothing of God's grace to 'handle them.'

Part of my problem was passed on through my busy mother. There were six of us. She was so busy. Another part was my low view of God's truth. If God said it, it is true. I did not believe what He said. I needed to have my view and heart changed to conform to His truth to learn to love what He loves.

I would often repeat something like this to myself. "Children are a blessing but also a big responsibility. They make a lot of work and messes. No more children! Only two. Two is enough."

God's dealing with me began when I became pregnant with number three. We were just moving to Pittsburgh. I had dreams and hopes of ministering alongside Paul showing hospitality, doing counseling together, visitation together, being free to pursue what I do not know. That idea of freedom versus being tied down to watch children was a strong battle. It was a struggle to accept that God had better ideas than me. I cannot say the battle was won all at once. It has been an ongoing process. At least, I came to accept that God's ways are better and wiser. So our third child was born in the fall of 1991.

The following spring God used a book that someone lent to me to turn my heart back around a little more. The book, *The Way Home* by

Mary Pride challenged many of my dearly held views. God used it to help me see my selfishness and how much I resisted God's ways. It showed me how much of the world's views I had swallowed as truth. I read this book just before number four was conceived.

I was really embarrassed to be pregnant with number four. I did not want to tell anyone. God still had a work to do on my attitude about family. He used this child to turn my heart around a little more. Daniel was born in 1993. It was then that we entrusted our family planning to the Lord. Trusting in the Lord to plan our family was an exercise in faith that had an impact on my attitude. I began to believe the truth— children are a blessing and a reward. They are not a burden or a bother. Believing the truth and putting His Word in my heart turned my heart back to my children. Instead of thinking what other people might think, I finally was learning to be more concerned about what God thinks.

What about the standard for church?

It is easy to make excuses for not giving to the Lord or not going to church. We keep a strong standard here. But honestly, we need to carefully determine how sick the child really is. Linda and I have made our share of 'excuses' (really lies) when we were young. We had some firsthand experience in this area. Here are some thoughts we use to help us deal with many real-life situations.

- Would we stay home from an engagement that we would really like to go to if we were feeling like this?
- If we agree the child has a debilitating sickness, then we make sure they have time to recover without television and the extras.

Just imagine how difficult it would be if our children figured out that when they stay home from church, they can watch a video. We would be readying our home for an invasion of Sunday morning flu.

Money decisions

We are fairly straightforward with our children when it comes to our finances. We tell them how it is. We state how we have given such and such an amount of money away. We tell them what missionaries we gave the money to. We want them to see how to properly make decisions even when it is not easy.

The older ones know that we have made a decision not to spend it on them. Some might conclude that this would push our children away from us, but it does not. They respect our willingness to give to others.

They need to know that giving to the Lord's work is more important than a trip to Disney World. If, however, they saw us spending money on bad habits or selfish things then resentment would easily build up.

Time well spent

We do need to spend time with our children, though. This does not necessarily mean much time.

Just today I heard my daughter wanted to learn how to ride her bike. Well, the other children had their bikes running well, but her tire was flat. I figured it would be good to put air in her tire. These little things make a big difference to our children.

We do jobs together. We play together. We read books to the little children. I might read a book to everyone at mealtime. We sometimes have game night. Our vacations are typically on very low budgets, but we do swim, ride and walk together. One of my greatest joys as Dad is watching them learn how to swim on vacation.

Pause for Reflection:

Do you believe children are a blessing? Have you always believed this? What else do you need to learn to fully appreciate the truth of the Lord? If your children are a blessing, do you enjoy spending time with them?

Fostering Intergenerational Love

We love our parents, but it is sometimes difficult to get along with them during special times like when a grandchild is born. Some parents are like a dream come true. For others, it seems like the home becomes a war zone. If everything is fine between you and your parents, then this chapter is not for you. It is for those who are trying to train their children but find interference from their parents. Many people have not learned how to enjoy their relationships with their parents

We should expect to have differences of opinion. This is not rare, especially if they are not Christians. As children grow older, they begin to gain different perspectives from their parents. It is to be hoped that they will do things better than we did!

Paul had a difficult time growing up with his parents' divorces and all. These difficulties lead to deep problems within him. He had to learn how to love someone that had hurt him. He had to learn to forgive. Although this is so basic to the gospel message, it is so easily skipped over. These special times with our parents give us opportunities to make sure that all is okay. God does not want smoldering relationships in our families. They always cause personal problems in our own children.

Restoring our relationships is a necessity. Once corrected, however, we do not want to destroy the fragile foundation we now have. It is much easier to react in loud words or quietly burn in anger rather than use biblical principles to relate to our parents. Our own natural tendencies can ruin what little we have if we are not careful. God has the ways to make the best out of the most difficult circumstances.

Please remember, that unless our own sins are confessed, they will always remain as a barrier in our relationship between us and our parents. Only until we have confessed our sins, can we expect God to bless our relationship. Be honest and sincere. Although our parents might not say anything, they will appreciate it. There is one step after this. Treasure your parents. Get wisdom from them. Ask them about their lives. Respect and honor your parents for God has appointed them. Our honoring of them will reveal itself in how we seek wisdom from them.

Paul distinctly remembers how he had to take special steps to honor his father by asking for his advice, whether it was about this ministry or fixing the cruise control on the van. God blessed in unusual ways! This was and still is a faith-building exercise.

Pause for Reflection:
It is worthwhile to develop a good relationship with your parents. It is a command of the Lord. Your relationship with them has a big influence on your family even if you try not to let it. What are the problems preventing you from having a good relationship with your parents? How hard are you trying to improve it? Do you really honor them despite their faults and the past?

Regaining the Trust of our Teens
Many parents who have read this material have a young child that can benefit, but they wonder what they can do with their older child. Is it too late? Can one change an older child?

We have shared a good number of our mistakes in this book. We have come uncomfortably close to a child 'shutting' her heart to us. Maybe you have experienced this or something much worse. God's Word has a lot to guide us on how to regain the heart of our children.

We need to be prayerful parents. I have learned to pray for each child every day. I cannot say I have done this from the beginning. Shame on me. Who, however, has taught me this responsibility? It perhaps is always assumed and never stated. We believe in prayer because we believe in God. Praying for the world and not praying for one's own home is wrong. Prayer opens the door for miracles and can open the heart of a rebellious child.

We disagree with those who say that rebellion is a normal teenage experience. We fight against this notion because it is not normal, although it is typically American. It is part of the Western culture only because we give too many freedoms (without responsibility) to our children and do not know how to bring our children back under our authority. Instead of making room for teenage rebellion, we need to have high hopes of transferring adult responsibilities and attitudes to our children. Teenagers do go through many emotional, spiritual, intellectual and physical changes. We can, however, make a significant difference at this stage of their lives. Ignorance of our responsibility will cause greater upheaval.

Instead, we should work closely with that child and believe they can obey us even when their body chemistries are changing. They need to learn self-control over again with a new mix of hormones and a new awareness of their personal lives. We need to gently show them how to do this, slowly but surely. Before this is possible, however, we must believe that they can live godly teen lives. Otherwise, we will feel helpless. This sense of helplessness (or doubt) is Satan's tool to assist him in his work.

We have a way to go. Although our second daughter has just married, our third and fourth children have already entered their teens and we have a host of children following them. We will no doubt have our own challenges, but we have found that our older ones chose not to be friends with some who now have children out of wedlock and all sorts of life problems.

There was something about home and our genuine faith that kept them desirous of having a large godly family for themselves. They regularly meet with God and serve God in the church (Sunday School teachers, VBS helpers, worship team, etc.)

Make the home the greatest place possible, but remember this kind of home can only exist if you regularly and rightly discipline your child. Parents need to remember that correction is merely a means to keep a good relationship with the child. Correction compels the child to respect you as the parent. We have provided a number of practical steps and considerations in attempting to bring back older children.

There are two critical things to bring about this change in older children (and keep our children good as they get older):

- Sufficient humility to apologize for your mistakes and

- Genuine repentance so that the child can see real life changes in your own life.

Parents are usually caught off guard by this book. They were looking for ways to improve their children by changing their children. We have tried to point out that we the parents are the ones that really need to change. As we change to be more like Christ, our children will turn for the better.

We might still have much pride combined with many faults. We need to take one step at a time and by God's grace deal with them. When we do, we can then honestly, and hopefully, share with our children how wonderful it is to grow in Christ.

Secularism is no longer hiding its desire to seduce our children. Our only hope (and this is a grand hope) is to show how great God really is. Fortunately, God is willing to enter any home or heart to do this very thing. God always wants to make His glory known. God wants to show how great His design of the family is. Walk down the steps of brokenness, and you will find the rewards of humility. Look up toward God and seek His wisdom, love and gentleness. May this describe all of our hearts for the remainder of our days.

Conclusion: The step toward love

Parents talk about loving their children but, in the end, we see that we first must get that love from God and then model it. Human love and wisdom is insufficient. We feel it is good enough until we hit a problem. It never was good enough. We were just happy with mediocre living.

It is not good enough to feel good about how we are training our children. We do not have the resources to live out the kind of life on our own that is needed for raising children. In many cases, an adult's first dose of humility occurs when he is married. Things do not work out as easily as he thought. The second dose comes as a child. Young and old parents are stretched beyond themselves.

As parents, we must not be content with children that live good lives in front of us. We must push them to put on self-control and the fear of God so that they will live godly lives even when we are not around.

Good parenting is a process of discipleship both for the parents and the child. The earlier we learn this, the better. We can start learning from Him rather than taking the course over and over as we fail. As we learn to live out God's love, we pass it on to our children to learn. Love provides the warmth our cold hearts need. Love motivates us to move when we feel lazy, help when it is dangerous, sacrifice even though there is no immediate reward.

We can speak of a thousand wonderful principles built on God's Word, but, in the end, remember that truth must be conveyed in a context of love or it will be rejected as phony. This is because love is a summary of the principles of truth having to do with relating to others.

What was so special about Jesus? What made those around Him love to hear and talk to Him? Jesus was full of grace and truth (John 1:14). Jesus was able to combine rigid standards with a compassionate heart. (See the appendix.) Now it is our turn. As Romans 13:14 says, "Put on the Lord Jesus Christ." This is what our children need the most.

One more chance!

By implementing biblical principles early on, parents can avoid many of the difficult family problems: rudeness, arrogance, disobedience and outright rebellion. Be careful, however, with each new stage of a child's growth lies another opportunity to take the same biblical principles and apply them to the same child but in what seems totally new circumstances. By constant application, we succeed, but if we fail, then we will allow the very things that we rejected early on to enter our families.

Parents need to be diligent and never give up allowing God's life-changing truth to marvelously work in our lives and the lives of our children! After all, is this not the goal of parenting? We are charged with producing children, no matter what our excuses, that obey God and respect others.

Notes from Chapter #12

---

[1] A parent cannot change the nature of the child's heart. This is God's work. We can, however, and are responsible to train the responses of our children. Training them to live out godly responses is the greatest way to lead them to Christ by showing them the superiority of Christ's ways and spurring their conscience to seek Christ's forgiveness.

[2] A majority of people and theologians teach that moral accountability begins at the age of twelve. This is not scriptural and plainly does not make sense. We pretend our children are innocent when the children themselves know full well at a very early age when they have done wrong. "Joey took my toy and won't give it back to me!" Why not instead teach them that they are sinners so that they might seek the Savior?

[3] The most interesting aspect of this is that I believe strongly in the depravity of man. I just never have applied it to children. Perhaps it is because I never heard how the expression of man's sin could be hindered if parents rightly trained their children. Of course, this did not make their hearts any better. The positive result is that they are more sensitive to the Gospel. They know of their sin because they have not met God's standard.

[4] Every person is responsible to worship and love God and others. Christians have "good works" which God has prepared beforehand that they should walk in (Ephesians 2:10).

[5] God's instructions to Samson's parents is a good example of this need for specific training of our children. Although our children might not have such a specific calling, Ephesians 2:10 does highlight how God has a plan for each of His children, and we as parents are to prepare them for this. We must do a much better job than Samson's parents did, however. They completely failed. Samson had no vision for God's purpose for his life nor did he have a fear of God to generally guide his life.

[6] At times, parents have clear but ungodly goals. These children become specialists in idol worship which eventually destroys them (living for money, education, sports, etc.)

[7] Her Chinese name "Hwei Jen" beautifully reflects this.

[8] Many parents do not like Ezzo's suggested routines. Their scriptural basis is weak and so receive a lot of criticism. On the whole, however, their principles and advice are good.

[9] See an explanation of this in our book *'Building a Great Marriage.'*

[10] The idea is very pronounced in the scriptures. Just read Ephesians 4-5 and one will see a number of positive commands that keep one from doing the wrong thing. Put on the new self and put off the old.

[11] See the web page www.foundationsforfreedom.net/Topics/Family/Parenting009_Harmony.html for a clearer picture of this process.

[12] Modernists do not have any right to say anything to to others on how anyone including conservatives should or should not live and talk. They supposedly have no standards, right? www.foundationsforfreedom.net/Topics/Family/Parenting010_SecularBible.html.

[13] Check out the mini web series how God urged Paul to compel others in his family to follow God's standards, www.foundationsforfreedom.net/References/OT/Poetical/Psalms/Psalm036.1_12/Psalm036_1.html .

[14] Advanced Training Institute (ATI) has a remarkable curriculum. There are some weaknesses such as in Math but can easily be supplemented with other math materials such as Saxon. See http://ati.iblp.org for more information.

<u>Other Parenting Resources</u>

Reading sources can give us a big boost to get where we otherwise could not.

The Way Home by Mary Pride. (A feminist goes home. Very lively book. Helps the mother wrestle with God's Word about her role as a mother and wife).

The Family: God's Weapon for Victory by Robert Andrews. (Thorough picture of the whole family starting with courtship and marriage and thus provides a good context for Principles & Practices of Biblical Parenting. Instruction is aided by personal illustrations).

Growing Kids God's Way by Gary and Anne Marie Ezzo. (Practical and detailed. Seems to focus too much on some topics and miss others. Provide adequate discussion of false philosophies. Unfortunately, lacks good biblical instructions and therefore seems to be more of an opinion than it really is).

Train up a Child by Michael and Debbie Pearl. (Fun and yet dead serious. More practical than you might want! Unfortunately, many of us cannot be so radical and live out on a farm as the Amish but do not let that stop you from reading the material - www.nogreaterjoy.org).

Godly Beginnings for the Family by Paul and Linda Bucknell. (This series helps parents start right: filled with many practical advice for pre-birth, birth and post-birth accompanied by reading, handouts and clear illustrations on early training.)

Building a Great Marriage by Paul and Linda Bucknell. (Every marriage can be great if couples would just follow God's advice. The Lord is sincere in wanting each couple to have a beautiful marriage because it is in this way they bring glory to His Name. This book captures the main principles undergirding a great marriage).

Appendix 1
Biblical Parenting, Really?

Much discussion has come up over the past years on whether the phrase 'biblical parenting' is appropriate. Some people have problems even with the word 'parenting.' They prefer the more traditional term 'raising children.' This is not our concern. If neither term is offensive and somewhat clear, both can be equally used. Our concern here is with the problem using the word 'biblical.'

There are two major problems. First, people are offended to the point that they react rather than think. Second, our generation focuses so much on their opinion that they cannot hear the voice of God from the scriptures. We will answer both groups together.

People react against the whole notion that there is anything called biblical parenting. From my conversations and readings, it appears that some individuals are unwilling to examine their parenting practices by taking a close look at the scriptures. What is really the problem?

Now it is very possible that they have met up with people who are prideful on how their so-called 'biblical parenting' has worked for them. This will turn off anyone no matter what one may call it. Biblical parenting, if carefully followed, produces great results, but there is no need for pride. After all, where did the ideas come from? Are we not all beggars on the street? Yes, God designed the family. He prescribes how we should live and raise our children in a degenerate society. God's ideas work because they are from Him. We are humbled that God has taught us through the scriptures. Where would we be without His grace?

Another problem is that people believe that those who espouse biblical parenting are intolerant toward other views. One must distinguish between principle and practice here. Principles are our attempt to verbalize truth to our specific situations. We do not compromise these issues. We know God and trust His opinions are better than ours! We do, however, and this is crucial, closely examine whether the supposed principle is what God has said and designed. In a recent seminar, those in the class asked, "How do we know what is God's principles?" They are on the right track. We are seekers. We want the Holy Spirit to teach us. We are aggressive on learning.

Practices, however, are a more specific application of some general truth to a given situation. In this book, we often use the word 'rod' as the means to spank a child. The Bible uses the word rod (i.e. branch). We do not mean, however, that a rod is the only way to chastise a child or that those who spank with their hand are morally wrong.

In those days, they did not have PVC tubing or many other plastic kitchen stirrers to use. It is important that we see the nature of the rod, a young branch, and make sure we remember why it was used: flexible, something other than the hand, inexpensive and available.

However, the idea of discipline itself is biblical. It is a theme written all the way through the scriptures. If we refuse to entertain the truth of this principle, then we will desperately fail God and our children. These biblical principles need to be carefully thought through. Any God-given principle ignored in our families will not only generate disobedience but sad consequences. Remember, God shares these principles with us to bless us, not to trouble us. This leads us to our last comment on the attitudes people have towards biblical parenting.

We are not trying to set a law. Biblical parenting, rightly understood, is far from a legalistic way of doing things. If we understood Jesus' condemnation of legalism in the Pharisees, we would consider it a biblical truth that a system of self-righteousness always falls horribly short of God's expectations.

Our lives are too short to play the game, "I'm right," and "You're wrong." Instead, we need to join hands in seeking what God has revealed to us and how to live it out. The welfare of our children is at stake! Who are we fighting with? Other parents who care about their children? Certainly not! We are fighting with the evil forces that have propagated falsehood as truth. Many parents have unknowingly been hoodwinked and believe modern teachings are more 'loving.' Their unwillingness to evaluate their position against the scriptures will bring great harm to others.

Each moment we pretend that we are better than another is a complete waste. We need to get on with knowing God better through Christ Jesus and more closely adopt His ways. In this book we have tried to identify some biblical principles relevant to raising children. We are, however, still growing in our grasp of what these principles mean, how they are to be applied in specific situations and perhaps the most important of all, trying to get to know the God who stands behind these principles better. When we know God better, then we can appreciate and grasp His truths.

Far too many parents have shut God out of their parenting. They do not think or want to think that God has anything to say about how to raise their children. They think they do God a favor by redefining Him so that "He would never hit a child." They are gravely mistaken (See 2 Kings 2:23-24). The lives of their children are at stake. Let us together seek what He has to say!

I have seen wonderful families. What do I think to myself? I think that they have adopted some of God's biblical parenting principles, whether they know it or not. They might not even call themselves Christians. The point is that they conduct themselves more according to God's truths than others who call themselves Christians. Words in themselves are empty. We need to see the truth of God's principles ring alive in our lives. Only in this way will God be praised and our families be so happily blessed.

Appendix 2
Theology of Parenting

God

God's purposes for this earth and parenting are closely connected. The Lord glorifies His Name by showing His magnificent grace to His specially saved people. He adopts them into His great family where they reflect His image and share in His many riches in Christ Jesus.

First Adam
Plan #1

Second Adam
Plan #2

God created man in His own image, in the image of God He created him; male and female He created them ... Be fruitful and multiply, and fill the earth, and subdue it (Genesis 1:27-28).

Adam was originally called to reproduce others in God's image.

When Adam had lived one hundred and thirty years, he became the father of a son in his own likeness, according to his image, and named him Seth (Genesis 5:3).

After the fall, Adam's descendants carried his own stained image instead of God's holy image.

Therefore, just as through one man sin entered into the world, and death through sin, and so death spread to all men, because all sinned-- (Romans 5:12).

In the end people lived after their own ways and reflected the treacherous devil rather than God.

By this the children of God and the children of the devil are obvious: anyone who does not practice righteousness is not of God, nor the one who does not love his brother (1 John 3:10).

Without father, without mother, without genealogy, having neither beginning of days nor end of life, but made like the Son of God, he abides a priest perpetually (Hebrews 7:3).

God instead sent His own Son, Christ Jesus, into the world to accomplish His purpose of having sons.

And He (Christ) is the image of the invisible God, the first-born of all creation (Colossians 1:15).

People are born into God's family and brought into His kingdom through belief in Jesus Christ.

But as many as received Him, to them He gave the right to become children of God, even to those who believe in His name (John 1:12).

God is recreating His image in His people as they seek to be more like Christ and obey Him.

And have put on the new self who is being renewed to a true knowledge according to the image of the One who created him (Colossians 3:10).

Parents responsibly lead their children in the Lord's gracious and righteous ways that they might follow Christ.

And, fathers ... bring them up in the discipline and instruction of the Lord (Ephesians 6:4).

Appendix 3
A Parenting Flow Chart

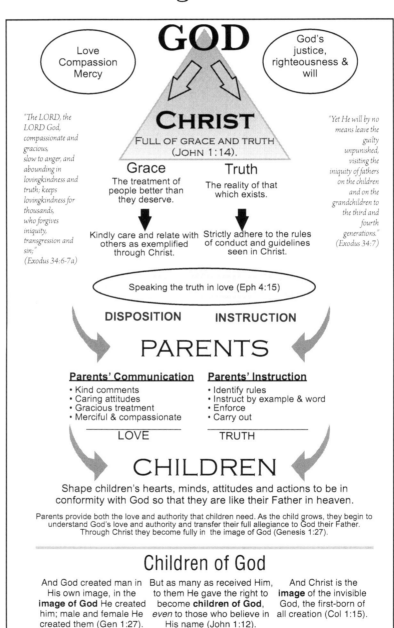

GOD

Love
Compassion
Mercy

God's
justice,
righteousness &
will

CHRIST
FULL OF GRACE AND TRUTH
(JOHN 1:14).

"The LORD, the LORD God, compassionate and gracious, slow to anger, and abounding in lovingkindness and truth; keeps lovingkindness for thousands, who forgives iniquity, transgression and sin;"
(Exodus 34:6-7a)

"Yet He will by no means leave the guilty unpunished, visiting the iniquity of fathers on the children and on the grandchildren to the third and fourth generations."
(Exodus 34:7)

Grace
The treatment of people better than they deserve.

Truth
The reality of that which exists.

Kindly care and relate with others as exemplified through Christ.

Strictly adhere to the rules of conduct and guidelines seen in Christ.

Speaking the truth in love (Eph 4:15)

DISPOSITION   **INSTRUCTION**

PARENTS

Parents' Communication
• Kind comments
• Caring attitudes
• Gracious treatment
• Merciful & compassionate

Parents' Instruction
• Identify rules
• Instruct by example & word
• Enforce
• Carry out

LOVE   TRUTH

CHILDREN

Shape children's hearts, minds, attitudes and actions to be in conformity with God so that they are like their Father in heaven.

Parents provide both the love and authority that children need. As the child grows, they begin to understand God's love and authority and transfer their full allegiance to God their Father. Through Christ they become fully in the image of God (Genesis 1:27).

Children of God

And God created man in His own image, in the **image of God** He created him; male and female He created them (Gen 1:27).

But as many as received Him, to them He gave the right to become **children of God**, *even* to those who believe in His name (John 1:12).

And Christ is the **image** of the invisible God, the first-born of all creation (Col 1:15).

308

Authors

Paul & Linda Bucknell, parents of eight children, have had much parenting experience. The large age spread of their children of over twenty years enables them to keep the whole parenting perspective in process. Their experiences as missionaries and pastor and pastor's wife, have provided them special responsibilities and insights for training, counseling families and holding parenting seminars. As founder of *Biblical Foundations for Freedom*, Paul has had many opportunities to train God's people in many places around the world. Paul has authored a variety of biblical training materials.

A Summary of Principles & Practices for Biblical Parenting

You can do it! God wants you to succeed in raising a godly family and has provided all you need to do it. We do not need to experiment with the many popular parenting methods only to discover later that it did not work and our children suffer for it. God the Designer of the family has and is passing His love and truth on to us!

By modeling and applying God's truth to the family, parents can expect good changes to take place. God designed the family and knows how it best functions even in a less than ideal world. We discern what God wants and through love and the training process pass His standards onto our children.

The earlier parents begin training, the better. Parents have an opportunity to prevent bad habits from forming by establishing godly attitudes early on. These in turn become such a rewarding part of our children's lives, filled with lovely memories and joy, that when they grow up, they adopt the same lifestyle. Teenage rebellion is not necessary. Parents can continue to develop a growing relationship with their older children through the many new situations they face in their adolescent years.

God Bless!

Happy Parenting!

Made in the USA
Charleston, SC
10 March 2012